366 Meaningful Marriage Minutes

ONE MINUTE CHRISTIAN DAILY DEVOTIONALS FOR COUPLES

LONDON C. MONROE, CMC

Contents

Introduction

~

Greetings and God's peace to you, my friends.

I commend you for starting this devotional journey, where each verse is explained, thoughts are shared on its relevance to marriage in contemporary times, and a prayer concludes the devotional.

The intent of this book is to provide an ongoing deepening spiritual connection between you and your significant other.

Throughout the daily scriptures provided, I aim to provide a deeper understanding of what those scriptures mean in God's design for marriage.

Your support means the world, and I wish you the best on your '366 Meaningful Marriage Minutes' journey.

With grace and gratitude,

~ London

January

AS THE NEW YEAR UNFOLDS, LET US OPEN OUR HEARTS TO THE POSSIBILITIES OF GROWTH, TRANSFORMATION, AND DIVINE GUIDANCE. MAY THE LIGHT WITHIN GUIDE OUR STEPS, AND MAY THE JOURNEY AHEAD BE FILLED WITH BLESSINGS, GRACE, AND MOMENTS OF PROFOUND CONNECTION WITH THE SACRED.

January 1

Genesis 2:24

"Therefore shall a man leave his father and his mother, and shall cleave unto his wife: and they shall be one flesh".

What Does This Mean For Us?

Therefore shall a man leave his father and his mother. This indicates the establishment of a new family unit. In today's context, it encourages couples to prioritize their marriage relationship above other relationships, including those with their parents.

And shall cleave unto his wife and they shall be one flesh. This expresses the profound unity and oneness in marriage. It encourages couples to be tightly bonded to each other, both emotionally and spiritually.

Modern Day Reflection

In today's world, external influences and distractions can challenge marital unity, Genesis 2:24 serves as a reminder of the importance of leaving and cleaving for a strong and enduring marriage.

Prayer for Strength in Oneness

Gracious Father, grant us the strength to be one flesh, deeply connected and united in our marriage. May our love be a testimony to Your design for the beauty of marital oneness. Amen.

January 2

Mark 10:8

"And they twain shall be one flesh: so then they are no more twain, but one flesh."

What Does This Mean For Us?

And they twain shall be one flesh. This reaffirms the divine design of marriage, where two individuals come together to form a deep, inseparable union. It encourages couples to embrace and celebrate the oneness that God intended for marriage.

So then they are no more twain, but one flesh. This emphasizes the transformation in marriage, where the individual identities of husband and wife are joined into a single, unified entity. It encourages couples to recognize and honor this transformation in their daily lives.

Modern Day Reflection

Where individualism and independence are often emphasized today, Mark 10:8 serves as a reminder of the beauty and strength found in the unity of marriage.

~

Prayer for Daily Recognition of Unity

Gracious God, as we navigate each day together, remind us that we are no longer two but one flesh. May our actions and decisions reflect the unity You have blessed us with. Amen.

January 3

Ecclesiastes 4:9

"Two are better than one because they have a good reward for their
labor."

What Does This Mean For Us?

Two are better than one. This highlights the idea that there is added value
and benefit in having a partner. In marriage, it speaks to the synergy that
comes from the collaboration of two individuals working together in
various aspects of life.

Because they have a good reward for their labor. This suggests that the
combined efforts of a married couple yield positive outcomes and
rewards. In life's challenges, having a supportive partner can enhance the
overall quality and satisfaction of the journey.

Modern Day Reflection

In today's world, where self-sufficiency is often emphasized, Ecclesiastes
4:9 encourages couples to recognize the strength and reward of their
partnership.

~

Prayer for Collaborative Strength

Heavenly Father, as we journey together in marriage, help us recognize
the strength of our partnership. May our combined efforts yield a good
reward, and may we always support and uplift each other. Amen.

January 4

Ephesians 4:3

"Endeavouring to keep the unity of the Spirit in the bond of peace."

What Does This Mean For Us?

Endeavoring to keep the unity of the Spirit. This highlights the active effort required to preserve and nurture the spiritual unity within a marriage. It encourages couples to intentionally work towards maintaining a connection that goes beyond the physical and emotional aspects, seeking unity in the spiritual realm.

In the bond of peace. The bond of peace signifies a harmonious and tranquil relationship. In the context of marriage, this suggests that unity is closely tied to a peaceful and harmonious coexistence where love and understanding prevail.

Modern Day Reflection

Where conflicts and distractions can strain relationships, Ephesians 4:3 encourages couples to prioritize spiritual unity and peace in their marriage.

～

Prayer for Harmony and Peace

Gracious God, as we navigate the journey of marriage, help us maintain a bond of peace. May our relationship be characterized by understanding, love, and the unity of Your Spirit. Amen.

January 5

Colossians 3:14
"And above all these things put on charity, which is the bond of perfectness."

What Does This Mean For Us?

And above all these things put on charity. In this context, Charity refers to love, not just any love, but selfless and unconditional love. The verse encourages individuals and couples to make love the overarching quality that encompasses and guides all other virtues and actions in their lives.

Which is the bond of perfectness. Love is described as the bond of perfectness, indicating that it can bring completeness and perfection to various aspects of life, including marriage. When love is the foundation, it binds individuals together in a way that transcends imperfections, creating a sense of unity and wholeness.

Modern Day Reflection

Today, relationships can face numerous challenges; Colossians 3:14 reminds couples to prioritize and cultivate a love that goes beyond surface-level feelings.

Prayer for Unconditional Love
Dear Lord, as we navigate the journey of marriage, help us prioritize love above all else. Let it be the bond that brings perfection and completeness to our relationship. May our love mirror Your perfect love. Amen.

January 6

1 Corinthians 1:10

"Now I beseech you, brethren, by the name of our Lord Jesus Christ, that ye all speak the same thing, and that there be no divisions among you; but that ye be perfectly joined together in the same mind and judgment."

What Does This Mean For Us?

Now I beseech you, brethren, by the name of our Lord Jesus Christ, that ye all speak the same thing. Paul begins with a plea, invoking the name of Jesus Christ as a source of authority and inspiration. The importance of unity and togetherness is highlighted through this invocation.

and that there be no divisions among you; but that ye be perfectly joined together in the same mind and judgment. Divisions can be detrimental to any relationship; here, the encouragement is to avoid divisions. The ultimate goal is perfect unity in mind and judgment. In the context of marriage, this encourages couples to share common values, goals, and perspectives, fostering a deep connection.

Modern Day Reflection

In today's world, where differences can create rifts, 1 Corinthians 1:10 encourages couples to work toward unity and active understanding.

Prayer for Shared Understanding

Lord Jesus, help us to be perfectly joined together in mind and judgment. May our shared values and perspectives strengthen the bond of our marriage. Guide us towards perfect unity. Amen.

January 7

Romans 12:16

"Be of the same mind one toward another. Mind not high things but condescend to men of low estate. Be not wise in your own conceits."

What Does This Mean For Us?

Be of the same mind one toward another. The emphasis on having a shared mindset encourages mutual understanding and agreement. In marriage, it suggests the importance of being on the same page, sharing common values, and aligning goals.

Mind not high things but condescend to men of low estate. This advises humility and avoiding pride. In the context of marriage, it encourages spouses to treat each other with humility, not seeking to elevate oneself above the other but embracing equality and understanding.

Be not wise in your own conceits. The caution against self-centered wisdom suggests the importance of listening and considering the perspectives of others. Marriage encourages openness and receptivity to each other's thoughts and ideas.

Modern Day Reflection

Where individualism can sometimes strain relationships, Romans 12:16 guides fostering a harmonious and understanding marriage.

~

Prayer for Humility And Understanding

Gracious God, help us be of the same mind toward one another, sharing common goals and values. Guide us in humility, and may our wisdom be rooted in understanding and love. Amen.

January 8

1 Peter 3:8

"Finally, be ye all of one mind, having compassion one of another, love as brethren, be pitiful, be courteous."

What Does This Mean For Us?

In the modern world, where relationships can face various challenges, 1 Peter 3:8 guides couples to build a foundation of unity, compassion, and courtesy.

Modern Day Reflection

In 1 Peter 3:8, the verse calls for a modern understanding of relationships within the Christian community, urging believers to be harmonious, sympathetic, compassionate, and humble. This verse emphasizes the importance of cultivating a community marked by empathy and unity, transcending differences and fostering an atmosphere of mutual support and understanding. In a contemporary context, 1 Peter 3:8 encourages individuals to approach their interactions with a spirit of kindness, acknowledging the diverse experiences and perspectives within the Christian community. It serves as a guiding principle for modern believers, urging them to build connections based on compassion and humility, creating a community where love and understanding prevail, despite the complexities of the world.

Prayer for Unity and Compassion

Gracious God, help us to be pitiful and courteous toward each other, fostering a spirit of understanding and respect. May our love be marked by consideration and kindness. Amen.

January 9

Philippians 2:2

"Fulfil ye my joy, that ye be likeminded, having the same love, being of
one accord, of one mind."

What Does This Mean For Us?

Fulfil ye my joy. The Apostle Paul expresses his joy in the unity and likemindedness of the Philippians. In marriage, this encourages couples to
find joy in their unity and shared purpose.

That ye be likeminded. Unity of mind is a recurring theme in the Bible
and is crucial in marriage. It emphasizes being on the same page, sharing
common values, and having mutual understanding.

Having the same love. Love is foundational in marriage. The call to have
the same love underscores the importance of a shared commitment to
love, respect, and care for each other.

Being of one accord, of one mind. These phrases reinforce the idea of
unity and harmony in marriage. Couples are encouraged to be in
agreement, not just in actions but also in the way they think and
approach life together.

Modern Day Reflection

In the modern world, where remaining single-minded is often
emphasized, Philippians 2:2 challenges couples to cultivate a shared
mindset and love that brings fulfillment and joy.

Prayer for Shared Love and Harmony

Gracious God, guide us to have the same love and be of one mind in our
marriage. May our unity and harmony reflect the joy that comes from
living in accordance with your Word. Amen.

<h1 style="text-align:center">January 10</h1>

Psalm 133:1

"Behold, how good and how pleasant it is for brethren to dwell together in unity!"

What Does This Mean For Us?

Behold, how good and how pleasant it is. The psalmist is drawing attention to the beauty and desirability of unity. In the context of marriage, this verse underscores the goodness and joy that come from a harmonious and unified relationship.

for brethren to dwell together in unity. While originally referring to brethren (brothers), the principle extends to any close relationship, including marriage. The idea is that living together in unity is not just beneficial but is also a source of goodness and pleasantness.

Modern Day Reflection

Relationships are always at risk of becoming fractured and can face various challenges; Psalm 133:1 encourages couples to recognize the inherent goodness and joy that come from dwelling together in unity within the sacred bond of marriage.

Prayer for Joyful Togetherness

Heavenly Father, as we navigate life together, grant us the grace to dwell in unity. May our marriage be a source of goodness and joy, bringing pleasantness to our journey. Amen.

January 11

Proverbs 17:1

"Better is a dry morsel, and quietness therewith, than a house full of
sacrifices with strife."

What Does This Mean For Us?

Better is a dry morsel, and quietness therewith. This part emphasizes the
value of peace and contentment over material abundance. It suggests
that having a simple and peaceful life, even if it means having little, is
better than a lavish lifestyle filled with conflict.

than a house full of sacrifices with strife. Despite having a house full of
offerings or sacrifices, the presence of strife or discord diminishes the
value of those sacrifices. It highlights the importance of harmony and
unity in the home, which is more valuable than outward displays of
religious observance.

Modern Day Reflection

In the context of marriage, this verse encourages couples to prioritize
peace and unity over material possessions or external displays. It speaks
to the richness of a relationship characterized by tranquility and
understanding.

Prayer for Harmony In Marriage

Heavenly Father, grant us the wisdom to cherish the quietness and
peace in our home. May our love be a source of richness, surpassing the
abundance of material possessions. Let our sacrifices be those of love
and understanding. Amen.

January 12

Proverbs 18:22

"Whoso findeth a wife findeth a good thing, and obtaineth favour of the Lord."

What Does This Mean For Us?

Whoso findeth a wife findeth a good thing. This part emphasizes the value and goodness of finding a wife. It implies that a marital relationship is a blessing and a source of goodness in one's life.

and obtaineth favour of the Lord. The verse suggests that finding a wife is not only a good thing in itself but also brings favor from the Lord. It underscores the divine approval and blessing that comes with a committed and loving marital relationship.

Modern Day Reflection

In the context of marriage, this verse encourages couples to see their union as a divine blessing and a source of goodness in their lives.

Prayer for Gratitude In Marriage

Gracious Lord, as we navigate the journey of marriage, grant us your favor and guidance. May our relationship be filled with the goodness that comes from your blessings. Help us build a marriage that reflects your love and grace. Amen.

January 13

Song of Solomon 6:3

"I am my beloved's, and my beloved is mine: he feedeth among the lilies.

What Does This Mean For Us?

I am my beloved's, and my beloved is mine. This expression of mutual ownership and belonging underscores the deep connection between the spouses. It reflects a sense of unity, commitment, and exclusivity in the marital relationship.

he feedeth among the lilies. The imagery of feeding among the lilies symbolizes a beautiful and nurturing environment. In the context of marriage, it suggests that the relationship is a source of sustenance, growth, and beauty.

Modern Day Reflection

In the contemporary world, this verse encourages couples to embrace the idea of mutual belonging and commitment, finding nourishment and beauty in their shared journey.

❧

Prayer for Beauty and Growth In Marriage

Loving God, we thank you for the unity we share as a couple. May our commitment to each other deepen, and may our relationship be a source of strength and nourishment. Please help us to cherish and care for the bond we have with you. Amen.

January 14

1 Corinthians 7:4

"The wife hath not power of her own body, but the husband: and likewise also the husband hath not power of his own body, but the wife.

What Does This Mean For Us?

This verse emphasizes the mutual ownership and shared responsibility within the marital relationship. It highlights that spouses are not independent entities but are intricately connected, both physically and emotionally. It underscores the importance of unity, mutual consideration, and the idea that the needs and desires of one spouse are not to be neglected by the other.

Modern Day Reflection

In today's world, this verse encourages couples to approach their marriage with a spirit of selflessness, recognizing the significance of prioritizing each other's needs and maintaining a balanced and mutual relationship.

Prayer for Shared Responsibilities In Marriage

Gracious God, help us to understand the depth of our connection in marriage. May we always consider each other's needs with love and selflessness. Guide us in maintaining a balance that reflects the unity and mutual respect You desire for our marriage. Amen.

January 15

1 Corinthians 11:3

"But I would have you know, that the head of every man is Christ; and the head of the woman is the man; and the head of Christ is God."

What Does This Mean For Us?

This verse delves into the concept of authority and submission, establishing a hierarchy where Christ is the head of every man, man is the head of the woman, and God is the head of Christ. In the context of marriage, it doesn't imply inferiority but emphasizes roles and responsibilities. It encourages a harmonious order and mutual respect within the marriage relationship.

Modern Day Reflection

1 Corinthians 11:3 encourages couples to recognize and appreciate their marriage's complementary roles. It promotes a partnership where both spouses work together, each contributing their unique strengths for the well-being of the marriage.

Prayer for Partnership and Harmony in Marriage
Dear Lord, as we navigate the journey of marriage, teach us to appreciate the strengths and contributions of each other. May our union be a testament to harmony and unity, where we complement and support one another for the greater good of our marriage. Amen..

January 16

Ephesians 5:21
"Submitting yourselves one to another in the fear of God."

What Does This Mean For Us?

This verse emphasizes mutual submission to the fear of God. In the context of marriage, it encourages both partners to yield to and consider each other willingly. It forms the foundation for a relationship built on humility, respect, and shared reverence for God.

Modern Day Reflection

In today's world, this verse encourages couples to foster a climate of mutual respect and cooperation. It discourages a power struggle within the marriage but promotes an environment where both spouses willingly serve and consider the needs of the other.

~

Prayer for Shared Reverence
Gracious Lord, teach us to submit to one another in love, respecting and considering each other's needs. May our marriage reflect Your divine design, where humility and mutual service strengthen our bond. Amen.

January 17

Ephesians 5:31
"For this cause shall a man leave his father and mother and shall be joined unto his wife, and they two shall be one flesh."

What Does This Mean For Us?

In the context of God's encouragement in marriage, this verse echoes the divine design for the unity and oneness of a husband and wife. It reflects the profound commitment and bond that marriage creates, emphasizing that spouses are to prioritize and cleave to each other.

Modern Day Reflection

Ephesians 5:31 encourages couples to recognize the significance of leaving the parental home to establish a new family unit. It emphasizes marriage's unity and intimacy, calling for a deep and exclusive connection between spouses.

Prayer for a Strong Foundation
Holy Jesus, as we embark on this journey of marriage, help us to leave behind all that hinders us and to submit to each other. May our marital union reflect the oneness You designed, filled with love, understanding, and unity. Amen.

January 18

Colossians 3:18-19

"Wives, submit yourselves unto your own husbands, as it is fit in the Lord. Husbands, love your wives and be not bitter against them."

What Does This Mean For Us?

In the context of God's encouragement in marriage, these verses provide guidance for the roles of spouses. It emphasizes the importance of mutual respect, submission, and love within the marital relationship.

Modern Day Reflection

Colossians 3:18-19 encourages a balance of responsibilities and a foundation of love and respect in marriage. The call for wives to submit is not about inferiority but about mutual understanding and respect within the framework of God's design. Husbands are called to love their wives selflessly, without bitterness, fostering a relationship built on God's principles.

Prayer for Harmony In Marriage

Loving God, grant us the strength to love without reservation or bitterness. May our marriage be a testament to the sacrificial love Christ has shown us, fostering a bond that withstands the test of time. Amen.

January 19

Proverbs 31:12
"She will do him good and not evil all the days of her life."

What Does This Mean For Us?

This verse, often referring to the virtuous wife, underscores the idea of consistently doing good to one's spouse throughout their life. It encourages a continuous and intentional effort to treat each other with kindness and goodness in marriage.

Modern Day Reflection

In the context of treating your spouse well, Proverbs 31:12 challenges us to adopt a daily commitment to the well-being and goodness of our partner. This verse inspires couples to prioritize acts of kindness, support consistently, and love throughout their shared journey. It calls for a modern-day reflection on the importance of intentional and enduring efforts to bring joy, encouragement, and positive influence into each other's lives, fostering a relationship built on continuous goodwill and love.

Prayer for Mutual Honor In Marriage

Heavenly Father, We come before you with gratitude for the love that binds us together. Bless our union, Lord, and grant us the wisdom to navigate the complexities of life as a couple. May our actions and words reflect our love and respect for each other. Help us to treat one another with kindness, understanding, and patience. Lord, grant us the strength to face challenges hand in hand and the humility to seek forgiveness when needed. In Your name, we pray. Amen.

January 20

1 Corinthians 12:25
"That there should be no schism in the body; but that the members
should have the same care one for another."

What Does This Mean For Us?

In 1 Corinthians 12:25, Paul emphasizes the idea of unity within the body of Christ, suggesting that there should be no division among its members, but rather mutual care and concern for one another.

Modern Day Reflection

God provides much encouragement in our marriage, and it's wholly apparent in this verse which emphasizes the idea of unity and care within the body, which can be extended to the unity of a married couple. It encourages a harmonious relationship where both partners care deeply for each other, fostering a sense of togetherness and oneness.

Prayer for Mutual Support In Marriage
Heavenly Father, grant us the grace to support and care for one another
in our marriage. May our relationship be free from division and always
be mindful of each other's needs. Amen.

January 21

Romans 15:5-6

"Now the God of patience and consolation grant you to be likeminded one toward another according to Christ Jesus: That ye may with one mind and one mouth glorify God, even the Father of our Lord Jesus Christ."

What Does This Mean For Us?

This passage from Romans 15:5-6 encourages people to be united in their thoughts and attitudes, following the example of Christ. The prayer is for harmony and agreement among followers of Jesus so that, with a shared purpose and voice, they can give glory to God, the Father of their Lord Jesus Christ. It emphasizes the importance of unity in worship and service.

Modern Day Reflection

In the context of God's encouragement in marriage, these verses underscore the importance of unity and harmony between partners. The call to be "likeminded" encourages mutual understanding and agreement, aligning thoughts and actions according to the example set by Christ. The ultimate purpose is to glorify God with a unified heart and voice.

Prayer for Mutual Agreement In Marriage

Gracious Father, grant us the patience and consolation to be likeminded in our marriage. May our thoughts and actions align with the love and grace of Christ, glorifying You in unity. Amen.

January 22

Galatians 3:28

"There is neither Jew nor Greek, there is neither bond nor free, there is neither male nor female: for ye are all one in Christ Jesus."

What Does This Mean For Us?

In the context of God's encouragement in marriage, this verse emphasizes the equality and oneness of individuals in Christ. It dismisses distinctions based on ethnicity, social status, or gender, affirming that all believers are united in Christ.

Modern Day Reflection

For a couple, this verse encourages mutual respect, acknowledging that in Christ, there are no hierarchies that diminish the worth or role of either partner.

~

Prayer for Mutual Respect In Marriage
Dear Lord, Thank You for making us one in Christ, transcending worldly distinctions. May we honor and respect each other as equal partners in Your love. Amen.

January 23

Philippians 4:2
"I beseech Euodias, and beseech Syntyche, that they be of the same mind in the Lord."

What Does This Mean For Us?

In the context of God's encouragement in marriage, this verse underscores the importance of unity and shared purpose within the community of believers. In a marital context, it encourages spouses to strive for harmony, especially when faced with disagreements or differences of opinion.

Modern Day Reflection

For a couple, this verse prompts them to seek common ground and understanding, fostering an environment of peace and oneness within their marriage.

~

Prayer for Unity In Marriage
Loving God, we pray that you will help us find common ground and understanding in our marriage, just as you helped Euodias and Syntyche. Let Your peace reign in our hearts and home. Amen.

January 24

Colossians 2:2-3

"That their hearts might be comforted, being knit together in love, and unto all riches of the full assurance of understanding, to the acknowledgment of the mystery of God, and of the Father, and of Christ; In whom are hid all the treasures of wisdom and knowledge."

What Does This Mean For Us?

In the context of God's encouragement in marriage, these verses emphasize the importance of unity, love, and a shared understanding in the couple's hearts. The "mystery of God" refers to the depth and richness of God's plan, which includes the bond and partnership between a husband and wife.

Modern Day Reflection

This passage encourages couples to find comfort in their shared love and to seek a deep understanding of each other and God's purpose for their marriage.

~

Prayer for Wisdom and Knowledge in Marriage

Gracious Father knit our hearts together in love and guide us to the riches of understanding in Your plan for our marriage. May we find comfort in the mystery of Your love. Amen.

January 25

Colossians 2:19

"And not holding the Head, from which all the body by joints and bands having nourishment ministered, and knit together, increaseth with the increase of God."

What Does This Mean For Us?

In the context of God's encouragement in marriage, this verse underscores the importance of staying connected to Christ, the head of the body (the Church). Just as a body is nourished and grows through its joints and organs, a marriage thrives when rooted in a connection with Christ.

Modern Day Reflection

Colossians 2:19 encourages married couples to keep Christ at the center of their marriage. By doing so, they can experience growth and increase, not just in worldly terms, but in ways that align with God's design for their relationship.

Prayer for Spiritual Growth in Marriage

Heavenly Father, help us stay connected to Christ, the head of our marriage. May our union be a reflection of Your design, continually growing and increasing in the ways that honor You. Amen.

January 26

1 Peter 4:8
"And above all things have fervent charity among yourselves: for charity shall cover the multitude of sins."

What Does This Mean For Us?

In the context of God's encouragement in marriage, this verse emphasizes the importance of fervent love (charity) within the relationship. Love has the power to cover a multitude of sins, suggesting that a strong foundation of love can overcome challenges and imperfections in a marriage.

Modern Day Reflection

This passage encourages couples to dig deep within themselves to prioritize and cultivate a deep, selfless love for each other. It's a reminder that love, when practiced with sincerity and dedication, can be a unifying force that helps overcome the inevitable shortcomings in any relationship.

Prayer for Fervent Love in Marriage
Gracious Father, instill in us a fervent love, one that covers and forgives. May our charity towards each other be a reflection of Your enduring love, overcoming any challenges we may face. Amen.

January 27

John 17:23

"I in them, and thou in me, that they may be made perfect in one; and that the world may know that thou hast sent me, and hast loved them, as thou hast loved me."

What Does This Mean For Us?

In the context of God's encouragement in marriage, this verse highlights the concept of unity and oneness. The idea of Christ being in believers and believers being in Him emphasizes a profound unity. For a married couple, this unity can serve as a reflection of the divine unity, expressing the profound connection between spouses.

Modern Day Reflection

This verse encourages a couple to strive for a unity that goes beyond the physical and emotional realms, seeking a spiritual oneness that mirrors the unity between Christ and believers. The love shared between a couple should be a testimony to the world of the divine love that unites them.

Prayer for Divine Love in Marriage

Heavenly Father, as You abide in us, help us to abide in each other. Let our love be a beacon of Your love, showing the world the unity and perfect love that comes from You. Amen.

January 28

Romans 12:5

"So we, being many, are one body in Christ, and every one members one of another."

What Does This Mean For Us?

In the context of God's encouragement in marriage, this verse underscores the concept of unity within the body of believers, symbolized as one body in Christ. Applied to marriage, it implies that a husband and wife, as believers, are interconnected members of a spiritual union. The emphasis is on the mutual dependence and support that each partner provides to the other.

Modern Day Reflection

Today, this verse encourages a married couple to recognize and embrace their interdependence. It suggests that the strength of their union lies in their shared commitment to Christ and in their willingness to be supportive members of one another's lives.

Prayer for Spiritual Unity in Marriage

Heavenly Father bind us together as one body in Christ. May our marriage be a testament to the oneness we share in You, supporting and encouraging each other as interconnected members of a divine union.
Amen.

January 29

1 Corinthians 10:17

"For we being many are one bread, and one body: for we are all partakers of that one bread."

What Does This Mean For Us?

1 Corinthians 10:17 underscores the unity of believers through communion. The verse emphasizes that though many individuals partake, they become one body in Christ through the shared bread. This symbolic act represents Christians' collective unity and oneness in the Body of Christ. The communion is not merely a ritual but a profound expression of the believers' shared identity and fellowship with Christ and each other.

Modern Day Reflection

In today's world, this verse encourages a married couple to recognize the sacred unity in their relationship. It speaks to the idea that, like partaking in one bread symbolizes shared spiritual sustenance among believers, the marriage bond represents a shared life, purpose, and spiritual journey.

Prayer for Shared Spiritual Journey in Marriage

Gracious Lord, bind us together as one body in our marriage. May our union be a testament to the shared spiritual sustenance we find in You, journeying together as partakers of the same bread. Amen.

January 30

1 Corinthians 12:12

"For as the body is one, and hath many members, and all the members of that one body, being many, are one body: so also is Christ."

What Does This Mean For Us?

We welcome the constant encouragement of God in marriage, and this verse draws a powerful analogy between the unity of believers in the body of Christ and the unity of a married couple. It emphasizes the diversity of gifts and roles within the body, highlighting that though individuals may have distinct roles, they are still part of one unified body. Applied to marriage, it suggests that a husband and wife, with their unique qualities and roles, form a unified entity—a singular body in Christ.

Modern Day Reflection

In today's world, this verse encourages a married couple to appreciate and celebrate their differences, recognizing that each partner contributes unique gifts and strengths to the marriage. It invites them to view their union as a reflection of the diverse yet unified body of Christ.

Prayer for Mutual Contribution in Marriage

Gracious God, thank you for the unique gifts and roles we bring to our marriage. May we, as one body, shine forth the richness of Christ in our union. Amen.

January 31

Ephesians 2:14-15

"For he is our peace, who hath made both one, and hath broken down the middle wall of partition between us; Having abolished in his flesh the enmity, even the law of commandments contained in ordinances; for to make in himself of twain one new man, so making peace."

What Does This Mean For Us?

As we continually welcome God's encouragement in marriage, this verse beautifully illustrates Christ as the source of unity and peace. The imagery of breaking down walls and making two into one speaks directly to the idea of unity in marriage. It suggests that Christ's work reconciles differences and brings about a new creation—a unified entity.

Modern Day Reflection

Applied to marriage, this verse encourages a couple to recognize Christ as the foundation of their unity. It calls them to break down any metaphorical walls that may divide them and embrace the oneness that Christ desires for them.

Prayer for Oneness With Christ in Marriage

Gracious Lord, in your name, we seek unity. Make us a new creation in our marriage, founded on the peace that comes from Christ. Let your love bind us together as one. Amen.

AS WINTER BEGINS TO WANE AND NATURE AWAKENS, MAY OUR HEARTS ALSO STIR WITH A RENEWED SENSE OF HOPE AND LOVE. IN THIS MONTH OF TRANSITION, LET US EMBRACE THE WARMTH OF COMPASSION, AND MAY THE BLOSSOMING OF OUR SPIRITS MIRROR THE UNFOLDING BEAUTY OF THE WORLD AROUND US. MAY FEBRUARY BE A TIME OF DEEPENING CONNECTIONS, BOTH WITH OTHERS AND WITH THE DIVINE, AS WE JOURNEY FORWARD WITH GRACE AND GRATITUDE.

February 1

Ephesians 2:19-22

"Now therefore ye are no more strangers and foreigners, but fellowcitizens with the saints, and of the household of God; And are built upon the foundation of the apostles and prophets, Jesus Christ himself being the chief corner stone; In whom all the building fitly framed together groweth unto an holy temple in the Lord: In whom ye also are builded together for an habitation of God through the Spirit."

What Does This Mean For Us?

In the context of God's encouragement in marriage, this passage emphasizes the idea of believers as part of God's household, built upon a foundation with Christ as the cornerstone. The imagery of a building highlights the idea that the couple, as fellow citizens in the household of God, is being constructed into a holy temple. This suggests a divine partnership, where God is intricately involved in building and dwelling within the marriage.

Modern Day Reflection

Applied to marriage, this verse encourages the couple to see their union as a sacred dwelling place for God. The emphasis on being "fitly framed together" underscores the importance of unity and cooperation in the marital relationship.

≈

Prayer For Unity and Cooperation in Marriage

Heavenly Father, In our journey together, make us fitly framed, united in love and purpose. Let our marriage be a habitation for your presence. Amen.

February 2

Ephesians 4:13

"Till we all come in the unity of the faith, and of the knowledge of the Son of God, unto a perfect man, unto the measure of the stature of the fulness of Christ.

What Does This Mean For Us?

In the context of God's encouragement in marriage, this verse speaks about the journey toward spiritual maturity and unity in the faith. It suggests that individuals, including a married couple, are on a path of growth and development, aiming to attain the fullness of Christ's stature.

Modern Day Reflection

Applied to marriage, this verse encourages the couple to seek spiritual unity and maturity together. The aspiration is not only for individual growth but for a shared journey toward a deeper understanding of the faith and the likeness of Christ.

Prayer For Spiritual Unity in Marriage

Gracious Lord, as we walk this journey of faith together, grant us unity and understanding. May our marriage reflect the fullness of Christ's love. Amen.

February 3

Philippians 1:27

"Only let your conversation be as it becometh the gospel of Christ: that whether I come and see you, or else be absent, I may hear of your affairs, that ye stand fast in one spirit, with one mind striving together for the faith of the gospel."

What Does This Mean For Us?

In the context of God's encouragement in marriage, this verse encourages a couple to align their lives with the principles of the Gospel. The call to "stand fast in one spirit, with one mind striving together" implies a unity of purpose and effort. For a married couple, this could mean jointly pursuing a life that reflects the values and teachings of the Gospel.

Modern Day Reflection

Philippians 1:27 advises believers to conduct themselves in a manner worthy of the gospel of Christ, emphasizing unity, steadfastness, and collaboration in spreading the message of faith. In a modern context, it encourages individuals to live in a way that reflects the principles and teachings of their beliefs, fostering a sense of community and resilience amidst challenges. It prompts believers to be a positive influence on the world around them, promoting unity and embodying the values they hold dear.

Prayer For Shared Pursuit of Faith in Marriage

As a couple, we strive together for the faith of the gospel. Guide us in unity of mind and spirit as we navigate this journey of marriage. Amen.

February 4

Philippians 2:1-4

"If there be therefore any consolation in Christ, if any comfort of love, if any fellowship of the Spirit, if any bowels and mercies, Fulfil ye my joy, that ye be likeminded, having the same love, being of one accord, of one mind. Let nothing be done through strife or vainglory; but in lowliness of mind let each esteem other better than themselves. Look not every man on his own things, but every man also on the things of others".

What Does This Mean For Us?

In this passage, Paul encourages believers to embody the spirit of Christ in their relationships. It underscores the importance of unity, selflessness, and humility within the Christian community, values that are equally applicable to marital relationships.

Modern Day Reflection

In the context of marriage, the call for "likemindedness" emphasizes the need for a shared vision and purpose. Couples are encouraged to operate with a collective mindset, fostering mutual understanding and agreement. The injunction to "esteem other better than themselves" echoes the selflessness required in marriage, where each partner prioritizes the well-being and happiness of the other.

Prayer For Consolation in Marriage

As this couple continues on the journey of marriage, may they find consolation in Christ, comfort in love, and fellowship in the Spirit. Grant them the grace to be likeminded, united in love and purpose.

Amen.

<h1 style="text-align:center">February 5</h1>

Ephesians 5:33

"Nevertheless let every one of you in particular so love his wife even as himself; and the wife see that she reverence her husband."

What Does This Mean For Us?

In this verse, Paul provides a concise yet profound summary of the roles and dynamics within a Christian marriage. The emphasis is on love and reverence, highlighting the reciprocal nature of the marital relationship.

Modern Day Reflection

In a contemporary context, this verse encourages couples to foster a relationship built on love, mutual respect, and understanding. For husbands, it underscores the importance of selfless love, active listening, and a commitment to the growth and happiness of their wives. For wives, it emphasizes the significance of recognizing and appreciating the roles and efforts of their husbands.

Prayer For Blessings in Marriage

Gracious God, we ask for your continued blessings to strengthen our marriage. Bless us with a love that knows no bounds. May our love be a source of security and warmth for each other, and may our lives bring honor and strength to our union. In our journey together, let us continually seek your guidance and grace. Amen.

February 6

1 Peter 3:7
"Likewise, ye husbands, dwell with them according to knowledge,
giving honor unto the wife, as unto the weaker vessel, and as being heirs
together of the grace of life; that your prayers be not hindered."

What Does This Mean For Us?

In this verse, Peter guides husbands, urging them to understand and
honor their wives. It emphasizes the shared inheritance of God's grace
and the importance of treating each other with respect and
consideration.

Modern Day Reflection

This verse encourages couples to cultivate understanding, respect, and
equality in their marriage. It emphasizes that, despite differences, both
partners are valuable in God's eyes and should be honored as such. The
linkage between marital harmony and prayer underscores the spiritual
interconnectedness of the couple.

❧

Prayer For Respect in Marriage
Lord God, please bless our marriage founded on mutual understanding
and respect. May our relationship be a reflection of the unity and
equality we desire for our children. As we journey together, may our
prayers rise before you unhindered. Amen.

February 7

Colossians 3:19

"Husbands, love your wives, and be not bitter against them."

What Does This Mean For Us?

This verse from Colossians is a concise yet powerful directive to husbands, urging them to love their wives and avoid harboring bitterness towards them.

Modern Day Reflection

In the context of contemporary marriages, this verse remains profoundly relevant. It calls for a love that goes beyond mere sentiment, one that actively seeks the well-being and flourishing of the spouse. The warning against bitterness underscores the importance of addressing conflicts with grace and forgiveness.

Prayer For Reconciliation in Marriage

Dear Lord, bless our marriage with a patient, kind, and enduring love. May we each be a source of support and understanding to each other, and may forgiveness and reconciliation characterize our relationship.
Amen.

February 8

1 Corinthians 7:3-4

"Let the husband render unto the wife due benevolence: and likewise also the wife unto the husband. The wife hath not power of her own body, but the husband: and likewise also the husband hath not power of his own body, but the wife."

What Does This Mean For Us?

This passage addresses the mutual responsibility and intimacy within the marital relationship. It emphasizes the concept of conjugal rights and the interconnectedness of spouses.

Modern Day Reflection

In the contemporary context, this passage encourages couples to approach physical intimacy with respect, communication, and a genuine desire to meet each other's needs. It emphasizes the idea that a healthy marital relationship involves a mutual exchange of love, care, and physical intimacy.

Prayer For Intimacy in Marriage

Gracious God, we pray that we may always approach each other with love and benevolence in our physical intimacy. May our union be a reflection of the deep connection you desire for us. Amen.

February 9

Philippians 2:3
"Let nothing be done through strife or vainglory; but in lowliness of mind let each esteem other better than themselves."

What Does This Mean For Us?

This verse from Philippians calls for humility and selflessness in all actions, urging believers to prioritize others above themselves. It sets a foundation for understanding and practicing genuine love and consideration, values that are equally relevant in marriage.

Modern Day Reflection

In the context of marriage, this verse encourages spouses to approach their relationship with humility, avoiding conflicts rooted in selfishness or a desire for personal recognition. It promotes a mindset where each partner considers the needs and feelings of the other as more significant than their own.

Prayer For Humility in Marriage
Gracious God, as we continue to navigate the journey of marriage, please continue to instill the spirit of humility in us. May we continually strive to esteem each other higher than ourselves, fostering a love that reflects our selfless nature. Amen.

February 10

Romans 12:10

"Be kindly affectioned one to another with brotherly love; in honour preferring one another."

What Does This Mean For Us?

Romans 12:10 advocates for a relationship characterized by affectionate love and mutual honor. It calls spouses to prioritize each other, demonstrating a deep and sincere love that goes beyond mere obligation.

Modern Day Reflection

In a world often marked by busyness and individual pursuits, this biblical principle challenges couples to intentionally show affection and prioritize their spouse. It's a call to create a marriage where each partner feels valued, cherished, and honored.

Prayer For Selfless Love in Marriage
Heavenly Father, as a couple, we walk through the journey of marriage. May our love be marked by kindness and genuine affection. Help us both to honor and prefer one another, and continue to build a relationship that reflects the beauty of selfless love. Amen.

February 11

1 Thessalonians 5:11

"Wherefore comfort yourselves together, and edify one another, even as also ye do."

What Does This Mean For Us?

This verse encourages believers to find comfort and build each other up. The context of mutual support and encouragement is a valuable principle that can be applied to marriage.

Modern Day Reflection

In a world filled with challenges and uncertainties, this biblical principle speaks to the importance of creating a home where spouses find solace and encouragement in one another. It's a call for couples to be each other's biggest supporters and builders.

~

Prayer For Strength in Marriage

Heavenly Father, grant us as a couple the ability to find comfort in each other's presence. May our marriage be a source of strength and encouragement, and may we build each other up in love. Amen.

February 12

Galatians 5:13

"For, brethren, ye have been called unto liberty; only use not liberty for
an occasion to the flesh, but by love serve one another."

What Does This Mean For Us?

This verse emphasizes the idea of freedom in Christ but cautions against
using that freedom for selfish desires. Instead, believers are encouraged
to serve one another in love. In the context of marriage, Galatians 5:13
suggests that the freedom and liberty experienced in Christ should be
expressed through selfless service and love within the marital
relationship. It promotes an atmosphere where both partners willingly
serve and prioritize each other's well-being.

Modern Day Reflection

In a world that often emphasizes individual rights and freedoms, this
biblical principle challenges couples to channel their freedom into acts
of love and service within their marriage. It invites them to embrace a
selfless approach to building a strong and healthy relationship.

Prayer For Inspiration in Marriage

Loving God as we walk our marriage journey, please continue to inspire
us to serve each other with genuine love and humility. May our
relationship be a reflection of the freedom found in Christ. Amen.

February 13

James 3:17

"But the wisdom that is from above is first pure, then peaceable, gentle, and easy to be entreated, full of mercy and good fruits, without partiality, and without hypocrisy."

What Does This Mean For Us?

This verse describes the characteristics of divine wisdom, highlighting its purity, peaceful nature, gentleness, approachability, mercy, goodness, impartiality, and sincerity. James 3:17 encourages couples to seek and apply God's wisdom in their relationship. It sets a standard for the qualities that should characterize their interactions—purity, peace, gentleness, and sincerity.

Modern Day Reflection

In a world often marked by conflicts and challenges in relationships, this verse guides couples to approach their marriage with divine wisdom. It calls for a relationship built on purity, understanding, and a genuine desire for each other's well-being.

Prayer For Wisdom in Marriage

Loving God, As we navigate the journey of marriage, fill our hearts with the divine wisdom described in James 3:17. May our relationship reflect the peace, gentleness, and sincerity that come from seeking your guidance. Amen.

February 14

Proverbs 15:1

"A soft answer turneth away wrath: but grievous words stir up anger."

What Does This Mean For Us?

This proverb emphasizes the power of gentle and kind words in diffusing conflicts. It contrasts the positive impact of a calm response with the destructive nature of harsh and grievous words. Today, Proverbs 15:1 advises couples to respond to each other with gentleness and understanding. It highlights the potential for soft words to de-escalate conflicts and prevent the stirring up of anger.

Modern Day Reflection

In a world where communication can be strained, especially in the intensity of marital disagreements, this verse serves as a guide for couples. It encourages them to choose their words carefully, opting for kindness and understanding even in challenging moments.

Prayer For Disagreement and Peace in Marriage

Gracious God, grant us the grace to respond with soft words in times of disagreement. May our communication be infused with kindness and understanding, turning away wrath and fostering peace. Amen.

February 15

Proverbs 31:11

"The heart of her husband doth safely trust in her, so that he shall have no need of spoil."

What Does This Mean For Us?

This verse from the famous Proverbs 31 describes the virtuous woman. The heart of her husband safely trusts in her, indicating a deep sense of security and confidence in her character and actions. Proverbs 31:11 encourages trust as a foundation. It speaks to the security and confidence a spouse should have in their partner, creating a relationship built on mutual respect and reliance.

Modern Day Reflection

In the complexities of modern relationships, trust remains a cornerstone. This verse prompts couples to cultivate a relationship where trust is nurtured and maintained, fostering a sense of safety and security.

Prayer For Trust in Marriage

Heavenly Father, as we journey through the highs and lows of marriage, instill in us the value of trust. May our relationship be a testament to the security found in mutual reliance. Amen.

February 16

Matthew 7:12

"Therefore all things whatsoever ye would that men should do to you,
do ye even so to them: for this is the law and the prophets."

What Does This Mean For Us?

Commonly known as the Golden Rule, this verse encourages treating others as you would like to be treated. It emphasizes the principles of reciprocity and kindness. In the marital context, this principle underscores the importance of mutual respect, understanding, and consideration. It suggests that the way you treat your spouse should reflect the kindness and consideration you desire in return.

Modern Day Reflection

Applying the Golden Rule in marriage fosters an environment of love and empathy. It encourages spouses to be mindful of each other's needs, promoting a harmonious relationship.

Prayer For the Golden Rule in Marriage

Loving God, help us as a couple to embody the spirit of Matthew 7:12 in our marriage. May our actions be rooted in love, creating a bond built on mutual understanding and consideration. Amen.

February 17

Ephesians 4:2
"With all lowliness and meekness, with longsuffering, forbearing one another in love."

What Does This Mean For Us?

This verse highlights the virtues of humility, gentleness, patience, and the ability to endure with love. It encourages believers to maintain unity through these qualities. In the context of marriage, Ephesians 4:2 encourages spouses to approach their relationship with humility, gentleness, and patience. It promotes a culture of understanding, forgiveness, and enduring love within the marital bond.

Modern Day Reflection

In a world often marked by haste and impatience, embodying the spirit of Ephesians 4:2 can strengthen a marriage. It suggests that, in the face of challenges, spouses should exercise patience, bear with each other's imperfections, and navigate difficulties with love.

Prayer For Virtue in Marriage
Gracious Father, bless us as a couple with the virtues of humility, gentleness, and patience. May our love endure, and may we navigate the challenges of marriage with a spirit of forbearance. Amen.

February 18

1 Corinthians 10:24

"Let no man seek his own, but every man another's wealth."

What Does This Mean For Us?

This verse encourages selflessness and a focus on the well-being of others. In the context of marriage, it advises against selfishness and emphasizes the importance of considering one another's needs and happiness.

Modern Day Reflection

In a marital context, this verse encourages spouses to prioritize each other's welfare, fostering a relationship built on mutual respect and care. Rather than focusing solely on personal desires, couples can embrace a selfless attitude, striving to enhance each other's lives. For example, making decisions with the partner's best interest in mind, actively listening to each other's concerns, and being supportive in times of need can contribute to a stronger and more respectful marriage.

Prayer For Selflessness in Marriage

Heavenly Father, we approach you, inspired by the selflessness in 1 Corinthians 10:24. Guide us in our marriage to seek each other's well-being, placing the needs of our partner above our own. May our love be characterized by compassion, understanding, and mutual respect.
Amen.

February 19

Romans 13:10

"Love does no harm to a neighbor. Therefore love is the fulfillment of the law."

What Does This Mean For Us?

This verse underscores the importance of love and highlights that true love involves avoiding harm and prioritizing the well-being of others.

Modern Day Reflection

Romans 13:10 encourages spouses to cultivate a love that goes beyond mere sentiment and encompasses actions that promote the happiness and welfare of their partner. It advises against actions that might cause harm, emphasizing the fulfillment of the law through love. In practical terms, this can mean respecting boundaries, communicating with kindness, and making choices that contribute positively to the relationship.

$\sim$

Prayer For Cultivation of Love in Marriage

Eternal God, we humbly gather in reflection on Romans 13:10, recognizing the transformative power of love. May our actions in our marriage align with a love that does no harm, fulfilling the spirit of your law. Grant us the wisdom to navigate challenges with kindness and understanding. Amen.

February 20

1 Corinthians 13:4-5

"Charity suffereth long, and is kind; charity envieth not; charity vaunteth not itself, is not puffed up, Doth not behave itself unseemly, seeketh not her own, is not easily provoked, thinketh no evil;"

What Does This Mean For Us?

This iconic passage on love emphasizes patience, kindness, humility, and forgiveness.

Modern Day Reflection

These verses encourage spouses to embody a love that goes beyond mere feelings and involves active, selfless behavior. Couples can apply this wisdom by practicing patience during challenging times, showing kindness in their interactions, and letting go of resentment. By embracing these qualities, a marriage can flourish with mutual respect and understanding.

Prayer For Honor in Marriage

Eternal God, as we reflect on 1 Corinthians 13:4-5, we are reminded of the transformative nature of love. Grant us the strength to be patient and kind, to set aside envy and pride. May our actions reflect a love that honors and seeks the best for one another, free from anger and grudges. Amen.

February 21

Colossians 4:6

"Let your speech be always with grace, seasoned with salt, that ye may know how ye ought to answer every man."

What Does This Mean For Us?

This verse encourages believers to communicate with grace and wisdom, ensuring their words are both thoughtful and impactful.

Modern Day Reflection

In relation to marriage, this verse underscores the importance of respectful and considerate communication between spouses. By approaching conversations with grace and seasoning them with wisdom, couples can navigate challenges and disagreements in a way that fosters understanding and mutual respect.

Prayer For Conversation in Marriage

Heavenly Father, we come before you, inspired by the wisdom in Colossians 4:6. May our conversations be filled with grace, seasoned with the wisdom that comes from your Word. Guide us in our communication, that we may answer each other with love and understanding. Amen.

February 22

Hebrews 13:4

"Marriage is honourable in all, and the bed undefiled: but
whoremongers and adulterers God will judge."

What Does This Mean For Us?

This verse emphasizes the sanctity of marriage and the importance of
keeping the marital relationship pure and free from any form of
infidelity or impurity.

Modern Day Reflection

Hebrews 13:4 encourages couples to honor the sacred covenant of
marriage, fostering an environment of trust, fidelity, and mutual respect.
By upholding these values, couples can strengthen their bond and create
a foundation of love and commitment.

~

Prayer For Purity in Marriage

Heavenly Father, we come before you, inspired by the wisdom in
Hebrews 13:4. Grant us the strength to honor the sanctity of our
marriage, keeping our commitment pure and free from any harm. May
your love guide us in maintaining a relationship built on trust and
fidelity. Amen.

February 23

Philippians 4:5

"Let your moderation be known unto all men. The Lord is at hand."

What Does This Mean For Us?

This verse encourages individuals to demonstrate gentleness in their interactions with others, promoting a spirit of kindness and consideration. In the context of marriage, it calls for spouses to treat each other with gentleness, fostering an environment of mutual respect and understanding.

Modern Day Reflection

In strengthening the bond of marriage, Philippians 4:5 can guide couples to prioritize gentleness in their communication and actions. By being mindful of each other's feelings and perspectives, spouses can strengthen their connection and build a foundation of respect. In today's world, where external pressures can be challenging, practicing gentleness within the marriage helps create a supportive and harmonious relationship.

∽

Prayer For Gentleness in Marriage

Eternal God, as we reflect on Philippians 4:5, we seek your guidance in cultivating gentleness in our marriage. Help us treat each other with kindness, knowing that your presence is near. Amen.

February 24

Romans 15:7

"Wherefore receive ye one another, as Christ also received us to the glory of God."

What Does This Mean For Us?

This verse emphasizes the importance of mutual respect and acceptance. Just as Christ welcomed us despite our imperfections, the spouses should embrace each other, recognizing and appreciating their unique qualities. This verse encourages a loving and understanding attitude, fostering an environment where both partners feel accepted and valued.

Modern Day Reflection

In today's fast-paced world, it's easy to overlook each other's strengths and weaknesses. Embracing the spirit of this verse can strengthen the marital bond by promoting empathy and creating a foundation of love and respect. Remember that a healthy marriage requires acknowledging and celebrating each other's differences, just as Christ embraced us.

Prayer For Mutual Respect in Marriage

Dear Heavenly Father, grant us the wisdom to receive and accept one another in our marriage, just as you have welcomed us. Help us to cherish the uniqueness in our partner and to build a foundation of love and respect. May our home be a reflection of your glory, filled with understanding and compassion. In Jesus' name, we pray. Amen.

February 25

1 Corinthians 8:9

"But take heed lest by any means this liberty of yours become a stumbling block to them that are weak."

What Does This Mean For Us?

In the context of marriage, this verse advises exercising caution in our choices, especially when exercising our freedom in the relationship. It encourages spouses to be mindful of how their actions and decisions may affect their partner. For a couple seeking to strengthen their marriage, this verse emphasizes the importance of considering each other's feelings, vulnerabilities, and individual needs.

Modern Day Reflection

In a world where personal freedom is often celebrated, it reminds us that true strength in a marriage comes from a mutual understanding and respect for each other's sensitivities and boundaries.

Prayer For Mindfulness in Marriage

Dear Heavenly Father, help us navigate the complexities of our marriage with wisdom and love. May our actions and choices not become stumbling blocks for each other but rather be a source of support and encouragement. Grant us the grace to honor and respect each other's vulnerabilities, fostering a bond that reflects your love. In Jesus' name, we pray. Amen.

February 26

Leviticus 27:30

"And all the tithe of the land, whether of the seed of the land, or of the fruit of the tree, is the Lord's: it is holy unto the Lord."

What Does This Mean For Us?

In marriage, this verse highlights the sanctity of shared resources. Just as the tithe is dedicated to the Lord, a portion of our joint earnings should be consecrated to the well-being of our marriage and the service of others.

Modern Day Reflection

Leviticus 27:30 encourages couples to approach financial decisions holistically, recognizing that their partnership involves not just the practical aspects of budgeting but a spiritual commitment to each other and the greater good.

Prayer For Good Stewardship in Marriage

Heavenly Father, help us see our shared finances as sacred. May our use of resources reflect our commitment to You and strengthen the bond of love in our marriage. Guide us in stewarding our joint blessings for Your glory. Amen.

February 27

Colossians 3:13

"Forbearing one another, and forgiving one another, if any man have a quarrel against any: even as Christ forgave you, so also do ye."

What Does This Mean For Us?

In the context of marriage, this verse underscores the importance of forbearance and forgiveness. It encourages spouses to be patient and understanding with each other, acknowledging that conflicts may arise. Drawing parallels to Christ's forgiveness, it emphasizes the need for a compassionate and forgiving spirit within the marriage.

Modern Day Reflection

Today, where relationships are often tested by various stressors, this verse reminds couples that forgiveness is a cornerstone for a healthy and resilient marriage. By extending the same grace that Christ showed us, spouses can overcome challenges and build a foundation of mutual respect and understanding.

Prayer For Compassion in Marriage

"Gracious God, teach us the art of forbearance and forgiveness in our marriage, mirroring the compassion Christ showed us. Help us to navigate conflicts with grace, seeking understanding and extending forgiveness. May our home be a haven of love and reconciliation. In Jesus' name, we pray. Amen."

February 28

1 Peter 2:17

"Honour all men. Love the brotherhood. Fear God. Honour the king."

What Does This Mean For Us?

this verse encourages a broader perspective of honor and respect, extending beyond the marital relationship to encompass a sense of reverence for all people. For a couple seeking to strengthen their marriage in today's world, it suggests that the foundation of mutual respect begins with a genuine regard for humanity and a shared commitment to love and honor each other.

Modern Day Reflection

This verse prompts spouses to see the inherent worth in one another and to approach their relationship with a reverence for the divine. By embodying honor, love, and fear of God within their marriage, the couple can foster an environment of mutual respect that transcends the challenges of contemporary life.

~

Prayer For Reverence in Marriage

Lord, teach us to honor and love each other in our marriage, recognizing the value in every person. Grant us the wisdom to approach our relationship with a sense of awe and reverence for You. May our home be a sanctuary of mutual respect, reflecting the love and grace You bestow upon us. Amen.

February 29 (Leap Year)

Proverbs 14:21
"He that despiseth his neighbor sinneth: but he that hath mercy on the
poor, happy is he."

What Does This Mean For Us?

In the context of marriage, this verse underscores the significance of showing kindness and mercy toward one another. It suggests that harboring contempt or disregard for each other harms the marital relationship.

Modern Day Reflection

For a couple seeking to strengthen their marriage in today's world, this verse calls for a conscious effort to treat each other with respect and empathy. It emphasizes that true happiness in marriage is found in acts of compassion and understanding. In the midst of life's challenges, spouses can strengthen their bond by choosing mercy over contempt, fostering an environment of mutual respect and love.

Prayer For Kindness and Mercy in Marriage
"Heavenly Father, guide us in showing kindness and mercy to one another in our marriage. May our hearts be filled with compassion, and may we choose understanding over contempt. Grant us the strength to build a relationship rooted in respect and love. In Jesus' name, we pray.
Amen."

March

AS SPRING EMERGES AND THE EARTH
STIRS WITH LIFE, MAY OUR SOULS BE
REFRESHED WITH THE PROMISE OF NEW
BEGINNINGS. LIKE THE BLOSSOMING
FLOWERS, LET OUR HEARTS OPEN TO
GROWTH, RESILIENCE, AND THE BEAUTY
OF DIVINE POSSIBILITIES.

March 1

Leviticus 19:18

"Thou shalt not avenge, nor bear any grudge against the children of thy people, but thou shalt love thy neighbour as thyself: I am the Lord."

What Does This Mean For Us?

In the context of marriage, this verse emphasizes the importance of love, forgiveness, and the absence of resentment.

Modern Day Reflection

For a couple seeking to strengthen their marriage in today's world, this verse encourages them to let go of grudges and practice love that transcends personal grievances. It challenges spouses to treat each other with the same care and consideration they would extend to themselves, fostering an environment of mutual respect and understanding. In a society where conflicts can easily escalate, this biblical principle offers a timeless guide for building a resilient and loving marital foundation.

Prayer For The Absence of Resentment in Marriage

Heavenly Father, teach us to love each other as ourselves, free from avenging and grudges. May our marriage be a testament to forgiveness and understanding, reflecting Your boundless love. Grant us the strength to cultivate a relationship rooted in mutual respect. In Jesus' name, we pray. Amen.

March 2

1 Corinthians 16:14
"Let all your things be done with charity."

What Does This Mean For Us?

In the context of marriage, this verse underscores the significance of conducting all aspects of life with love. For a couple seeking to strengthen their marriage in today's world, this verse serves as a guiding principle.

Modern Day Reflection

It challenges spouses to approach every interaction, decision, and communication with a foundation of love and respect. In a society where external pressures can strain relationships, this biblical teaching encourages the couple to prioritize empathy, kindness, and understanding within their marriage. By embodying charity, or selfless love, in their daily interactions, they can foster a relationship that withstands challenges and grows stronger over time.

Prayer For Empathy in Marriage
Dear Heavenly Father, guide us in conducting every aspect of our marriage with charity, with selfless love. May our words and actions be infused with kindness and empathy. Grant us the strength to navigate challenges with grace and to build a foundation of mutual respect. In Jesus' name, we pray. Amen

March 3

Galatians 6:2
"Bear ye one another's burdens, and so fulfil the law of Christ."

What Does This Mean For Us?

This verse highlights the importance of mutual support and empathy. It encourages spouses to share and lighten each other's burdens, embodying Christ's teachings of love and selflessness.

Modern Day Reflection

This biblical principle is a powerful reminder for a couple seeking to strengthen their marriage. By actively shouldering each other's challenges, whether big or small, they foster a sense of unity and understanding. In practical terms, it means being there for each other during tough times, offering a listening ear, and providing unwavering support. Through such actions, the couple fulfills the law of Christ, creating a foundation of mutual respect and love.

Prayer For Relief of Burden in Marriage
Heavenly Father, guide us in bearing each other's burdens in our marriage, following the example set by Christ. May our love be manifested in actions of support and understanding. Strengthen our bond through empathy, and help us navigate life's challenges together. In Jesus' name, we pray. Amen.

March 4

1 Thessalonians 4:9

"But as touching brotherly love ye need not that I write unto you: for ye yourselves are taught of God to love one another."

What Does This Mean For Us?

1 Thessalonians 4:9 emphasizes the divine guidance in cultivating a love that goes beyond the surface. It suggests that the couple, having a foundation of brotherly love, has already been taught by God to extend that love within the marriage.

Modern Day Reflection

This biblical teaching encourages spouses to go beyond mere obligations and actively nurture a deep, respectful, and God-inspired love for each other. It prompts the couple to reflect on the divine source of their love and seek to embody it in their actions, words, and interactions.

Prayer For Embodiment in Marriage

Dear Heavenly Father, thank you for teaching us the essence of brotherly love in our marriage. May our hearts be open to your guidance as we strive to love one another deeply and genuinely. Strengthen our bond with your divine love, and help us navigate the challenges of life with grace and mutual respect. In Jesus' name, we pray. Amen.

March 5

1 John 4:11
"Beloved, if God so loved us, we ought also to love one another."

What Does This Mean For Us?

In the context of marriage, this verse emphasizes the reciprocity of love. It suggests that the couple, having experienced the divine love of God, should mirror that love in their relationship.

Modern Day Reflection

In our modern world, relationships can face numerous challenges. This biblical teaching calls the spouses to love each other not just as a response to their partner's actions but as a conscious choice. It challenges them to extend love even in moments of difficulty, mirroring the unconditional love they have received from God. By embodying this principle, the couple can cultivate a marriage built on mutual respect, understanding, and enduring love.

∼

Prayer For A Safe Journey in Marriage
Lord, teach us to love one another as you have loved us. May our marriage be a reflection of the divine love we have received. Grant us the strength to navigate life's journey together with unwavering love, respect, and understanding. Amen.

March 6

Deuteronomy 7:13

"And he will love thee, and bless thee, and multiply thee: he will also bless the fruit of thy womb, and the fruit of thy land, thy corn, and thy wine, and thine oil, the increase of thy kine, and the flocks of thy sheep, in the land which he sware unto thy fathers to give thee."

What Does This Mean For Us?

This verse emphasizes God's love and blessings, not only in the form of material abundance but specifically extending to fertility and the blessings of children. It reaffirms God's covenant promise to multiply His people.

Modern Day Reflection

In the context of starting a family, this verse inspires confidence in God's faithfulness to bless the fruit of the womb. It encourages couples to trust in God's provision for their family life, not only in terms of children but also in all aspects of their lives. It calls for a deep reliance on God's promises and a recognition of His blessings in every area of family life.

Prayer For Promise of Love and Blessing in Marriage

Heavenly Father, we trust in Your promises of love and blessing. May our family be a testament to Your faithfulness, and may we experience the blessings of children and abundance in all aspects of our lives. Guide us as we navigate the journey of starting a family, and may it be a journey filled with Your grace. Amen.

March 7

Romans 15:1-2

"We then that are strong ought to bear the infirmities of the weak, and not to please ourselves. Let every one of us please his neighbour for his good to edification."

What Does This Mean For Us?

In Romans 15:1-2, the verse encourages a selfless and considerate approach. It advises the stronger partner to bear with the weaknesses of the other, emphasizing the importance of sacrificing personal preferences for the benefit and growth of the relationship.

Modern Day Reflection

In today's world, where individualism can sometimes overshadow partnership, this biblical teaching guides the couple to prioritize each other's well-being. It challenges them to go beyond self-interest and actively seek the betterment of their spouse, creating an atmosphere of mutual respect and support within their marriage.

Prayer For Mutual Edification in Marriage

Heavenly Father, help us embody the spirit of selflessness in our marriage, bearing each other's burdens and seeking mutual edification. May our actions reflect a genuine concern for our partner's well-being, fostering a relationship rooted in respect and love. In Jesus' name, we pray. Amen.

March 8

Proverbs 15:18

"A wrathful man stirreth up strife: but he that is slow to anger appeaseth strife."

What Does This Mean For Us?

This proverb emphasizes the impact of our emotions on interpersonal relationships. It suggests that a easily angered or hot-tempered person tends to create conflict and stir up strife.

Modern Day Reflection

The verse encourages married couples to be mindful of their emotions and responses, promoting a more peaceful and harmonious interaction with others. It suggests that maintaining a calm demeanor and not giving in to quick anger can contribute to a more positive and serene atmosphere in our relationships. It's a timeless piece of wisdom about the importance of emotional control to promote peace and understanding as a married couple.

~

Prayer For Common Ground in Marriage

Dear Heavenly Father, We come before you with grateful hearts for our gift of marriage. We acknowledge that in life's journey together, there may be moments when our tempers are tested and emotions run high. We seek your guidance in cultivating a spirit of patience and compassion towards one another. May our marriage be a testimony to the power of love and understanding Bind us together, Lord, with cords of love that cannot be easily broken. Amen.

March 9

1 Peter 5:5

"Likewise, ye younger, submit yourselves unto the elder. Yea, all of you be subject one to another and be clothed with humility: for God resisteth the proud, and giveth grace to the humble."

What Does This Mean For Us?

In the union of marriage, this verse emphasizes the importance of mutual submission and humility. It encourages spouses to approach their relationship with a humble and respectful attitude, valuing each other's perspectives and submitting to one another.

Modern Day Reflection

In the world today, where individualism can sometimes overshadow partnership, this biblical teaching guides the couple to prioritize humility over pride. It prompts them to actively seek to understand and honor each other, creating an environment of mutual respect and cooperation within their marriage.

~

Prayer For Humility in Marriage

Heavenly Father, teach us to submit to one another in humility within our marriage. May our hearts be clothed with humility, fostering an atmosphere of mutual respect and understanding. Keep us from pride, and may our relationship be marked by grace and cooperation. In Jesus' name, we pray. Amen.

March 10

Ephesians 4:32

"And be ye kind one to another, tenderhearted, forgiving one another, even as God for Christ's sake hath forgiven you."

What Does This Mean For Us?

On the subject of marriage, this verse emphasizes the virtues of kindness, tenderheartedness, and forgiveness. It encourages spouses to cultivate a compassionate and forgiving attitude toward each other, mirroring the divine forgiveness bestowed upon them.

Modern Day Reflection

All too often, stress and misunderstandings can strain relationships. This biblical teaching guides the couple to prioritize empathy and forgiveness. It prompts them to extend grace to their partner, fostering an environment of mutual respect and understanding within their marriage.

Prayer For Grace in Marriage

Lord, teach us to be kind, tenderhearted, and forgiving in our marriage, following the example of Your forgiveness. May our hearts be open to empathy and grace, and may our relationship be a testament to mutual respect and understanding. Strengthen our bond as we navigate life together. Amen.

March 11

Proverbs 5:15-19

"Drink waters out of thine own cistern, and running waters out of thine own well. Let thy fountains be dispersed abroad, and rivers of waters in the streets. Let them be only thine own, and not strangers' with thee. Let thy fountain be blessed: and rejoice with the wife of thy youth."

What Does This Mean For Us?

On the subject of faithfulness in marriage, this passage advises couples to find satisfaction and fulfillment within their own marital relationship. It uses the metaphor of "drinking waters from your own well" to emphasize the exclusivity and intimacy of the marital bond.

Modern Day Reflection

In many marriages today, external temptations can strain relationships. Proverbs 5:15-19 urges the couple to cherish and rejoice in the unique connection they share, guarding against the intrusion of outside influences. It encourages a commitment to faithfulness and mutual joy within the covenant of marriage.

Prayer For Faithfulness in Marriage

Lord, grant us the strength to draw satisfaction and joy from our marital bond. May our love be exclusive and steadfast, guarding against any temptations that may threaten our faithfulness. Bless our marriage, and fill our hearts with gratitude for the unique connection we share. Amen.

March 12

Hebrews 13:4

"Marriage is honorable in all, and the bed undefiled: but whoremongers and adulterers God will judge."

What Does This Mean For Us?

In the context of faithfulness in marriage, this verse underscores the sanctity and honor of the marital relationship. It emphasizes the purity and exclusivity of the marital bed, cautioning against infidelity and immorality.

Modern Day Reflection

In today's world, where external pressures and temptations can challenge marital fidelity, this biblical teaching encourages the couple to uphold the sanctity of their union. It serves as a reminder that faithfulness in marriage is not only a commitment to each other but also a reverence for the divine institution of marriage. By honoring the sanctity of their union, the couple strengthens their marital bond and guards against actions that may compromise the trust and fidelity essential for a thriving relationship.

Prayer For Sanctity in Marriage

Heavenly Father, we seek Your guidance in upholding the sanctity of our marriage. Grant us the strength to honor each other and keep our marital bed undefiled. Protect us from outside influences that may threaten our fidelity. In Jesus' name, we pray. Amen.

March 13

Matthew 19:6
"Wherefore they are no more twain, but one flesh. What therefore God hath joined together, let not man put asunder."

What Does This Mean For Us?

In the context of faithfulness in marriage, this verse underscores the sacred and inseparable nature of the marital union. It emphasizes that when a couple is joined in marriage, they become one entity in the eyes of God. This unity carries a divine sanctity, urging the couple to protect and preserve their oneness against any forces that may seek to divide them.

Modern Day Reflection

Where external challenges and temptations can strain marital bonds In today's world, this biblical teaching encourages spouses to nurture a sense of indivisibility and commitment. By recognizing and cherishing the oneness ordained by God, the couple strengthens their resolve to remain faithful and devoted to each other.

Prayer For Indivisibility in Marriage
Heavenly Father, we acknowledge the sacred oneness You have bestowed upon our marriage. Grant us the strength to protect and nurture this union against any forces that may seek to divide us. May our commitment and faithfulness be a testament to the unity You have ordained. In Jesus' name, we pray. Amen.

March 14

Proverbs 20:6-7

"Most men will proclaim everyone his own goodness, but a faithful man who can find? The just man walketh in his integrity: his children are blessed after him."

What Does This Mean For Us?

This verse reflects on the rarity and value of true faithfulness. It suggests that while many may boast of their virtues, finding genuine faithfulness is a rare treasure. The emphasis on integrity and the blessings upon the offspring underscore the enduring impact of faithfulness.

Modern Day Reflection

Many external influences can challenge marital fidelity, in the world today. This biblical teaching encourages the couple to strive for true faithfulness, recognizing it as a precious foundation for a blessed and enduring marriage.

Prayer For Virtue in Marriage

Lord, help us embody the rare virtue of true faithfulness in our marriage. May our commitment be a shining example to others, and may our love leave a legacy of blessings for our children and generations beyond. Strengthen our bond, and may our fidelity endure through all seasons of life. Amen.

<h1 style="text-align:center">March 15</h1>

Malachi 2:14-16

"Yet ye say, Wherefore? Because the Lord hath been witness between thee and the wife of thy youth, against whom thou hast dealt treacherously: yet is she thy companion, and the wife of thy covenant. And did not he make one? Yet had he the residue of the spirit. And wherefore one? That he might seek a godly seed. Therefore take heed to your spirit, and let none deal treacherously against the wife of his youth. For the Lord, the God of Israel, saith that he hateth putting away: for one covereth violence with his garment, saith the Lord of hosts: therefore take heed to your spirit, that ye deal not treacherously."

What Does This Mean For Us?

In the context of faithfulness in marriage, this passage highlights God's witness to the covenant of marriage. It condemns treacherous behavior and emphasizes the importance of preserving the sacred bond between spouses.

Modern Day Reflection

Malachi 2:14-16 underscores the responsibility to nurture a relationship that aligns with God's design, fostering faithfulness and a godly legacy.

~

Prayer For Upheld Covenants in Marriage

Heavenly Father, we acknowledge Your witness to our marriage covenant. May our union be a source of godly legacy, and help us take heed to our spirits, guarding against treacherous actions. In Jesus' name, we pray. Amen.

March 16

1 Corinthians 6:18-20

"Flee fornication. Every sin that a man doeth is without the body, but he that committeth fornication sinneth against his own body. What? know ye not that your body is the temple of the Holy Ghost which is in you, which ye have of God, and ye are not your own? For ye are bought with a price: therefore glorify God in your body, and in your spirit, which are God's."

What Does This Mean For Us?

In the context of faithfulness in marriage, this passage emphasizes the sacredness of the marital union and the significance of honoring the body as a temple of the Holy Spirit. It encourages individuals to flee from sexual immorality, recognizing that such actions not only violate the sanctity of the body but also go against God's design for marriage.

Modern Day Reflection

In today's world, where external influences can challenge marital fidelity, this biblical teaching guides the couple to cherish their bodies and recognize them as vessels of God's presence, fostering faithfulness within the marriage.

~

Prayer For Commitment in Marriage

Heavenly Father, help us flee from any actions that may dishonor the sanctity of our bodies and marriage. May we recognize our bodies as temples of Your Holy Spirit, bought with a price. Strengthen our commitment to glorify You in our bodies and spirits. In Jesus' name, we pray. Amen.

March 17

Proverbs 12:22

"Lying lips are abomination to the Lord: but they that deal truly are his delight."

What Does This Mean For Us?

In the context of trust, faithfulness, and sanctity in marriage, this verse highlights the abhorrence of deceit and the delight in truthfulness. It underscores the importance of honesty and integrity within the marital relationship.

Modern Day Reflection

In modern day, where trust forms the bedrock of a strong marriage, this biblical teaching guides the couple to cultivate a foundation of openness and transparency. It urges them to deal truly with each other, avoiding deceit and fostering an environment where trust can thrive. By embracing truthfulness, the couple strengthens their marital bond and upholds the value of faithfulness in both words and actions.

Prayer For Truth in Marriage

Lord, grant us the wisdom to deal truly with each other in our marriage. May our honesty and transparency delight Your heart. Strengthen our trust, and may our commitment be marked by the integrity that honors You. Amen.

March 18

Proverbs 3:3-4

"Let not mercy and truth forsake thee: bind them about thy neck; write them upon the table of thine heart: So shalt thou find favour and good understanding in the sight of God and man."

What Does This Mean For Us?

In the context of faithfulness in marriage, this verse encourages the couple to embrace a foundation of mercy and truth within their relationship. It advises them to bind these virtues close to their hearts, fostering an environment of understanding and favor both in the eyes of God and humanity.

Modern Day Reflection

In today's fast-paced and often hectic world, where misunderstandings and conflicts can strain marriages, this biblical teaching guides the couple to prioritize mercy and truth. By cultivating an atmosphere of compassion and honesty, they strengthen their bond, creating a relationship that reflects divine principles and earns the respect of those around them.

❧

Prayer For Conflict Resolution in Marriage

Lord, guide us in cultivating mercy and truth in our marriage. May these virtues shape our interactions, bringing favor and understanding not only in Your sight but also in the sight of those we encounter. Strengthen our commitment to embody these principles in our relationship. Amen.

March 19

Ephesians 5:25

"Husbands, love your wives, even as Christ also loved the church and gave himself for it."

What Does This Mean For Us?

This verse instructs husbands to love their wives sacrificially, mirroring Christ's love for the church. It emphasizes selfless and unconditional love, where a husband's commitment goes beyond mere emotion and extends to a willingness to sacrifice for the well-being of his wife.

Modern Day Reflection

Today, external pressures can strain marital bonds. This biblical teaching guides husbands to exemplify a love that withstands challenges. It encourages them to prioritize their wives' needs, fostering an environment of security and faithfulness within the marriage.

Prayer For Exemplification of Love in Marriage

Lord, help me embody the sacrificial love that Ephesians 5:25 teaches. May my love for my spouse be a reflection of Christ's love for the church. Strengthen our marriage, and guide us to prioritize each other's well-being. May our commitment deepen, and our love endure through all seasons of life. Amen.

March 20

1 Timothy 3:2

"A bishop then must be blameless, the husband of one wife, vigilant, sober, of good behaviour, given to hospitality, apt to teach."

What Does This Mean For Us?

Regarding faithfulness in marriage, this verse, though originally addressing the qualifications for a bishop, conveys the principle of marital fidelity. It emphasizes the importance of being the spouse of one partner, highlighting the value of faithfulness in a position of leadership.

Modern Day Reflection

For couples seeking to strengthen their marriage in today's world, this biblical teaching underscores the commitment to marital exclusivity and the virtues that support a faithful relationship. It encourages spouses to be vigilant, sober, and of good behavior, fostering an environment of trust and dedication within their marriage.

Prayer For Virtuous Embodiment in Marriage

Heavenly Father, guide us in our commitment to marital fidelity. May we be vigilant, sober, and of good behavior in our relationship. Strengthen our bond of exclusivity and trust, and help us embody the virtues that support a faithful marriage. In Jesus' name, we pray. Amen.

March 21

Titus 1:6
"If any be blameless, the husband of one wife, having faithful children not accused of riot or unruly."

What Does This Mean For Us?

This verse outlines the qualification for a church elder or overseer, emphasizing the importance of being the spouse of one partner. It underscores the value of marital fidelity and extends the principle to the behavior of their children.

Modern Day Reflection

For couples seeking to strengthen their marriage, this biblical teaching highlights the interconnectedness of marital faithfulness and the impact it has on the family unit. It encourages spouses to prioritize their commitment to each other, fostering an environment of stability and faithfulness that extends to their children.

Prayer For Stability in Marriage
Heavenly Father, guide us in our commitment to marital fidelity and family stability. May our marriage be blameless, and our children be faithful and well-behaved. Strengthen our bond and help us prioritize our commitment to each other and our family. In Jesus' name, we pray. Amen.

March 22

1 Corinthians 13:6
"Rejoiceth not in iniquity, but rejoiceth in the truth."

What Does This Mean For Us?

In the context of faithfulness in marriage, this verse from the famous "love chapter" underscores the importance of truth and honesty in a relationship. It suggests that genuine love does not find joy in wrongdoing but rather celebrates and cherishes the truth.

Modern Day Reflection

For a couple seeking to strengthen their marriage in today's world, where trust and transparency are vital, this biblical teaching encourages them to find joy in truthfulness. It guides them to build a foundation of openness and honesty, fostering an environment of trust and faithfulness in their relationship.

$\sim$

Prayer For Transparency and Truth in Marriage
Lord, guide us to rejoice in the truth within our marriage. May our love be marked by transparency and honesty, and may we find joy in the authenticity of our connection. Strengthen our commitment to truthfulness, fostering trust and faithfulness in our relationship. Amen.

March 23

Psalm 101:2-3

"I will behave myself wisely in a perfect way. O when wilt thou come unto me? I will walk within my house with a perfect heart. I will set no wicked thing before mine eyes: I hate the work of them that turn aside; it shall not cleave to me."

What Does This Mean For Us?

This biblical teaching encourages married couples to be intentional in their actions within the confines of their home. It guides them to be vigilant against external temptations, fostering an environment of faithfulness and righteousness within their marriage.

Modern Day Reflection

In the context of faithfulness in marriage, this psalm expresses the commitment to righteous behavior and the rejection of anything wicked. For a couple striving to strengthen their marriage in today's world, where external influences can impact fidelity,

Prayer For Vigilance in Marriage

Heavenly Father, grant us the wisdom to behave wisely within our home and marriage. May our hearts be perfect and set against anything wicked. Help us to reject influences that can harm our commitment to each other, and may our home be a sanctuary of faithfulness. In Jesus' name, we pray. Amen.

March 24

1 Thessalonians 4:3-5
"For this is the will of God, even your sanctification, that ye should abstain from fornication: That every one of you should know how to possess his vessel in sanctification and honour; Not in the lust of concupiscence, even as the Gentiles which know not God."

What Does This Mean For Us?

This biblical teaching guides couples to honor the sanctity of their relationship. It encourages them to possess their bodies and emotions with sanctification and honor, resisting temptations that may lead to unfaithfulness.

Modern Day Reflection

In the context of faithfulness in marriage, this passage emphasizes the divine call to sanctification and abstaining from immoral conduct. For a couple seeking to strengthen their marriage in today's world, external pressures and cultural norms can challenge fidelity.

Prayer For Fidelity in Marriage
Heavenly Father, lead us in the path of sanctification within our marriage. Grant us the strength to abstain from anything that may harm our fidelity. May our union be marked by honor and sanctity, reflecting Your will in our relationship. In Jesus' name, we pray. Amen.

<h1 style="text-align:center">March 25</h1>

Colossians 3:9-10

"Lie not one to another, seeing that ye have put off the old man with his deeds; And have put on the new man, which is renewed in knowledge after the image of him that created him."

What Does This Mean For Us?

In God's promotion of faithfulness in marriage, this verse emphasizes the importance of truthfulness and the transformation that occurs when embracing a new way of life.

Modern Day Reflection

For a couple seeking to strengthen their marriage in today's world, where honest communication is vital, this biblical teaching encourages them to abandon deceitful practices and embrace a renewed commitment to truth. It guides them to build a foundation of openness and transparency, fostering an environment of trust and faithfulness within their relationship.

Prayer For Renewed Commitment in Marriage

Heavenly Father, help us to be truthful and transparent in our marriage. May we put off deceitful behaviors and embrace the newness of commitment to truth. Strengthen our bond of trust and renew our knowledge of each other in Your image. In Jesus' name, we pray. Amen.

March 26

Proverbs 28:20

"A faithful man shall abound with blessings: but he that maketh haste to be rich shall not be innocent."

What Does This Mean For Us?

Proverbs 28:20 signifies and underscores the connection between faithfulness and the abundance of blessings.

Modern Day Reflection

For a couple striving to strengthen their marriage in today's world, where external pressures may tempt a pursuit of worldly desires, this biblical teaching encourages them to prioritize faithfulness over hasty pursuits. It suggests that genuine blessings come to those who remain faithful in their commitment. This verse guides the couple to focus on the richness of their relationship rather than hastily seeking external achievements, fostering an environment of loyalty and fulfillment within their marriage.

～

Prayer For Blessings in Marriage

Lord, guide us to prioritize faithfulness in our marriage. May we cherish the richness of our relationship over hasty pursuits, and may blessings abound in our commitment to each other. Amen.

March 27

1 Peter 4:8

"And above all things have fervent charity among yourselves: for charity shall cover the multitude of sins."

What Does This Mean For Us?

In the context of faithfulness in marriage, this verse emphasizes the importance of fervent love or charity in a relationship, which has the power to cover a multitude of sins.

Modern Day Reflection

For a couple seeking to strengthen their marriage in today's world, where conflicts and mistakes can strain fidelity, this biblical teaching encourages them to prioritize deep and sincere love for each other. It guides them to cultivate a love that forgives and overlooks faults, fostering an environment of understanding and faithfulness within their relationship.

Prayer For Lasting Love in Marriage

Lord, grant us a lasting love in our marriage that covers any mistakes or shortcomings. Help us to forgive and understand each other deeply, strengthening our commitment to love and faithfulness. Amen.

March 28

Proverbs 6:32-33

"But whoso committeth adultery with a woman lacketh understanding: he that doeth it destroyeth his own soul. A wound and dishonour shall he get; and his reproach shall not be wiped away."

What Does This Mean For Us?

This verse highlights the severe consequences of adultery, emphasizing the destruction it brings to one's soul, along with wounds, dishonor, and irreparable reproach.

Modern Day Reflection

For a couple striving to strengthen their marriage in today's world, where temptations may challenge fidelity, this biblical teaching serves as a warning against the devastating impact of infidelity. It encourages them to prioritize understanding, commitment, and the preservation of their sacred union, fostering an environment of trust and faithfulness within their relationship.

~

Prayer For Trust and Fidelity in Marriage

Heavenly Father, guide us in understanding the sanctity of our marriage. Protect us from the pitfalls of infidelity and help us build a bond based on trust and faithfulness. Shield our union from wounds and dishonor. In Jesus' name, we pray. Amen.

March 29

Matthew 5:28

"But I say unto you, That whosoever looketh on a woman to lust after her hath committed adultery with her already in his heart."

What Does This Mean For Us?

In the context of faithfulness in marriage, Matthew 5:28 underscores the importance of purity not just in actions but also in thoughts.

Modern Day Reflection

For a couple working to strengthen their marriage in today's world, where external influences and temptations can strain fidelity, this biblical teaching emphasizes the need to guard against lustful thoughts. It encourages them to cultivate a mindset of purity and fidelity, fostering an environment of emotional faithfulness within their relationship.

∼

Prayer For Temptation in Marriage

Lord, guide us in cultivating pure thoughts within our marriage. Help us to guard against temptations and lustful desires, fostering an environment of emotional faithfulness. Strengthen our commitment to each other. Amen.

March 30

Proverbs 17:17

"A friend loveth at all times, and a brother is born for adversity."

What Does This Mean For Us?

Proverbs 17:17 highlights the enduring nature of true friendship and love.

Modern Day Reflection

Couples seeking to strengthen their marriage where challenges and uncertainties may arise, Proverbs 17:17 encourages them to be not only spouses but also true friends to each other. It emphasizes the importance of steadfast love during both joyous and challenging times, fostering an environment of unwavering commitment and faithfulness within their relationship.

~

Prayer For True Friendship in Marriage

Lord, guide us in cultivating a friendship that withstands all times. May our love be unwavering, embracing both joy and adversity. Strengthen our commitment to each other, and may our marriage reflect the enduring nature of true friendship. Amen.

<h1 style="text-align:center">March 31</h1>

<h2 style="text-align:center">Proverbs 14:22</h2>

"Do they not err that devise evil? But mercy and truth shall be to them that devise good."

What Does This Mean For Us?

In the context of faithfulness in marriage, this verse underscores the importance of choosing a path of goodness and righteousness over actions that may lead to harm.

Modern Day Reflection

For a couple working to strengthen their marriage in today's world, this biblical teaching encourages them to devise good and merciful actions toward each other. It guides them to prioritize integrity and kindness, fostering an environment of trust and faithfulness within their relationship.

$\sim$

Prayer For Mercy and Truth in Marriage

Heavenly Father, guide us in choosing the path of goodness and righteousness in our marriage. May mercy and truth be our guiding principles, strengthening our commitment to each other. Protect us from harmful influences, and help us build a relationship based on trust and faithfulness. In Jesus' name, we pray. Amen.

April

IN THE TAPESTRY OF LIFE, APRIL WEAVES A STORY OF REBIRTH AND RENEWAL. MAY OUR SPIRITS BE LIFTED, MUCH LIKE THE BUDS ON THE TREES, AS WE EMBRACE THE UNFOLDING CHAPTERS OF GROWTH, TRANSFORMATION, AND THE ETERNAL CYCLE OF CREATION.

April 1

Proverbs 28:10

"Whoso causeth the righteous to go astray in an evil way, he shall fall himself into his own pit: but the upright shall have good things in possession."

What Does This Mean For Us?

In today's context of faithfulness in marriage, this verse emphasizes the consequences of leading others astray and the rewards for maintaining righteousness.

Modern Day Reflection

Proverbs 28:10 warns against leading others astray through deceitful means, emphasizing the consequences of dishonesty and manipulation. In a contemporary context, this verse serves as a reminder of the ethical imperative to uphold truth and integrity in all interactions. It cautions against engaging in deceptive practices that harm others or erode trust within relationships and society. The wisdom from Proverbs encourages individuals to prioritize honesty, transparency, and accountability in their words and actions, fostering a culture of trustworthiness and ethical behavior in personal and professional realms.

Prayer For Protection of Outside Influence in Marriage

Lord, grant us the strength to remain faithful and upright in our marriage. Guard us against any influences that may cause us to stray from righteousness. May our commitment to each other bring forth blessings and good things in our journey together. Amen.

April 2

1 Corinthians 4:2

"Moreover it is required in stewards, that a man be found faithful."

What Does This Mean For Us?

In the context of strengthening marriage, this verse underscores the importance of being trustworthy and reliable stewards of the marital bond.

Modern Day Reflection

For a couple working to strengthen their marriage in today's world, where distractions and challenges can test their fidelity, this biblical teaching encourages them to prioritize faithfulness in their roles as stewards of their relationship. It calls them to be dependable and true to each other, fostering a foundation of trust and commitment.

Prayer For Faithful Stewardship in Marriage

Heavenly Father, guide us in being faithful stewards of our marriage. May we be reliable and trustworthy in our commitment to each other. Help us navigate challenges with unwavering faithfulness, and let our love be a testimony of your grace. In Jesus' name, we pray. Amen.

April 3

James 4:4

"Ye adulterers and adulteresses, know ye not that the friendship of the world is enmity with God? Whosoever therefore will be a friend of the world is the enemy of God."

What Does This Mean For Us?

This verse emphasizes the dangers of worldly influences that can lead individuals away from their commitment to each other and, ultimately, from their spiritual values.

Modern Day Reflection

Where external pressures and temptations are abundant, this biblical teaching urges them to be vigilant against influences that could undermine their fidelity. It encourages couples to prioritize their commitment to each other over other worldly distractions.

Prayer For Protection in Marriage

Lord, guard our marriage from the enticements of the world. Strengthen our commitment to each other and fortify us against anything that may jeopardize our faithfulness. Let our love be a reflection of your enduring faithfulness. Amen.

April 4

1 Corinthians 10:13

"There hath no temptation taken you but such as is common to man: but God is faithful, who will not suffer you to be tempted above that ye are able; but will with the temptation also make a way to escape, that ye may be able to bear it."

What Does This Mean For Us?

In the context of strengthening the bonds of marriage, this verse reassures the couple that, no matter the challenges they face, God provides a way out of temptation and empowers them to withstand it. It emphasizes the importance of relying on God's faithfulness to navigate the trials that might test the commitment of the marriage.

Modern Day Reflection

For a couple seeking to strengthen their bond, this verse encourages them to trust in God's guidance and to lean on their faith when facing difficulties.

Prayer For Times of Trial in Marriage

Lord, in times of trial, remind us of your unwavering faithfulness. Strengthen our resolve to stay faithful to each other, and guide us away from any paths that may lead us astray. May our marriage be a testament to your sustaining love. Amen.

April 5

Ephesians 4:25

"Wherefore putting away lying, speak every man truth with his
neighbour: for we are members one of another."

What Does This Mean For Us?

In the verse Ephesians 4:25, it emphasizes the importance of honesty
and transparency. It encourages the couple to build their relationship on
a foundation of truth, as they are interconnected as members of one
another. Being truthful and open fosters trust and strengthens the
marital bond.

Modern Day Reflection

In modern times, where external pressures can strain relationships, this
verse reminds the couple that being truthful with each other is crucial
for maintaining a faithful and resilient marriage.

Prayer For Honesty in Marriage

Gracious God, help us to cultivate a relationship built on honesty and
transparency. May we speak the truth to each other in love, fostering
trust and understanding. Guard our hearts against deceit, and
strengthen our commitment to a faithful and enduring marriage. In
Jesus' name, we pray. Amen.

April 6

Colossians 3:8

"But now ye also put off all these; anger, wrath, malice, blasphemy, filthy communication out of your mouth."

What Does This Mean For Us?

In the context of faithfulness in marriage, this verse advises the couple to discard negative emotions and harmful communication patterns. Anger, malice, and inappropriate speech can erode the fabric of a marriage, leading to misunderstandings and fractures. By putting away these destructive elements, the couple can create a space for love, respect, and faithfulness to flourish.

Modern Day Reflection

Colossians 3:8 advises against harboring negative emotions and destructive behaviors such as anger, rage, malice, and slander. In a contemporary context, this verse encourages individuals to cultivate a positive and compassionate mindset, avoiding harmful expressions of frustration or resentment. It emphasizes the importance of fostering a spirit of kindness, understanding, and forgiveness in our interactions with others.

Prayer For Kindness in Marriage

Gracious God, guide us in putting away any negativity that may harm our marriage. May our communication be filled with kindness, understanding, and love. Strengthen our commitment to each other, fostering a faithful and enduring bond. In your name, we pray. Amen.

April 7

Matthew 5:32

"But I say unto you, That whosoever shall put away his wife, except for the cause of fornication, causeth her to commit adultery: and whosoever shall marry her that is divorced committeth adultery."

What Does This Mean For Us?

In the context of living as a marital unit in marriage, this verse emphasizes the sanctity and permanence of the marital bond. It encourages couples to approach marriage with commitment and fidelity, highlighting the gravity of divorce and remarriage.

Modern Day Reflection

Matthew 5:32 addresses the issue of divorce, stating that whoever divorces his wife, except in cases of marital unfaithfulness, causes her to commit adultery. This verse underscores the seriousness and permanence of the marriage covenant, encouraging individuals to approach marriage with a commitment to its sacred nature. It advises against divorce except in cases of serious breach of marital fidelity. It urges couples to work through challenges, prioritize communication, and seek reconciliation rather than resorting to divorce unless absolutely necessary.

Prayer For Commitment in Marriage

Heavenly Father, grant us the wisdom and strength to honor the sacred commitment of marriage. Help us to navigate challenges with love, understanding, and fidelity. May our union be a testament to your grace and the enduring bond of marriage. Amen.

April 8

Proverbs 11:13

"A talebearer revealeth secrets: but he that is of a faithful spirit concealeth the matter."

What Does This Mean For Us?

In the context of faithfulness in marriage, this verse underscores the importance of trust and discretion. It encourages spouses to cultivate a faithful spirit, one that values the confidentiality of their partner.

Modern Day Reflection

In today's world, where privacy is often challenged, this verse emphasizes the role of trust in building a strong and enduring marital relationship.

❧

Prayer For Spousal Privacy in Marriage

Gracious God, help us to nurture a faithful spirit in our marriage. Grant us the wisdom to guard each other's trust and to be discreet with the matters of our hearts. May our relationship be built on a foundation of honesty and confidentiality. Amen.

April 9

Proverbs 20:22

"Say not thou, I will recompense evil; but wait on the Lord, and he shall save thee."

What Does This Mean For Us?

Proverbs 20:22 advises against seeking revenge and encourages leaving justice to the divine. Instead, the wisdom from Proverbs prompts individuals to trust in a higher sense of justice and focus on personal growth and reconciliation rather than perpetuating a cycle of resentment. Proverbs 20:22 additionally advocates for a mindset of forgiveness and the belief that ultimately, justice is best served through grace and understanding.

Modern Day Reflection

In a contemporary context, this verse advocates for forgiveness and letting go of the desire for personal retaliation. It suggests that harboring grudges or seeking vengeance can be detrimental to one's own well-being and relationships.

Prayer For Reconciliation in Marriage

Gracious Lord, in moments of hurt and frustration, help us to resist the urge for retaliation. Grant us the patience to wait on You and trust in Your saving grace to heal our wounds. May our marriage be a testament to Your enduring love. Amen.

April 10

Proverbs 25:19

"Confidence in an unfaithful man in time of trouble is like a broken tooth, and a foot out of joint."

What Does This Mean For Us?

For the couple working to strengthen their marriage, this verse underscores the significance of building trust and dependability in their relationship. It serves as a reminder that faithfulness is foundational for a marriage to withstand the tests of time.

Modern Day Reflection

Proverbs 25:19 states that putting confidence in an unreliable person in a time of trouble is like a broken tooth or a foot out of joint. In the modern world, this verse remains relevant as a cautionary reminder about the importance of discernment in relationships and partnerships. It advises against relying on those who prove to be unreliable or untrustworthy, especially during challenging times. In contemporary terms, Proverbs 25:19 encourages individuals to choose their alliances wisely, whether in personal or professional spheres, and to invest trust in those who demonstrate consistency, reliability, and integrity.

Prayer For XXX in Marriage

Heavenly Father, guide us in strengthening our marriage through trust and faithfulness. Protect us from the pitfalls of unfaithfulness and grant us the grace to be reliable sources of support for one another. In Your name, we pray. Amen.

April 11

1 Corinthians 15:33

"Be not deceived: evil communications corrupt good manners."

What Does This Mean For Us?

This verse highlights the importance of surrounding oneself with positive influences. The company one keeps can significantly impact behavior and values. For the couple striving to strengthen their marriage, it suggests being mindful of the relationships they nurture and ensuring supportive and virtuous individuals surround them.

Modern Day Reflection

Where external influences are overly abundant through various media and social connections, the verse encourages you as a couple to be discerning about the information and influences they allow into their lives. By making intentional choices in your relationships and communication, you can protect the sanctity of your marriage.

Prayer For Positive Influences in Marriage

Heavenly Father, guide us in selecting influences that uplift and strengthen our marriage. Shield us from harmful communications, and may our interactions be a source of goodness and love. In Your name, we pray. Amen.

April 12

2 Timothy 2:22

"Flee also youthful lusts: but follow righteousness, faith, charity, peace, with them that call on the Lord out of a pure heart."

What Does This Mean For Us?

This verse advises against succumbing to impure desires and instead encourages the pursuit of righteousness, faith, love, and peace. For the couple seeking to fortify their marriage, it underscores the importance of avoiding temptations that may threaten the fidelity of their relationship and emphasizes the virtues that should guide their actions.

Modern Day Reflection

2 Timothy 2:22 advises to pursue righteousness, faith, love, and peace, along with those who call on the Lord with a pure heart. In the contemporary world, this verse encourages individuals to seek positive and uplifting relationships and surround themselves with like-minded individuals who share values of integrity, faith, and compassion. It promotes a focus on personal growth and cultivating connections that contribute to a supportive and virtuous community.

❧

Prayer For Spiritual Pursuit in Marriage

Lord, help us flee from temptations that may harm our marriage. Guide us in the pursuit of righteousness, faith, love, and peace. Surround us with those who share our commitment to a pure and faithful relationship. Amen

April 13

Revelation 2:10

"Fear none of those things which thou shalt suffer: behold, the devil shall cast some of you into prison, that ye may be tried; and ye shall have tribulation ten days. Be thou faithful unto death, and I will give thee a crown of life."

What Does This Mean For Us?

In the context of faithfulness in marriage, this verse encourages steadfastness and loyalty, even in the face of challenges and trials. It emphasizes the importance of remaining faithful to one another, no matter the difficulties that may arise.

Modern Day Reflection

For the couple seeking to strengthen their marriage, this verse serves as a reminder that endurance and unwavering commitment lead to a reward —symbolized by the "crown of life." In today's world, where marriages may face various trials, this verse inspires the couple to persevere through difficulties, trusting that their faithfulness will be rewarded.

Prayer For Challenges in Marriage

Lord, in the face of challenges, help us remain faithful to each other. Grant us the strength to endure trials and tribulations in our marriage. May our commitment be unwavering, and may we find the crown of life in our enduring love. Amen.

April 14

Ruth 1:16-17

"Where you go, I will go, and where you stay, I will stay. Your people will be my people, and your God my God."

What Does This Mean For Us?

In this verse, Ruth, a daughter-in-law, speaks to her mother-in-law Naomi, declaring her unwavering devotion. This commitment showcases the essence of partnership and selflessness in marriage, where spouses pledge to stand by each other's side through thick and thin.

Modern Day Reflection

The verse encourages a married couple to cultivate a deep sense of commitment and unity. It reminds them that, just as Ruth embraced Naomi's journey, they should face life's challenges together, embracing each other's paths and forging a shared destiny.

Prayer For Spousal Support in Marriage

Heavenly Father, as we reflect on Ruth 1:16-17, we seek your guidance in fostering unwavering commitment in our marriage. May we emulate Ruth's loyalty, standing by each other's side in all circumstances. Amen

April 15

1 Corinthians 7:39

"A wife is bound to her husband as long as he lives. But if her husband dies, she is free to be married to whom she wishes, only in the Lord."

What Does This Mean For Us?

In 1 Corinthians 7:39, the Apostle Paul discusses the principle of marriage and widowhood. This verse emphasizes the sanctity of marriage and the commitment involved. The verse encourages a couple to cherish the sacred bond of marriage and recognize the gravity of their commitment to each other. It reminds them that their union is a lifelong covenant, reflecting their enduring love.

Modern Day Reflection

In the complexities of modern life, where relationships face various challenges, 1 Corinthians 7:39 serves as a reminder to prioritize and honor marital commitment. Couples are encouraged to grow in understanding, forgiveness, and resilience, ensuring their marriage stands strong despite external pressures.

Prayer For Resilience in Marriage

Lord, inspired by the wisdom of 1 Corinthians 7:39, we pray for the grace to honor the sacred bond of marriage. May our union be a testament to enduring love, and may we navigate life's journey together in harmony and commitment. Amen.

April 16

Ecclesiastes 5:4-5

"When you vow a vow to God, do not delay paying it, for he has no pleasure in fools. Pay what you vow. It is better that you should not vow than that you should vow and not pay."

What Does This Mean For Us?

This verse underscores the importance of honoring commitments and vows, especially in marriage. This verse encourages a couple to prioritize the fulfillment of their marital vows. It emphasizes the significance of trust, integrity, and follow-through in building a strong and lasting marriage.

Modern Day Reflection

In the journey of strengthening a marriage, couples are urged to keep their promises to each other intentionally. Whether big or small, honoring commitments contributes to a foundation of trust and reliability, fostering a healthy relationship.

Prayer For Keeping Promises in Marriage

Lord, inspired by the wisdom of Ecclesiastes 5:4-5, we pray for the grace to be true to our promises in marriage. Please help us to prioritize and fulfill our commitments, cultivating a strong foundation for our relationship. Amen.

April 17

Proverbs 16:3

"Commit thy works unto the Lord, and thy thoughts shall be established."

What Does This Mean For Us?

This verse underscores the importance of seeking divine guidance and committing one's actions and plans to God. It encourages the couple to entrust their relationship to God, seeking His wisdom and guidance in their endeavors. When couples face various challenges and decisions, this verse emphasizes the role of faith and surrender to a higher power in building a resilient and thriving marriage.

Modern Day Reflection

To strengthen their marriage, the couple is encouraged to make God an integral part of their decision-making process. By committing their actions and plans to the Lord, they can find a source of strength and direction, fostering a relationship grounded in faith.

Prayer For Faith in Marriage

Heavenly Father, as we reflect on Proverbs 16:3, we commit our marriage to You. Grant us the wisdom to seek Your guidance in all our endeavors, that our thoughts and actions may be established according to Your will. Amen.

April 18

Psalm 37:5

"Commit thy way unto the Lord; trust also in him, and he shall bring it to pass."

What Does This Mean For Us?

Psalm 37:5 emphasizes the importance of surrendering one's plans and desires to God, trusting that He will bring about the best outcomes. In the context of marriage, it suggests that by entrusting their relationship to the Lord, the couple can find reassurance and guidance in their journey together.

Modern Day Reflection

Couples can apply this wisdom by committing their marriage, decisions, and aspirations to God, cultivating a foundation of trust and reliance on His guidance. By doing so, they may find a source of peace and direction, enhancing the resilience of their marital bond.

Prayer For Peace and Direction in Marriage

Heavenly Father, inspired by Psalm 37:5, we commit our marriage into Your hands. May we trust in Your guidance, and may Your wisdom bring forth blessings and harmony in our relationship. Amen.

April 19

Matthew 19:5

"For this cause shall a man leave father and mother, and shall cleave to his wife: and they twain shall be one flesh."

What Does This Mean For Us?

In the context of your marriage, this verse underscores the idea that a husband and wife are meant to be deeply connected, prioritizing their commitment to each other above other relationships. It's a call for unity and loyalty, emphasizing the oneness of the marital bond.

Modern Day Reflection

This verse encourages the couple to prioritize and nurture their connection in today's world, where various external pressures can strain a marriage. It's a reminder that, just as leaving one's family signifies a new, primary commitment, spouses should prioritize and strengthen their marital bond. In facing challenges, the couple can reflect on how they can truly be "one flesh" by supporting and understanding each other.

Prayer For Nurturing in Marriage

Heavenly Father, grant us the strength to prioritize and nurture our marriage. Help us leave behind distractions and focus on being deeply connected as one flesh. May our commitment to each other grow stronger each day, and may we find joy and fulfillment in our union.
Amen.

April 20

Proverbs 5:21
"For the ways of man are before the eyes of the Lord, and he pondereth all his goings."

What Does This Mean For Us?

This verse carries a compassionate message, highlighting the understanding that God observes our journeys with a caring eye, knowing every step we take. In the realm of marriage, it's a reassurance that your efforts to navigate this shared path are acknowledged by a higher presence.

Modern Day Reflection

In the modern complexities of relationships, where challenges abound, Proverbs 5:21 becomes a comforting beacon. It encourages couples to approach their marriage with kindness, compassion, and a commitment to uphold values that resonate with the divine perspective.

Prayer For Integrity in Marriage
Heavenly Father, as we reflect on this verse, we open our hearts to Your understanding gaze. Grant us the wisdom to navigate our marriage with love, compassion, and integrity. May our journey be a testament to the values that honor You. Amen.

April 21

Proverbs 20:25
"It is a snare to the man who devoureth that which is holy and after vows to make inquiry."

What Does This Mean For Us?

This verse carries the timeless wisdom of being cautious and deliberate in our actions, especially regarding commitments and promises. In the context of marriage, it urges couples to approach their vows and promises with sincerity and thoughtful consideration.

Modern Day Reflection

In the contemporary landscape of relationships, where external pressures and distractions can be abundant, Proverbs 20:25 resonates as a reminder for couples to honor the sacredness of their commitments. It encourages them to make decisions in their marriage with a sense of reverence and responsibility.

∼

Prayer For Responsibility in Marriage
Lord, in the light of Proverbs 20:25, we seek Your guidance in preserving the holiness of our marriage vows. Help us make inquiries before making decisions, ensuring our actions align with the sacred promises we've exchanged. May our marriage be a reflection of Your enduring love. Amen.

April 22

Proverbs 3:5-6

"Trust in the Lord with all your heart and lean not on your own understanding; in all your ways submit to him, and he will make your paths straight."

What Does This Mean For Us?

This verse encourages us to trust in the Lord with all our hearts and not rely on our own understanding. In the context of marriage, it's a reminder to lean on God for guidance and wisdom rather than solely on our own perspectives. Trusting in each other is crucial, but the foundation of that trust should ultimately rest on a shared trust in a higher power.

Modern Day Reflection

In today's world, where relationships face various challenges, this verse suggests that relying on a divine source of wisdom can bring stability and understanding. For couples navigating complex issues, it encourages them to seek spiritual guidance, fostering a deeper connection.

Prayer For Uncertainty in Marriage

O Lord, as we reflect on Proverbs 3:5-6, guide us in our marriage. May our trust in you deepen our bond and provide clarity in times of uncertainty. We seek your wisdom as we navigate the complexities of life together. Amen.

April 23

1 Corinthians 13:7

"Love bears all things, believes all things, hopes all things, endures all things."

What Does This Mean For Us?

1 Corinthians 13:7 beautifully describes the essence of love, stating that it bears all things, believes all things, hopes all things, and endures all things. In the context of marriage, this verse emphasizes the enduring strength of love, urging couples to withstand challenges, believe in each other, and maintain hope in the face of difficulties. It sets a standard for love that perseveres and remains steadfast, even when faced with trials.

Modern Day Reflection

In today's world, where marriages encounter various trials, this verse encourages couples to cultivate a resilient love. For example, during times of financial stress or personal struggles, it prompts spouses to support and believe in one another, fostering a love that can weather any storm.

Prayer For The Bond of Marriage

Lord, in contemplating 1 Corinthians 13:7, we seek your grace to embed these qualities of love in our marriage. Grant us the strength to bear, believe, hope, and endure, creating a bond that withstands the tests of time. Amen.

April 24

Romans 12:11

"Never be lacking in zeal, but keep your spiritual fervor, serving the Lord."

What Does This Mean For Us?

This verse from Romans 12:11 encourages believers to maintain enthusiasm and passion in their spiritual lives while dedicating themselves to serving the Lord. It emphasizes the importance of a vibrant and committed relationship with God.

Modern Day Reflection

In today's fast-paced world, where couples juggle various responsibilities, Romans 12:11 invites spouses to prioritize and invest intentional effort into their marriage. For instance, amid busy schedules and external pressures, it encourages couples to maintain an enthusiastic and dedicated approach to their relationship, ensuring that love remains a priority.

Prayer For Enthusiasm in Marriage

Lord, in contemplating Romans 12:11, we seek your guidance in infusing our marriage with passion and dedication. Grant us the strength to prioritize our love and serve each other with enthusiasm.
Amen.

April 25

Psalm 141:3

"Set a watch, O Lord, before my mouth; keep the door of my lips."

What Does This Mean For Us?

This verse from Psalm is a prayer for guidance and control over one's speech. It acknowledges the power of words and seeks divine help in using language wisely and positively. In modern times, this verse remains relevant as a reminder of the impact our words can have on others and the importance of speaking with mindfulness and kindness.

Modern Day Reflection

In today's world, where communication takes various forms, Psalm 141:3 remains relevant in both verbal and digital interactions. It reminds couples to choose their words wisely, whether in face-to-face conversations or through the channels of social media. By being intentional about their communication, spouses can contribute to a healthier, more respectful, and understanding marriage.

Prayer For Understanding in Marriage

Heavenly Father, as we reflect on Psalm 141:3, grant us the wisdom to use our words to nurture love and understanding in our marriage. May our communication be a source of strength and encouragement. Amen.

April 26

Proverbs 4:23

"Keep thy heart with all diligence; for out of it are the issues of life."

What Does This Mean For Us?

Proverbs 4:23 offers timeless wisdom, emphasizing the significance of protecting one's heart and thoughts. It encourages individuals to be mindful of the influences they allow into their lives—whether through relationships, media, or experiences—recognizing that the condition of the heart shapes one's actions and decisions. It speaks to the importance of maintaining emotional and spiritual well-being in a world filled with various influences.

Modern Day Reflection

In the contemporary context, where external pressures and distractions abound, Proverbs 4:23 remains relevant. Couples can apply this wisdom by actively nourishing their relationship with positive influences, open communication, and shared values. By doing so, they can fortify the emotional bond that sustains their marriage.

Prayer For Preserving Vows in Marriage

Heavenly Father, as we reflect on Proverbs 4:23, we ask for the strength to guard our hearts and protect the wellspring of love in our marriage. May our actions and influences be aligned with the values that strengthen our bond. Amen.

April 27

Proverbs 19:21

"Many are the plans in a person's heart, but it is the Lord's purpose that prevails."

What Does This Mean For Us?

This verse underscores the idea that human plans and aspirations may be numerous, but ultimately, it is the divine purpose that prevails. Additionally, this verse encourages humility, acknowledging that while we may have our own plans and ambitions, it's essential to be open to the guidance and direction that a higher purpose may provide. It speaks to the idea of surrendering control and trusting in a greater, overarching plan for our lives.

Modern Day Reflection

Proverbs 19:21 guides spouses to embrace flexibility and trust in the unfolding of their shared destiny. Recognizing that God's purpose extends beyond their individual aspirations, couples can find solace and strength in facing the unknown together.

Prayer For Purpose in Marriage

Lord, we entrust our marriage into your hands, acknowledging that your purpose surpasses our understanding. Help us to align our hearts with your divine plan and find peace in your sovereign will. Amen.

April 28

Jeremiah 29:11

"For I know the plans I have for you, declares the Lord, plans for welfare and not for evil, to give you a future and a hope."

What Does This Mean For Us?

This verse reassures us that God has a purpose and plan for our lives. In the context of marriage, it implies that God's intention is for the well-being of the couple, offering hope and a promising future.

Modern Day Reflection

For couples seeking to strengthen their marriage, this verse encourages them to trust in God's overarching plan, especially during challenging times, and believe that He has a positive trajectory for their relationship.

Prayer For Challenges in Marriage

Heavenly Father, as we ponder Jeremiah 29:11, we place our marriage in your hands, trusting in your plans for our welfare. Grant us the faith to navigate uncertainties, and may our union be a reflection of the hope and future you have promised. Amen.

April 29

Hebrews 7:2

"To whom also Abraham gave a tenth part of all; first being by interpretation King of righteousness, and after that also King of Salem, which is, King of peace."

What Does This Mean For Us?

This verse highlights Abraham's act of giving a tenth to Melchizedek, emphasizing the connection between generosity and the qualities of righteousness and peace.

Modern Day Reflection

In marriage, it suggests that our acts of giving, whether in finances or emotional support, should be rooted in righteousness and contribute to the peace within our relationship. Generosity becomes a pathway to righteousness and harmony within the marriage bond.

~

Prayer For Giving in Marriage

Lord, help us to emulate Abraham's spirit of giving, tying our generosity to righteousness and peace in our marriage. May our acts of kindness and support reflect Your love and contribute to the peace that surpasses understanding. Amen.

April 30

Colossians 3:23

"And whatsoever ye do, do it heartily, as to the Lord, and not unto men."

What Does This Mean For Us?

This verse encourages a wholehearted and sincere approach to all endeavors, viewing them as acts of service to the Lord. In the context of marriage, it suggests that spouses should invest genuine effort and commitment in their relationship, treating it as a sacred duty.

Modern Day Reflection

Colossians 3:23, viewed through a modern lens, encourages a work ethic grounded in a sense of purpose and dedication. The verse advises couples to approach their work as if they are serving the Lord, emphasizing the idea that every task, no matter how mundane, holds significance. In a contemporary context, this verse speaks to the value of mindfulness and intentionality in our professional lives. It encourages individuals to bring passion and diligence to their work, recognizing it as an opportunity to contribute positively to the world.

Prayer For Sincerity in Marriage

Lord, in light of Colossians 3:23, we pray for the wisdom to invest our energies into our marriage with sincerity. May our love for each other be a testimony to the love and dedication we have for You. Grant us the grace to navigate our journey with purpose and commitment. Amen.

May

AS MAY UNFOLDS ITS VIBRANT TAPESTRY,
LET US BE REMINDED OF THE
INTERCONNECTEDNESS OF ALL LIVING
THINGS. MAY OUR ACTIONS MIRROR THE
BLOSSOMING FLOWERS, RADIATING
KINDNESS, JOY, AND A SPIRIT OF UNITY TO
ALL WHOM WE ENCOUNTER.

May 1

1 Corinthians 7:3

"Let the husband render unto the wife due benevolence: and likewise also the wife unto the husband."

What Does This Mean For Us?

This verse emphasizes the importance of mutual care and intimacy within the marriage relationship. Additionally, it reminds the couple that fulfilling each other's needs, both emotionally and physically, is a vital aspect of building a strong and harmonious marriage. It encourages open communication and a willingness to meet each other's needs.

Modern Day Reflection

In 1 Corinthians 7:3, the verse emphasizes the importance of mutual conjugal rights within the context of marriage. In a modern perspective, it underscores the idea of a balanced and considerate relationship, where both partners are encouraged to fulfill each other's needs and maintain a healthy physical and emotional connection. It acknowledges the significance of intimacy in marriage, promoting a framework that values the well-being and fulfillment of both individuals within the sacred bond of matrimony.

Prayer For Benevolence in Marriage

Lord, in light of 1 Corinthians 7:3, we seek Your guidance in understanding and meeting each other's needs. Grant us the wisdom to express love and benevolence towards one another, fostering a connection that grows stronger with each passing day. Amen.

May 2

James 5:12

"But above all things, my brethren, swear not, neither by heaven, neither by the earth, neither by any other oath: but let your yea be yea; and your nay, nay; lest ye fall into condemnation."

What Does This Mean For Us?

This verse advises against making unnecessary oaths and emphasizes the importance of straightforward communication. It encourages honesty and integrity in our words and actions.

Modern Day Reflection

In marriage, this verse reminds couples to prioritize honesty and simplicity in their communication. Avoiding unnecessary oaths and being truthful in all matters fosters trust and transparency. It encourages spouses to build a relationship where a simple "yes" or "no" can be relied upon, creating a foundation of mutual respect and integrity.

Prayer For Simplicity in Marriage

Lord, help us to be people of honesty and integrity in our marriage. May our words be true, and our promises be kept. Guide us to communicate with transparency and simplicity, building a foundation of trust in our relationship. Amen.

May 3

1 Corinthians 7:10-11

"And unto the married I command, yet not I, but the Lord, Let not the wife depart from her husband: But and if she depart, let her remain unmarried or be reconciled to her husband: and let not the husband put away his wife."

What Does This Mean For Us?

This passage advises married couples not to separate, but if they do, reconciliation is preferable over remaining unmarried.

Modern Day Reflection

The verse addresses the issue of marital relationships, advising that married couples should not seek separation and, if they do, should aim for reconciliation. From a modern perspective, these verses highlight the commitment required in marriage, urging couples to navigate challenges with a focus on unity and reconciliation rather than opting for hasty divorce. It encourages a mindset that prioritizes working through differences and seeking solutions together, recognizing the enduring nature of marital bonds. The passage promotes a modern understanding of marriage as a partnership that requires effort, communication, and a commitment to overcoming obstacles for the sake of a strong and lasting relationship.

Prayer For Difficulties in Marriage

Lord, we seek Your guidance in our marriage journey. Grant us the patience to navigate difficulties and the strength to choose reconciliation over separation. May our love be resilient and enduring. Amen.

May 4

Proverbs 3:7-8

"Be not wise in thine own eyes: fear the Lord, and depart from evil. It shall be health to thy navel, and marrow to thy bones."

What Does This Mean For Us?

This verse advises against arrogance and self-reliance, urging the fear of the Lord and avoidance of evil. In the context of marriage, it emphasizes the importance of humility, mutual respect, and a shared commitment to virtuous living. Applying these principles can contribute to the health and vitality of the marriage, fostering a harmonious and supportive partnership.

Modern Day Reflection

Proverbs 3:7-8 imparts the wisdom of humility and reverence in a contemporary context, advising individuals not to be wise in their own eyes but to fear the Lord and turn away from evil. In modern terms, it encourages a mindset that values humility over arrogance and acknowledges the limitations of human understanding. The verse suggests that a respectful and humble posture towards life, coupled with a conscious avoidance of harmful actions, leads to spiritual and physical well-being. It invites people to trust in a higher wisdom and to navigate life with a sense of awe and reverence, fostering a holistic approach that encompasses both spiritual and practical aspects of daily living.

Prayer For Health in Marriage

Lord, grant us the grace to embrace humility and righteousness in our marriage. May our love be a beacon of health and vitality, reflecting Your divine wisdom. Amen.

May 5

Mark 10:14

"But when Jesus saw it, he was much displeased, and said unto them, Suffer the little children to come unto me, and forbid them not: for of such is the kingdom of God."

What Does This Mean For Us?

This verse reflects Jesus' love for children and His desire for them to be embraced in His presence. It highlights the purity and innocence of children as a model for the kingdom of God.

Modern Day Reflection

In the context of starting a family, this verse encourages parents to recognize the significance of children in the kingdom of God. It calls for a nurturing and welcoming environment for children within the family, acknowledging their innocence and potential for spiritual growth. It prompts couples to approach parenthood with the understanding that children are a precious part of God's plan and should be embraced with love and openness.

Prayer For Parenthood in Marriage

Gracious Lord, help us to approach parenthood with the same love and openness that You demonstrated for children. May our home be a welcoming place for little ones, and may we guide them on their journey towards You. Bless our family and may it be a reflection of Your kingdom. Amen.

May 6

Proverbs 28:20
"A faithful man shall abound with blessings: but he that maketh haste
to be rich shall not be innocent."

What Does This Mean For Us?

This verse speaks to the value of faithfulness and patience, emphasizing that genuine blessings come to those who remain steadfast. In the context of marriage, it suggests that a faithful and patient approach to the relationship will yield abundant blessings, while impatience and a rush for worldly gains may lead to undesirable consequences.

Modern Day Reflection

Proverbs 28:20, in a modern context, emphasizes the significance of diligent and purposeful work in achieving prosperity. The verse suggests that those who are eager to get rich quickly may face consequences, but those who steadily pursue their goals with integrity will experience lasting success. This verse serves as a reminder that sustainable success often comes from a combination of effort, honesty, and a commitment to personal and professional development, discouraging shortcuts that may compromise one's integrity or long-term stability.

Prayer For Patience in Marriage
Lord, grant us the wisdom to cultivate faithfulness and patience in our
marriage, as Proverbs 28:20 teaches. May our commitment to each other
lead to a life filled with Your abundant blessings. Amen.

May 7

Joshua 24:15

" And if it seem evil unto you to serve the Lord, choose you this day
whom ye will serve; whether the gods which your fathers served that
were on the other side of the flood, or the gods of the Amorites, in
whose land ye dwell: but as for me and my house, we will serve
the Lord."

What Does This Mean For Us?

This powerful verse emphasizes the importance of choosing a firm
foundation for one's household. In the context of marriage, it
encourages couples to unite in their commitment to serving a common
purpose, fostering a home that is centered on shared values and a
spiritual connection.

Modern Day Reflection

This verse challenges individuals and families to make a conscious and
committed choice to prioritize their allegiance to God. In today's fast-
paced and diverse world, it encourages a deliberate decision to live in
accordance with one's faith, fostering a home environment centered
around spiritual values and principles.

Prayer For Common Purpose in Marriage

Heavenly Father, in the spirit of Joshua 24:15, we commit to building
our marriage on the foundation of serving You. Guide us to create a
home filled with love, understanding, and devotion to Your teachings.
Amen.

May 8

Philippians 4:13
"I can do all things through Christ which strengtheneth me."

What Does This Mean For Us?

This verse serves as a source of encouragement, reminding the couple that, with faith and the support of their spiritual foundation, they have the strength to overcome challenges in their marriage. In today's world, where couples face various pressures, this verse encourages a resilient mindset and reliance on the divine strength available to them.

Modern Day Reflection

This verse serves as a source of inspiration and empowerment, encouraging individuals to face life's challenges with the confidence that comes from a deep and abiding connection to Christ. In the complexities of the modern world, it instills a sense of resilience and determination, reminding believers that their strength is not solely self-derived but drawn from a higher power. It promotes a mindset of overcoming obstacles, pursuing goals, and navigating life's journey with the assurance that, through faith, one has the strength to endure and triumph in various aspects of life. Philippians 4:13 is a timeless reminder of the transformative power of faith and reliance on Christ in the midst of life's trials and triumphs.

$\sim$

Prayer For Strength in Marriage
Heavenly Father, grant us the strength to navigate the challenges of our marriage. May Your love and guidance empower us to overcome obstacles and grow stronger together. Amen.

May 9

Hebrews 13:4

"Marriage is honourable in all, and the bed undefiled: but
whoremongers and adulterers God will judge."

What Does This Mean For Us?

Hebrews 13:4 emphasizes the sanctity of marriage and the importance
of keeping the marital relationship pure. In today's world, where
external influences can strain marital bonds, this verse encourages the
couple to honor and cherish their commitment, recognizing the divine
significance of their union.

Modern Day Reflection

Hebrews 13:4 holds contemporary significance by emphasizing the
sanctity of marriage and the call to maintain fidelity and purity within
the marital relationship. In a modern context, this verse underscores the
value of commitment, trust, and faithfulness in marriages, urging
individuals to honor the sacred bond of matrimony. It speaks to the
importance of upholding moral integrity and cherishing the intimate
aspects of marriage within the boundaries set by God. This also
encourages a steadfast commitment to the principles of love, fidelity,
and purity, recognizing them as essential components of a healthy and
God-honoring marriage.

~

Prayer For Purity in Marriage

Heavenly Father, we thank You for the sanctity of marriage as
highlighted in Hebrews 13:4. Help us honor and respect each other,
keeping our commitment pure and untarnished by outside influences.
Amen.

<h1 style="text-align:center">May 10</h1>

<h2 style="text-align:center">Mark 10:9</h2>

"What therefore God hath joined together, let not man put asunder."

<h2 style="text-align:center">What Does This Mean For Us?</h2>

This verse underscores the divine bond in marriage, emphasizing the permanence and sacredness of the union. In the contemporary world, where challenges may strain marital ties, this verse encourages the couple to approach their relationship with a sense of commitment and determination to overcome obstacles.

<h2 style="text-align:center">Modern Day Reflection</h2>

Mark 10:9 calls for a deep commitment to the covenant of marriage, urging individuals to approach their relationships with reverence and a determination to overcome obstacles. In a society where the sanctity of marriage is sometimes questioned or undermined, Mark 10:9 encourages a resolute stand against forces that seek to separate what God has joined together, emphasizing the value of enduring love and mutual commitment in the contemporary landscape of relationships.

<h3 style="text-align:center">Prayer For Mutual Love in Marriage</h3>

Lord, we seek Your guidance to fortify our marriage. May our love endure, and may we, as a couple, overcome adversities with unwavering faith and mutual support. Amen.

May 11

Malachi 2:15

"And did not he make one? Yet had he the residue of the spirit. And wherefore one? That he might seek a godly seed. Therefore take heed to your spirit, and let none deal treacherously against the wife of his youth."

What Does This Mean For Us?

Malachi 2:15 emphasizes the sacred nature of the marital union, highlighting God's intention for spouses to be united as one and to raise godly offspring. It calls for faithfulness and warns against betraying the covenant of marriage.

Modern Day Reflection

In the context of starting a family, this verse underscores the importance of a strong and faithful marital foundation. It encourages couples to prioritize the spiritual upbringing of their children and to guard against any form of betrayal or treachery within the marriage. The verse serves as a reminder of the responsibility to nurture a godly legacy through the union of husband and wife.

Prayer For Protection from Treachery in Marriage

Lord, guide us in building a strong and faithful marriage. May our union be a source of blessing for our children, and may our commitment to each other reflect Your love and faithfulness. Protect our marriage from any treachery, and help us raise a godly seed. Amen.

May 12

1 Thessalonians 5:24
"Faithful is he that calleth you, who also will do it."

What Does This Mean For Us?

This verse reassures us of God's faithfulness in fulfilling His promises. In the context of marriage, it encourages the couple to trust in the divine plan for their union. Just as God is faithful in His calling, the couple can rely on His guidance and support as they navigate the challenges and joys of married life.

Modern Day Reflection

In the midst of life's uncertainties, this verse serves as a comforting reminder that the source of our calling and purpose is rooted in a trustworthy and steadfast God. It encourages believers to rest in the confidence that God's faithfulness extends to every aspect of their lives, from the pursuit of purpose to the fulfillment of His plans. In the contemporary landscape of uncertainty and rapid change, 1 Thessalonians 5:24 instills a sense of peace and confidence, inspiring individuals to walk in faith, knowing that the faithful God who calls them will indeed bring His purposes to fruition in their lives.

Prayer For Confidence in Marriage
Heavenly Father, as we reflect on 1 Thessalonians 5:24, we place our trust in Your faithful guidance for our marriage journey. Strengthen our bond and lead us in love and understanding. Amen.

May 13

Proverbs 15:22

"Without counsel purposes are disappointed: but in the multitude of counsellors they are established."

What Does This Mean For Us?

The verse underscores the importance of seeking wise counsel in decision-making. In the context of marriage, it encourages the couple to communicate openly, seek advice when needed, and rely on the support of trusted individuals to strengthen their union.

Modern Day Reflection

In the contemporary context of Proverbs 15:22, the verse holds modern wisdom applicable in a world marked by complexity and interconnectedness. This verse underscores the importance of seeking guidance and diverse perspectives when making decisions in the contemporary context. It advocates for collaborative and informed decision-making, recognizing that many perspectives can offer valuable insights and contribute to the success of one's plans. In an era where individualism is celebrated, It advocates for collaborative and informed decision-making, recognizing that many perspectives can offer valuable insights and contribute to the success of one's plans.

Prayer For Trust in Others in Marriage

Heavenly Father, we acknowledge the wisdom in Proverbs 15:22. Bless our marriage with the guidance of trusted counselors and friends. May their insights help establish a strong foundation for our relationship.

Amen

May 14

Colossians 3:13

"Forbearing one another, and forgiving one another, if any man have a quarrel against any: even as Christ forgave you, so also do ye."

What Does This Mean For Us?

This verse emphasizes the importance of forgiveness in a marriage. It encourages the couple to bear with each other, understanding that conflicts may arise, and to practice forgiveness just as Christ forgave us. In today's world, where the pace of life can be hectic and numerous stressors, this verse reminds the couple of the healing power of forgiveness in nurturing a resilient and loving relationship.

Modern Day Reflection

Colossians 3:13 speaks to the contemporary imperative of cultivating a spirit of forgiveness and understanding in our interpersonal relationships. It advocates for a culture of reconciliation, urging people to let go of resentment and extend the same compassion they have experienced in their own journey of faith.

Prayer For Forgiveness in Marriage

Dear God, as we reflect on Colossians 3:13, grant us the strength to bear with one another and the grace to forgive, just as you have forgiven us. Help us cultivate a spirit of understanding and love in our marriage.
Amen.

May 15

Romans 8:28

"And we know that all things work together for good to them that love God, to them who are the called according to his purpose."

What Does This Mean For Us?

This verse reassures a couple that, in the grand tapestry of life, every experience—whether joyous or challenging—can contribute to their greater good when grounded in their love for each other and their shared commitment to God. In the complexities of today's world, this verse offers solace, reminding the couple that even in the face of trials, their love and faith can guide them toward a positive outcome.

Modern Day Reflection

This verse provides reassurance and a perspective shift, reminding believers that even in the midst of challenges and uncertainties, God is actively working for their ultimate good. It encourages individuals to trust in the divine orchestration of their lives, finding solace in the knowledge that every experience, whether joyful or challenging, contributes to God's greater purpose for those who are devoted to Him. In a world where adversity and unexpected turns are inevitable.

Prayer For Joy in Marriage

Lord, in times of joy and challenge, help us embrace the belief that, through our love and commitment, every experience contributes to our growth and strengthens our marriage. Amen.

<h1 style="text-align:center">May 16</h1>

<h2 style="text-align:center">Proverbs 16:9</h2>

"A man's heart deviseth his way: but the Lord directeth his steps."

What Does This Mean For Us?

This verse emphasizes the delicate balance between our own plans and the guidance of a higher power. In the context of marriage, it reminds the couple that while they may make plans and set goals, it is essential to surrender to the divine guidance that can lead them toward a fulfilling and purposeful journey together. In today's world, where uncertainties abound, this verse encourages the couple to seek direction from a higher source, trusting that their steps are being guided for a greater purpose.

Modern Day Reflection

In the digital age, where personal autonomy and decision-making are highly valued, this verse serves as a humbling reminder of the ultimate authority and guidance of the divine. Our modern pursuit of success and fulfillment encourages individuals to align their plans with a recognition that God ultimately shapes and directs the unfolding of their lives. It invites a posture of surrender, acknowledging that despite our best-laid plans, the Lord establishes the path, offering solace and assurance in the face of life's uncertainties.

Prayer For Guidance in Marriage

Heavenly Father, help us surrender our plans to Your divine guidance. May our steps be directed by Your wisdom as we navigate the path of marriage, trusting in Your purpose for our lives together. Amen.

May 17

Proverbs 12:22

"Lying lips are abomination to the Lord: but they that deal truly are his delight."

What Does This Mean For Us?

This verse underscores the value of honesty and integrity in relationships. In the context of marriage, it emphasizes the importance of open communication and transparency between partners. In today's world, where trust is a precious commodity, couples can find strength in cultivating a foundation of truthfulness, as it leads to a deeper connection and the delight of the divine in their union.

Modern Day Reflection

This verse resonates powerfully in the context of modern ethics and integrity. In a world where honesty is often challenged and truth can be subjective, this verse stands as a timeless call to uphold the value of trustworthiness. It asserts that God finds delight in those who embrace transparency and sincerity, while detesting the deception of lying. It serves as a moral compass, guiding individuals to embody integrity and reliability in their words and actions, fostering a culture where authenticity is esteemed, and falsehoods are rejected.

Prayer For Honesty and Integrity in Marriage

Lord, help us to be open and truthful in our marriage. May our commitment to honesty strengthen our bond, and may Your delight be upon our relationship as we navigate life's journey together. Amen.

May 18

Proverbs 19:14
"House and riches are the inheritance of fathers: and a prudent wife is
from the Lord."

What Does This Mean For Us?

This verse highlights the priceless value of a wise and discerning spouse. In the modern context, where material possessions often take precedence, it reminds couples that the true treasure lies in the qualities of character and wisdom. A prudent partner, a gift from the divine, brings immeasurable richness to a marriage.

Modern Day Reflection

In an era where material possessions are often prioritized, this verse emphasizes that a spouse characterized by wisdom and sound judgment is a divine gift. It underscores the importance of qualities such as prudence and discernment in a marital relationship, highlighting that true richness comes from worldly possessions and a life companion whose wisdom is rooted in the Lord. Additionally, it offers a perspective that values the spiritual and emotional wealth a prudent spouse brings, recognizing the profound impact of a harmonious partnership in navigating the complexities of contemporary life.

Prayer For Wisdom in Marriage
Heavenly Father, we seek Your guidance in cultivating wisdom and
prudence in our marriage. May our union be enriched by the qualities
that truly matter, and may Your blessings be upon our home. Amen.

May 19

Ephesians 5:25

"Husbands, love your wives, even as Christ also loved the church and gave Himself for it."

What Does This Mean For Us?

This verse emphasizes the sacrificial and unconditional love that husbands are called to exhibit in their marriages. It encourages husbands to go beyond traditional roles and embrace active, selfless love. Much like Christ's love for the church, husbands are called to prioritize their wives' well-being and growth, fostering a relationship built on love, respect, and support.

Modern Day Reflection

Ephesians 5:25 conveys a timeless call to husbands to emulate Christ's sacrificial love in their marriages. In the modern context, this verse champions selfless and unconditional love, urging husbands to prioritize the well-being and growth of their wives above all else. Additionally, recognizing that true love involves giving oneself completely for the sake of the other, Ephesians 5:25 inspires a contemporary vision of marriage where empathy, compassion, and a willingness to make sacrifices are foundational. All of these foster a harmonious and fulfilling union that reflects the profound love modeled by Christ for the Church.

Prayer For Selfless Love in Marriage

Lord, we pray for the strength to love each other with the same selflessness and devotion that Christ showed to the church. May our marriage be a reflection of Your boundless love. Amen.

May 20

Luke 11:42

"But woe unto you, Pharisees! for ye tithe mint and rue and all manner of herbs, and pass over judgment and the love of God: these ought ye to have done, and not to leave the other undone."

What Does This Mean For Us?

Luke 11:42 admonishes the Pharisees for emphasizing religious rituals like tithing without prioritizing essential virtues such as judgment and the love of God. It calls for a holistic approach to spirituality.

Modern Day Reflection

This verse warns against focusing solely on external expressions of commitment, like joint finances, without emphasizing deeper values such as understanding and Godly love. Balancing the practical aspects with the spiritual foundation ensures a truly fulfilling partnership.

Prayer For Godly Love in Marriage

Dear Lord, guide us in cultivating a marriage that goes beyond external gestures, one rooted in judgment, understanding, and Your boundless love. May our commitment be holistic, reflecting Your grace in every aspect of our relationship. Amen.

May 21

1 Peter 3:7

"Likewise, ye husbands, dwell with them according to knowledge, giving honor unto the wife, as unto the weaker vessel, and as being heirs together of the grace of life; that your prayers be not hindered."

What Does This Mean For Us?

1 Peter 3:7 emphasizes the importance of husbands honoring and understanding their wives, acknowledging their equal partnership in the marriage. Also, husbands are called to appreciate each partner's unique strengths, fostering an environment of love and unity.

Modern Day Reflection

In 1 Peter 3:7, husbands are instructed to treat their wives with understanding, showing them honor as the weaker vessel and fellow heirs of life's grace. In a contemporary context, this verse advocates for a partnership founded on mutual respect, recognizing equal worth and shared inheritance of grace between spouses. The verse also promotes a modern vision of marriage that values each spouse's unique strengths while emphasizing the importance of treating one another with dignity and understanding and acknowledging their shared journey of grace.

Prayer For Honor in Marriage

Heavenly Father, as we reflect on 1 Peter 3:7, we seek Your guidance to honor and understand each other in our marriage. Grant us the wisdom to navigate challenges together, recognizing the strength in our unity. Amen.

May 22

Ephesians 5:28-29

"So ought men to love their wives as their own bodies. He that loveth his wife loveth himself. For no man ever yet hated his own flesh, but nourisheth and cherisheth it, even as the Lord the church."

What Does This Mean For Us?

This verse emphasizes the profound connection between a husband and wife, drawing a parallel between marital love and self-love. Husbands are called to love their wives as an extension of themselves, caring for and nurturing the relationship. In today's world, it encourages husbands to prioritize the well-being and growth of the marriage, fostering an environment of love, support, and mutual care.

Modern Day Reflection

Ephesians 5:28-29 imparts a modern lesson on the dynamics of marital love, stating that husbands ought to love their wives as they love their own bodies. It also fosters a vision of marriage that rejects individualism in favor of a shared life where both spouses contribute to each other's growth and happiness, cultivating a bond characterized by love, understanding, and a commitment to shared well-being.

Prayer For Connection in Marriage

Lord, in light of Ephesians 5:28-29, we pray for a love that nourishes and cherishes, mirroring the selfless love You have shown us. May our marriage be a testament to the beauty of sacrificial love and mutual care. Amen.

May 23

1 Timothy 5:8

"But if any provide not for his own, and specially for those of his own house, he hath denied the faith, and is worse than an infidel."

What Does This Mean For Us?

This verse emphasizes the responsibility of husbands to provide for and care for their families. It underscores the importance of ensuring the well-being of one's household. Today, it speaks to the need for husbands to be actively involved in their families' financial and emotional support, fostering a stable and secure environment.

Modern Day Reflection

In 1 Timothy 5:8, the verse underscores the contemporary responsibility of providing for one's family, stating that those who do not provide for their own household have denied the faith and are worse than unbelievers. It addresses the societal obligation to provide financial support and emotional and physical care for one's household. It resonates as a call for modern individuals to embody the values of responsibility, care, and support within the family unit, recognizing that such actions reflect the essence of living out one's faith in a tangible and meaningful way.

Prayer For Care in Marriage

Lord, we pray for the ability to provide for our family, both materially and emotionally. May our efforts be guided by love and a commitment to the well-being of those entrusted to our care. Amen.

May 24

Genesis 2:18

"And the Lord God said, It is not good that the man should be alone; I will make him an help meet for him."

What Does This Mean For Us?

This verse highlights the divine design for companionship and partnership in marriage. It underscores the idea that spouses are meant to be helpers and companions to one another. In modern times, it speaks to the importance of mutual support, understanding, and collaboration in marriage, where couples work together to navigate life's challenges.

Modern Day Reflection

In Genesis 2:18, the verse highlights the divine recognition that it is not good for man to be alone, leading to the creation of a suitable partner for Adam. This verse speaks to the innate human need for companionship and connection in a modern context. It emphasizes the value of relationships and the idea that individuals are not meant to navigate life in isolation. It resonates as a reminder that, in our pursuit of purpose and happiness, meaningful relationships play a fundamental role, reflecting a universal truth about the human experience that transcends time and cultural changes.

Prayer For Collaboration in Marriage

Heavenly Father, we acknowledge the beauty of the partnership You designed for marriage. Help us to be true helpers to each other, supporting and uplifting one another in our journey together. Amen.

May 25

Proverbs 18:22

"Whoso findeth a wife findeth a good thing and obtaineth favour of the Lord."

What Does This Mean For Us?

The verse emphasizes the value of a wife as a precious gift and a source of divine favor. Additionally, it speaks to the profound importance of mutual appreciation and the recognition of the goodness and favor that marriage brings. Husbands are reminded to cherish and honor their wives, acknowledging the blessing they are in their lives.

Modern Day Reflection

The verse emphasizes the divine favor that comes with discovering a life partner, encouraging a perspective that views marriage not only as a human institution but as a source of blessing and fulfillment sanctioned by God. Proverbs 18:22 invites individuals to appreciate the goodness and favor that a harmonious marital bond brings, fostering a contemporary understanding of the sacred and enriching nature of a loving partnership built on mutual respect, companionship, and shared purpose.

Prayer For Appreciation in Marriage

Heavenly Father, we thank You for the gift of marriage and the favor it brings into our lives. Help us, as husband and wife, to appreciate and cherish each other, recognizing the goodness that comes from our union. Amen.

May 26

Romans 12:18

"If it be possible, as much as lieth in you, live peaceably with all men."

What Does This Mean For Us?

Romans 12:18 encourages married partners to actively pursue peace in their relationship, doing their part to maintain harmony whenever possible.

Modern Day Reflection

In marriage, it's a joint effort to create a peaceful and loving environment. This verse reminds us to seek resolutions, understanding, and compromise proactively. It's a call to be peacemakers within our own homes and presents opportunities to strengthen the marriage bond. The marriage becomes stronger When both partners attempt to maintain peace and harmony.

Prayer For Respect in Marriage

Heavenly Father, help us to be instruments of peace in our marriage. Grant us the patience to understand, the humility to apologize, and the love to bridge any gaps that may arise. May our home be a sanctuary of peace. Amen.

May 27

Genesis 14:20

"And blessed be the most high God, which hath delivered thine enemies into thy hand. And he gave him tithes of all."

What Does This Mean For Us?

This verse marks Abraham giving a tenth of his possessions to Melchizedek after a victorious battle, acknowledging God's role in his triumph and expressing gratitude through giving.

Modern Day Reflection

In marriage, it encourages couples to recognize and celebrate victories, big or small, together. Sharing the fruits of success, be it financial gains or personal achievements, reinforces a sense of unity and gratitude in the relationship.

~

Prayer For Victories in Marriage

Gracious God, help us to acknowledge and appreciate the victories in our marriage. May our shared gratitude lead to acts of generosity, strengthening the bond between us and glorifying Your name. Amen.

May 28

1 Peter 5:3

"Neither as being lords over God's heritage, but being ensamples to the flock."

What Does This Mean For Us?

This verse speaks to the idea that husbands should not lord over their wives but instead lead by example. It suggests that a husband should not exert dominance or control but rather demonstrate love, understanding, and righteousness to inspire a harmonious relationship. Instead of dictating, a husband can lead through actions that reflect the values they wish to see in the marriage.

Modern Day Reflection

The verse advises leaders to be examples to the flock, not lording over them but being models of humility. In a modern context, this verse speaks to the qualities expected of those in leadership positions. It encourages leaders to lead humbly, serving as role models who inspire and guide rather than dictating authority. In a world often characterized by hierarchical structures.

Prayer For Exemplary Leadership in Marriage

Lord, teach us to be humble leaders in our marriage. May we strive to exemplify patience, kindness, and selflessness. Let our actions be a source of inspiration for each other, fostering a partnership built on love and respect. Grant us the strength to overcome difficulties and grow closer through the values you've bestowed upon us. Amen.

May 29

Proverbs 11:24-25

"There is that scattereth, and yet increaseth; and there is that withholdeth more than is meet, but it tendeth to poverty. The liberal soul shall be made fat: and he that watereth shall be watered also himself."

What Does This Mean For Us?

Proverbs 11:24-25 encourages couples to approach their relationship with a mindset of generosity. Just as the verses speak about scattering and increasing, it suggests that in marriage, being open-handed with love, understanding, and support can lead to a richer, more fulfilling relationship. The more each partner gives of themselves, the more they receive in return, creating a harmonious and abundant marital environment. This mindset fosters a cycle of mutual blessing, contributing to the overall prosperity and well-being of the marriage.

Modern Day Reflection

In marriage, it urges couples to approach their union with a spirit of generosity, not only in material aspects but also in emotional support and understanding. The more we give, the more we receive, creating a flourishing environment for both partners.

Prayer For Spirit of Generosity in Marriage

Gracious God, instill in us a generous spirit within our marriage. May our acts of giving, whether big or small, lead to an abundance of love, understanding, and shared prosperity. Bless our union and make it a source of blessing to others. Amen.

May 30

Ephesians 5:22

"Wives, submit yourselves unto your own husbands, as unto the Lord."

What Does This Mean For Us?

This verse has been interpreted in various ways, but in the context of modern relationships, it suggests mutual respect and cooperation between spouses. It's not about dominance but rather emphasizes a harmonious partnership where each person complements the other.

Modern Day Reflection

Ephesians 5:22 instructs wives to submit to their husbands, a verse that, in a modern perspective, is often approached with nuance and reinterpretation. Rather than advocating for a one-sided authority, contemporary interpretations emphasize the concept of mutual submission and partnership within marriage. It invites a vision of marriage where both partners contribute to the relationship, respecting each other's strengths and perspectives.

Prayer For Partnership in Marriage

Lord, teach us the true meaning of partnership in marriage. May we, as husband and wife, submit to each other in love and respect. Grant us the strength to work together, appreciating the gifts and perspectives we each bring to our relationship. May our marriage be a reflection of your grace and unity. Amen.

May 31

Colossians 3:18

"Wives, submit yourselves unto your own husbands, as it is fit in the
Lord."

What Does This Mean For Us?

In understanding this verse, it's crucial to recognize that the concept of
submission doesn't imply inferiority but rather speaks to a respectful
cooperation and partnership within marriage. In today's context, it
suggests that wives should willingly work together with their husbands,
acknowledging each other's strengths and supporting one another in
their respective roles. It's about fostering a harmonious dynamic where
both spouses contribute to the well-being of the marriage.

Modern Day Reflection

The verse doesn't advocate for a rigid hierarchy but rather emphasizes
the importance of cooperation, understanding, and mutual support.
The verse encourages spouses to navigate their roles collaboratively,
recognizing and valuing each other's contributions. It invites a vision of
marriage where both partners, regardless of gender, work together as
equal and complementary parts of a unified whole.

Prayer For Respect and Cooperation in Marriage

Lord, grant us the wisdom to understand the true meaning of
partnership in marriage. Help us, as spouses, to support and
complement each other in our roles. May our relationship be
characterized by mutual respect and love, reflecting your divine design
for marriage. Amen.

June

AS THE SUN REACHES ITS ZENITH IN THE SKY, MAY OUR SOULS ALSO BASK IN THE WARMTH OF DIVINE LOVE. IN THIS MONTH OF ABUNDANCE, LET US BE GRATEFUL FOR THE BLESSINGS THAT SURROUND US AND SHARE THE OVERFLOW OF OUR HEARTS WITH THOSE IN NEED.

June 1

1 Peter 3:1-2

"Likewise, ye wives, be in subjection to your own husbands; that, if any obey not the word, they also may without the word be won by the conversation of the wives; While they behold your chaste conversation coupled with fear."

What Does This Mean For Us?

This passage suggests that a wife's behavior and character have the power to influence her husband positively, even if he may not share the same faith. It encourages wives to lead by example, fostering an environment of love, respect, and virtue in the marriage that can potentially lead to positive change in the spouse.

Modern Day Reflection

In a modern perspective, this verse is often seen as promoting qualities of patience, understanding, and a commitment to relational harmony. Rather than enforcing a rigid hierarchy, this passage is interpreted in contemporary terms as a call for relational wisdom, advocating for qualities that contribute to the well-being of the marital bond, emphasizing the transformative power of love and understanding within diverse partnerships.

Prayer For Well-Being in Marriage

Lord, help us cultivate a marriage where love and respect abound. May our character and actions contribute to the well-being of our relationship, creating a space for positive change. Grant us the grace to support and uplift each other, reflecting the beauty of your love in our marriage. Amen.

June 2

Proverbs 31:10-12

"Who can find a virtuous woman? for her price is far above rubies. The heart of her husband doth safely trust in her so that he shall have no need of spoil. She will do him good and not evil all the days of her life."

What Does This Mean For Us?

This passage highlights the immense value of a wife who is not only capable but also trustworthy and committed. The focus is on fostering a relationship where trust is the foundation, and the wife's actions bring continuous good to her husband.

Modern Day Reflection

Proverbs 31:10-12 describes the qualities of an excellent wife, portraying her as a woman of great value who brings immense good to her husband's life. The emphasis is not merely on traditional roles but on the qualities of trustworthiness, support, and industriousness. Rather than reinforcing outdated stereotypes, this verse serves as a celebration of the diverse and invaluable qualities that women bring to relationships, fostering an appreciation for the collaborative and equal nature of partnerships in the complexities of the modern world.

Prayer For Appreciation in Marriage

Lord, guide us in cultivating a marriage of trust and mutual support. May our love be steadfast, and our actions reflect the goodness that sustains our relationship. Grant us the grace to appreciate the unique qualities each of us brings to this partnership. Amen.

June 3

Titus 2:4-5

"That they may teach the young women to be sober, to love their husbands, to love their children, To be discreet, chaste, keepers at home, good, obedient to their own husbands, that the word of God be not blasphemed."

What Does This Mean For Us?

This passage highlights the virtues expected of wives, emphasizing love, discretion, chastity, and obedience. In today's context, it encourages wives to foster a loving and supportive atmosphere at home, embracing their roles with wisdom and grace. It doesn't prescribe subservience but rather a partnership where each spouse's strengths contribute to the well-being of the family.

Modern Day Reflection

Titus 2:4-5 encourages women to mentor and guide younger women in various aspects of life, including love for their husbands and children, self-control, purity, and homemaking. The passage encourages the passing down of wisdom, while fostering a community where women empower and guide one another. It promotes a vision of women supporting each other in personal growth and and pursuing virtuous living, recognizing the value of collective wisdom and shared experiences across generations.

Prayer For Grace in Marriage

Gracious Father, guide us as a couple to embody the virtues outlined in Titus 2:4-5. May our love for each other and our family be a testament to Your grace, and may our home be a place where Your love and wisdom shine. Amen.

June 4

Proverbs 21:19

"It is better to dwell in the wilderness, than with a contentious and an angry woman."

What Does This Mean For Us?

This verse uses vivid imagery to convey the challenges of living with a quarrelsome and angry woman. It suggests that even dwelling in the wilderness, often considered a desolate place, is preferable to dealing with constant contention and anger.

Modern Day Reflection

In the context of marriage, this verse emphasizes the detrimental impact of strife and anger on the home environment, underscoring the importance of cultivating peace and harmony within the marital relationship.

∼

Prayer For Patience in Marriage

Dear Lord, grant us the patience to navigate through disagreements and the wisdom to foster love and understanding in our marriage. May our home be a haven of peace and not a dwelling of contention. Amen.

June 5

Genesis 1:28

"And God blessed them, and God said unto them, Be fruitful, and multiply, and replenish the earth, and subdue it: and have dominion over the fish of the sea, and over the fowl of the air, and over every living thing that moveth upon the earth."

What Does This Mean For Us?

This verse is a divine commandment to Adam and Eve to multiply and fill the earth. It reflects God's design and intention for humanity to procreate and care for the world.

Modern Day Reflection

In the context of starting a family, this verse encourages couples to embrace the blessing of parenthood. It emphasizes the importance of bringing forth life, nurturing a family, and responsibly caring for the earth. As couples embark on the journey of having children or continuing to raise their children, this verse invites them to recognize the sacred nature of family and the role they play in shaping the future.

Prayer For Family in Marriage

Gracious Father, as we embark on the journey of starting a family or nurturing our existing family, may Your blessing be upon us. Grant us the wisdom to nurture and guide our children, and may our family contribute positively to the world around us. Amen.

June 6

1 Peter 3:5-6

"For after this manner in the old time the holy women also, who trusted in God, adorned themselves, being in subjection unto their own husbands: Even as Sara obeyed Abraham, calling him lord: whose daughters ye are, as long as ye do well, and are not afraid with any amazement."

What Does This Mean For Us?

This passage addresses the role of wives, emphasizing the virtues of trust, submissiveness, and reverence. It parallels the holy women of old, particularly highlighting Sarah's obedience to Abraham. In a contemporary context, the verse suggests that wives can contribute to a harmonious marriage by trusting their husbands, being supportive, and respecting their leadership.

Modern Day Reflection

In a modern context, these verses are often interpreted as a celebration of inner strength, humility, and resilience rather than prescribing a passive demeanor. It resonates with a contemporary understanding that values qualities like resilience, humility, and a steadfast spirit in navigating the complexities of life, promoting an inclusive perspective that transcends cultural and historical contexts.

Prayer For Union in Marriage

Dear Lord, grant us the wisdom to trust and support each other in our marriage, just as the holy women of old trusted in you. May our union be built on a foundation of love and respect. Amen.

June 7

Proverbs 14:1

"Every wise woman buildeth her house: but the foolish plucketh it down with her hands."

What Does This Mean For Us?

This verse underscores the impact of a wife on the home. A wise and understanding wife contributes to the building and stability of her household, while a foolish one can bring it to ruin. In today's context, it emphasizes the significance of a wife's role in creating a harmonious and supportive environment at home.

Modern Day Reflection

For the couple seeking to strengthen their marriage, this verse encourages the wife to play a positive and constructive role in building a strong foundation for their family. It prompts a reflection on the actions and choices that contribute to the well-being of the home.

Prayer For The Home in Marriage

Lord, help us as a couple to navigate challenges with wisdom and discernment. May our home be a haven of peace, built on the foundation of love and understanding. Amen.

June 8

Proverbs 31:26-27

"She openeth her mouth with wisdom, and in her tongue is the law of kindness. She looketh well to the ways of her household and eateth not the bread of idleness."

What Does This Mean For Us?

This verse describes the virtues of a capable and wise wife. It emphasizes her use of wisdom in speech and kindness in her actions. She is attentive to the needs of her household and avoids idleness. In today's world, this verse encourages wives to be proactive, wise communicators, and actively involved in the well-being of their families.

Modern Day Reflection

Proverbs 31:26-27 describes the qualities of a virtuous woman, emphasizing her wisdom and kindness. In a modern context, these verses are often understood as celebrating the strength found in a woman's character rather than narrowly defining her worth by traditional roles. It promotes a vision of strength rooted in character and virtue, acknowledging the diverse ways women contribute to the world, whether within their homes or in broader society, fostering a perspective that appreciates the multifaceted strengths women bring to the challenges of the modern world.

Prayer For Wisdom in Marriage

Lord, help us as a couple to be proactive in caring for our home and in our communication. May our actions and words reflect wisdom and kindness. Amen.

June 9

1 Timothy 2:11-12

"Let the woman learn in silence with all subjection. But I suffer not a woman to teach, nor to usurp authority over the man, but to be in silence."

What Does This Mean For Us?

These verses encourage mutual respect and collaboration in marriage rather than enforcing rigid gender roles. The emphasis is on learning, subjection, and understanding, promoting a relationship where both partners value each other's perspectives and strengths. For the couple, this means fostering a supportive environment where both can learn and grow together.

Modern Day Reflection

1 Timothy advises that women should learn in quietness and full submission, not having authority over men. Some interpret this passage as specific to the cultural and religious context of the time, while others grapple with its application today. It prompts reflections on fostering an environment of respect and equality. Modern interpretations often seek a balance between cultural relevance and maintaining the core principles of love, respect, and unity within the Christian community.

Prayer For Support of Each Other in Marriage

Heavenly Father, guide us in our journey as a married couple. Grant us the patience to listen, the humility to learn, and the strength to support each other. May our marriage be a testament to your love, where we find harmony in our unique roles and contribute to each other's happiness and well-being. Amen.

June 10

2 Corinthians 9:7

"Every man according as he purposeth in his heart, so let him give; not grudgingly, or of necessity: for God loveth a cheerful giver."

What Does This Mean For Us?

This verse encourages couples to approach giving, whether financial or emotional, with a willing and joyful heart, emphasizing that giving should reflect genuine love and generosity rather than obligation or reluctance.

Modern Day Reflection

2 Corinthians 9:7 calls for spouses to support and contribute to each other willingly and joyfully, fostering an atmosphere of love and generosity that extends beyond material possessions to include understanding, time, and emotional support.

~

Prayer For Generosity in Marriage

Heavenly Father, teach us to give wholeheartedly and joyfully in our marriage, both materially and emotionally. May our acts of generosity be fueled by love, strengthening our bond and bringing glory to Your name. Amen.

June 11

Matthew 23:23

"Woe unto you, scribes and Pharisees, hypocrites! for ye pay tithe of mint and anise and cummin and have omitted the weightier matters of the law, judgment, mercy, and faith: these ought ye to have done, and not to leave the other undone."

What Does This Mean For Us?

This verse reminds us that while tithing is important, it's equally crucial to prioritize justice, mercy, and faith in our relationships and interactions.

Modern Day Reflection

Matthew 23:23 provides married couples with a call to balance the tangible aspects of giving with the intangible—showing love, compassion, and faithfulness. Tithing with a heart full of mercy and faith strengthens the spiritual foundation of a marital partnership.

Prayer For Justice, Mercy and Faith in Marriage

Lord, help us honor You not only with our material possessions but also with our hearts. May our marriage be characterized by justice, mercy, and unwavering faith. Guide us in balancing the practical and spiritual aspects of our union. Amen.

June 12

Nehemiah 10:38

"And the priest the son of Aaron shall be with the Levites when the Levites take tithes: and the Levites shall bring up the tithe of the tithes unto the house of our God, to the chambers, into the treasure house."

What Does This Mean For Us?

In Nehemiah 10:38, this verse underscores the structured and cooperative aspect of tithing, emphasizing the importance of unity and joint responsibility in financial matters.

Modern Day Reflection

In our marriage, it encourages us to approach financial responsibilities as a team, recognizing that our combined efforts contribute to the well-being of our home. Just as the Levites worked together, may we harmonize our financial stewardship for the benefit of our relationship and shared goals.

Prayer For Tithing in Marriage

Lord God, guide us in aligning our financial responsibilities as a united front in our marriage. May our joint efforts bring abundance to our home and honor to Your name. Amen.

June 13

1 Corinthians 7:3-5

"Let the husband render unto the wife due benevolence: and likewise also the wife unto the husband. The wife hath not power of her own body, but the husband: and likewise also the husband hath not power of his own body, but the wife. Defraud ye not one the other, except it be with consent for a time, that ye may give yourselves to fasting and prayer, and come together again, that Satan tempt you not for your incontinency."

What Does This Mean For Us?

The verse addresses the mutual responsibilities within a marital relationship. The passage suggests that spouses should fulfill each other's physical needs and not deprive one another, except perhaps by mutual agreement and for a set time of prayer and fasting.

Modern Day Reflection

1 Corinthians 7:3-5 emphasizes that both partners must meet each other's needs and maintain a healthy and intimate connection. The verse promotes open communication and a mutual understanding of each other's desires, fostering a relationship where both spouses actively contribute to the well-being and satisfaction of the other.

Prayer For Intimate Connection in Marriage

Heavenly Father, teach us the importance of mutual submission in the intimate aspects of our marriage. May our union be a reflection of your design for the beauty and sanctity of marital intimacy. Amen.

June 14

1 Peter 3:8

"Finally, be ye all of one mind, having compassion one of another, love as brethren, be pitiful, be courteous."

What Does This Mean For Us?

In 1 Peter 3:8, the verse encourages believers to be harmonious, sympathetic, compassionate, and humble in their relationships with one another. It sets a tone for how members of the Christian community should interact, emphasizing qualities of unity, empathy, and humility. This verse calls for a spirit of kindness and understanding, fostering a sense of unity and support within the community of believers. It serves as a guiding principle for cultivating positive and compassionate relationships, promoting a harmonious and empathetic atmosphere among Christians.

Modern Day Reflection

1 Peter 3:8 promotes unity, compassion, and courtesy, which are essential principles for mutual submission in marriage. The verse encourages spouses to cultivate a shared mindset, demonstrating understanding and empathy toward each other. It emphasizes a relationship built on brotherly love, where kindness and consideration are central.

Prayer For Unity in Marriage

Dear God, help us cultivate unity of mind and compassion in our marriage. May our love for each other resemble that of brothers and sisters, marked by kindness and courtesy. Guide us in mutual submission, creating a harmonious and supportive relationship that reflects your love. Amen.

June 15

Psalm 128:3

"Thy wife shall be as a fruitful vine by the sides of thine house: thy children like olive plants round about thy table."

What Does This Mean For Us?

This poetic verse envisions the blessings of a flourishing family, comparing the wife to a fruitful vine and children to olive plants. It emphasizes the beauty and abundance that family life brings.

Modern Day Reflection

In the contemporary context, this verse paints a picture of a harmonious and thriving family. It speaks to the mutual support and growth within the household, where the partnership between spouses and the presence of children contribute to a fulfilling and abundant life. It encourages couples to see their family as a source of strength, joy, and shared blessings.

Prayer For Family Blessings in Marriage

Dear Lord, thank you for the vision of a flourishing family in Your word. As we journey through the blessings of marriage and parenthood, may our home be a place of abundance, joy, and mutual support. Bless our family as we grow together in Your love. Amen.

June 16

Proverbs 22:6

"Start children off on the way they should go, and even when they are old, they will not turn from it."

What Does This Mean For Us?

This verse emphasizes the significance of early guidance and training in a child's life. It encourages parents to instill values, wisdom, and a foundation of faith in their children from an early age.

Modern Day Reflection

Proverbs 22:6 in a modern context could be understood as an encouragement for parents and caregivers to actively and positively influence the upbringing of their children. The verse suggests that the early guidance and values instilled in a child's life can significantly shape their future. This verse underscores the impact of intentional parenting, emphasizing the long-term effects of nurturing a child in a way that aligns with positive values, ethics, and faith, contributing to their overall well-being and character development throughout their lives.

Prayer For Our Children in Marriage

Heavenly Father, we thank you for our family and the privilege of raising our children. Grant us the wisdom to lead by example and the patience to navigate the challenges of parenthood. May our home be a sanctuary of love and learning and may our family be a testament to your love. In Jesus' name, we pray. Amen.

June 17

James 5:7-8

"Be patient, then, brothers and sisters, until the Lord's coming. See how the farmer waits for the land to yield its valuable crop, patiently waiting for the autumn and spring rains. You too, be patient and stand firm, because the Lord's coming is near."

What Does This Mean For Us?

In these verses, James encourages believers to be patient and steadfast in their faith, drawing an analogy to a farmer patiently waiting for the crops. It encourages believers to remain resilient and unwavering in their faith, knowing that the ultimate fulfillment of God's purposes is imminent.

Modern Day Reflection

In our modern context, James 5:7-8 encourages us to maintain patience and steadfastness in our faith journey, much like a farmer patiently waits for the harvest. It speaks to the fast-paced nature of our lives, where instant results are often expected. It encourages us to endure life's challenges, trusting that God's promises will come to fruition.

Prayer For Faith in Marriage

Lord, We come before you with gratitude for the wisdom reminding us to be patient and steadfast in our faith. Grant us the patience to navigate life's challenges, trusting in Your perfect timing. May our hearts be attuned to Your guidance and find strength in the waiting. Amen.

June 18

Malachi 3:10

"Bring ye all the tithes into the storehouse, that there may be meat in mine house, and prove me now herewith, saith the Lord of hosts, if I will not open you the windows of heaven, and pour you out a blessing, that there shall not be room enough to receive it."

What Does This Mean For Us?

Malachi 3:10 calls believers to embrace a spirit of generosity by faithfully giving a tenth of their income, known as tithes, to support the community of faith, symbolized as the "storehouse." The verse challenges individuals to test God's faithfulness in this act of obedience, promising abundant blessings beyond measure.

Modern Day Reflection

In our contemporary context, Malachi 3:10 encourages a modern-day reflection on the principles of generosity, stewardship, and trust in God's provision. It invites believers to recognize the value of contributing to the needs of their faith community and beyond, whether through financial giving or other forms of support.

Prayer For Generosity in Marriage

Heavenly Father, as we come before you, grant us a spirit of generosity, recognizing that all we have is entrusted to us by You. Help us faithfully contribute to the needs of our faith community and those around us. May we live out lives of stewardship, acknowledging Your ownership of our resources. Guide us to embody the principles of this verse in our modern context. Amen.

June 19

Proverbs 15:1

"A gentle answer turns away wrath, but a harsh word stirs up anger."

What Does This Mean For Us?

This verse imparts timeless wisdom about the power of our words in interpersonal relationships. It encourages responding to others with gentleness and kindness, as it has the potential to diffuse conflict and soothe anger.

Modern Day Reflection

Proverbs 15:1 serves as a poignant reminder of our words' profound impact on relationships. This verse urges us to embrace a communication style characterized by gentleness and kindness, emphasizing that such an approach can diffuse tension and navigate conflicts constructively. In a time where words can travel instantly and be widely shared, the verse prompts us to cultivate a culture of understanding and empathy, recognizing that our choice of words can either heal or exacerbate wounds in the complex tapestry of human relationships.

Prayer For Our Words in Marriage

Heavenly Father, grant us the strength to respond to others with gentleness and kindness, especially in moments of conflict and tension. May Your Spirit guide our words, turning away wrath and fostering understanding. We surrender our communication to You, trusting in Your wisdom to guide us in every word we speak. Amen.

June 20

1 Peter 4:9

"Use hospitality one to another without grudging."

What Does This Mean For Us?

In this verse, the Apostle Peter encourages believers to practice hospitality willingly and without hesitation. The emphasis is on extending a welcoming and generous spirit to one another, emphasizing the importance of genuine and cheerful hospitality within the Christian community.

Modern Day Reflection

In our contemporary world, 1 Peter 4:9 calls us to cultivate a culture of genuine and open-hearted hospitality in our interactions. It challenges us to create spaces of warmth and generosity, not only within our homes but also in our communities and relationships. It prompts us to be intentional in our relationships, offering hospitality as a powerful expression of Christ's inclusive and selfless love in our modern lives.

Prayer For Hospitality in Marriage

Dear Lord, as we navigate the complexities of our modern world, we seek Your guidance in embodying the spirit of hospitality. Grant us the grace to extend genuine kindness and warmth to those around us, both within our homes and in our broader communities. May our hearts be open, and our actions reflect the love of Christ as we create spaces where others feel valued and welcomed. In our daily interactions, may Your love shine through us, making a tangible impact on those we encounter.
Amen.

June 21

Psalm 90:12

"So teach us to number our days, that we may apply our hearts unto wisdom."

What Does This Mean For Us?

The verse encourages us to approach life with a perspective of wisdom and awareness of our limited time. It prompts us to reflect on our days' brevity and seek divine guidance in using our time. Ultimately, it challenges us to live intentionally, making choices that contribute to our spiritual growth, the well-being of others, and the pursuit of God's purposes in the time we have been given.

Modern Day Reflection

In our modern reflection, Psalm 90:12 serves as a poignant reminder to navigate life with intentionality and wisdom. It encourages us to be mindful of the limited nature of time, urging a shift from a hurried pace to a thoughtful and purposeful existence. This verse prompts us to reflect on our priorities, emphasizing what truly matters—relationships, personal growth, and the pursuit of God's purposes.

Prayer For Purpose in Marriage

Heavenly Father, as we stand in the midst of our fast-paced and dynamic world, we echo the prayer of Psalm 90:12. Teach us to number our days, to recognize the brevity of life, and to approach each moment with wisdom and intentionality. May our days be marked by purpose and pursuit of Your divine wisdom. Amen.

June 22

James 1:19

"My dear brothers and sisters, take note of this: Everyone should be quick to listen, slow to speak and slow to become angry."

What Does This Mean For Us?

It encourages us to prioritize effective communication by being quick to listen and being willing to understand before responding. The instruction to be slow to speak advises caution in our words, promoting thoughtfulness and consideration in what we say. Additionally, the call to be slow to become angry emphasizes the value of patience, urging us to respond to situations calmly rather than impulsively.

Modern Day Reflection

This verse provides a timeless blueprint for effective and considerate communication. It prompts us to be intentional listeners, seeking to understand before being understood. The call to be slow to speak challenges us to navigate the fast-paced nature of marital conversations with thoughtfulness and restraint, avoiding hasty or careless words.

Prayer For Understanding in Marriage

Lord, grant us the humility to be quick to listen, the wisdom to be slow to speak, and the patience to be slow to become angry. May our interactions be marked by understanding, empathy, and a genuine desire to connect with others. In moments of tension, grant us the strength to respond with patience and kindness. May our communication be a source of unity and compassion in a diverse and dynamic world. Amen.

June 23

Galatians 5:13

"For, brethren, ye have been called unto liberty; only use not liberty for an occasion to the flesh, but by love serve one another."

What Does This Mean For Us?

In a contemporary context, it encourages believers to recognize and appreciate their freedom in Christ. It emphasizes that this freedom is not a license for self-indulgence but a call to selfless service. It speaks to a lifestyle marked by humility, putting the needs of others before our own desires. Essentially, this verse encourages believers to express their faith through tangible acts of love and service, positively impacting the world around them.

Modern Day Reflection

In the context of marriage today, Galatians 5:13 encourages a balance between freedom and responsibility. While spouses can express themselves and pursue individual goals, the verse emphasizes that this freedom should not be exploited for selfish desires. Instead, it calls for using freedom as an opportunity to serve one another in love. In a modern marital context, this verse encourages mutual submission by fostering an environment where both partners actively seek to support and serve each other with love.

Prayer For Liberty in Marriage

Dear God, guide us in using our freedom in marriage responsibly. May our actions be guided by love and serve each other selflessly. Help us balance individual liberty and mutual submission, creating a marriage marked by love and respect. Amen.

<h1 style="text-align:center">June 24</h1>

<h2 style="text-align:center">Proverbs 17:14</h2>

"The beginning of strife is as when one letteth out water: therefore leave off contention, before it be meddled with."

What Does This Mean For Us?

Proverbs 17:14 uses the metaphor of letting out water to describe the onset of strife. It advises to cease contention before it is stirred up or meddled with. This imagery reinforces the idea of preventing the overflow of conflict, emphasizing the importance of avoiding the initial sparks of discord to maintain peace and harmony.

Modern Day Reflection

In the context of modern marriages, Proverbs 17:14 serves as a timeless reminder of the destructive potential of unnecessary conflict. It prompts couples to recognize that the beginnings of strife, much like the first cracks in a dam, can lead to significant damage if not addressed wisely. It advocates for open communication, active listening, and a willingness to let go of minor grievances before they escalate into major disputes.

Prayer For Unnecessary Conflict in Marriage

Dear God, help us agree in our marriage. May we cultivate humility, avoiding pride and arrogance. Guide us in mutual submission, promoting a spirit of honesty and peace. Grant us the grace to live harmoniously with each other. Amen.

Proverbs 16:24

"Pleasant words are as an honeycomb, sweet to the soul, and health to the bones."

What Does This Mean For Us?

In the context of communication in marriage, Proverbs 16:24 highlights the impact of using kind and pleasant words. The verse compares such words to a honeycomb, emphasizing their sweetness and their positive effects on the soul and well-being.

Modern Day Reflection

In marriage, this verse encourages spouses to prioritize kindness and positivity in communication, recognizing that gentle and uplifting words contribute to a healthy and harmonious relationship.

Prayer For Communication in Marriage

Heavenly Father, teach us the value of pleasant words in our marriage. May our communication be a source of sweetness to each other's souls, promoting love and health in our relationship. Strengthen our commitment to speaking with kindness and positivity. Amen.

June 26

Ephesians 4:29

"Let no corrupt communication proceed out of your mouth, but that which is good to the use of edifying, that it may minister grace unto the hearers."

What Does This Mean For Us?

In the context of communication in marriage, Ephesians 4:29 advises against using harmful or corrupt language and encourages constructive and uplifting speech. The verse emphasizes the importance of words contributing positively to the listener's well-being.

Modern Day Reflection

Applied to marriage, this verse guides couples to communicate with kindness, choosing words that build each other up and contribute to the growth and grace within the relationship.

⁓

Prayer For Kind Language in Marriage

Heavenly Father, teach us the importance of wholesome communication in our marriage. May our words be a source of edification and grace to each other. Strengthen our commitment to using language that builds up and contributes to the growth of our relationship. Amen.

June 27

Matthew 6:14-15

"For if ye forgive men their trespasses, your heavenly Father will also forgive you: But if ye forgive not men their trespasses, neither will your Father forgive your trespasses."

What Does This Mean For Us?

These verses serve as a profound reminder in our Christian journey, emphasizing the interconnectedness of forgiveness in our relationships with God and others. It challenges us to extend the same mercy and forgiveness we receive from God to our spouse. This reciprocity highlights the transformative power of forgiveness, encouraging a release of resentment and a cultivation of reconciliation in our interactions.

Modern Day Reflection

Matthew 6:14-15 speaks directly to the challenges and complexities of human relationships. These verses prompt us to reflect on the reciprocal nature of forgiveness—highlighting that our experience of God's mercy is intimately connected to our ability to extend forgiveness to others. It encourages us to navigate conflicts with a spirit of mercy, recognizing that forgiveness is a virtue and a transformative force that can bring healing and restoration to our broken world.

Prayer For Forgiveness in Marriage

Lord, grant us the strength to forgive as we are forgiven. Break the chains of unforgiveness in our hearts, and help us cultivate a spirit of reconciliation and love. May our actions reflect the transformative power of Your mercy in our relationships. Amen.

June 28

Proverbs 18:13

"He that answereth a matter before he heareth it, it is folly and shame unto him."

What Does This Mean For Us?

Proverbs 18:13 urges spouses to practice active and patient listening before responding. The verse highlights the folly and shame in prematurely answering or passing judgment without fully understanding the matter at hand.

Modern Day Reflection

This verse guides couples to foster a culture of attentive and empathetic listening, promoting a deeper understanding of each other's perspectives and experiences.

Prayer For Patient Listening in Marriage

Heavenly Father, guide us in embodying the wisdom found in Proverbs 18:13. May patient listening and understanding mark our communication in marriage. Grant us the humility to withhold judgment until we fully hear each other's hearts. Strengthen our commitment to fostering a relationship where communication reflects love and respect. Amen.

June 29

Ephesians 4:15

"But speaking the truth in love, may grow up into him in all things, which is the head, even Christ."

What Does This Mean For Us?

In the context of communication in marriage, Ephesians 4:15 emphasizes the importance of speaking the truth with love. This verse encourages spouses to communicate openly and honestly but to do so in a way that is infused with love and respect. It implies that truthful communication when rooted in love, fosters growth and unity in the relationship.

Modern Day Reflection

In today's world, this verse guides couples to navigate difficult conversations with a commitment to both truth and love, fostering an environment where communication contributes to the spiritual and emotional growth of the marriage.

Prayer For Openness in Marriage

Dear Lord, teach us the wisdom of Ephesians 4:15 in our marriage. May our communication be characterized by truth spoken in love. Strengthen our commitment to honesty and openness, creating a space where our words contribute to the growth and unity of our relationship. Amen.

June 30

James 4:8

"Come near to God and he will come near to you. Wash your hands, you sinners, and purify your hearts, you double-minded."

What Does This Mean For Us?

This verse from the Book of James encourages believers to draw close to God through repentance and purification. It uses the imagery of washing hands and purifying hearts to convey the need for both outward and inward transformation. The promise is that as individuals seek God with sincerity and turn away from sin, God will draw near to them in a reciprocal relationship.

Modern Day Reflection

James 4:8 invites believers to approach God with sincerity and a desire for transformation. It recognizes the need for both external actions and internal attitudes to align with a life of faith. The call to "wash your hands" symbolizes the tangible actions of repentance and turning away from sinful behaviors, while "purify your hearts" speaks to the inner transformation and the importance of genuine motives. It serves as a reminder that drawing near to God involves a holistic commitment to both our outward actions and the purity of our innermost thoughts and intentions.

Prayer For Repentance in Marriage

Lord, draw us near to You as we seek to cleanse our actions and purify our hearts. May our repentance be genuine, and our desire for transformation leads us into a closer relationship with You. Amen.

Be the Inspiration for Married Couples Everywhere!

"Choose a love blessed by divine grace, and your marriage will be a sacred journey." – Unknown

Ask yourself this question: How often have you wished to reconnect spiritually with your partner? I'd hazard a guess that the answer is similar to "quite often" – if anything.

Don't get me wrong, there's lots of time every day to interact with your partner, but the sad truth is that, for the most part, it's easier to focus on whatever life challenges are taking center stage for one or both partners' attention, which can have a negative effect on your Christian marriage vows.

Time carved out every day between married couples to focus, reflect, and pray about the world around you and the effects that world may have on your marriage isn't only necessary; it's vital. Simply remaining connected and on the same emotional level as your spouse has proven to be instrumental in spiritually recognizing both partners are foundationally invested and committed to their vows and to God.

Many married couples like you need this foundation, and I'd humbly ask your help to ensure they get it. Don't worry – it'll take less than five minutes, and you don't need to leave the house!

Spreading this essential spiritual guidance is as simple as leaving an honest book review online.

By leaving a review of this book on Amazon, you'll make sure other married couples find the book and discover the foundational simplicity of taking just one minute a day to block out the world and focus on each other.

It really is that simple – book reviews are how we validate resources we're looking for, and just a few sentences from you can have a real impact.

By leaving a review of *'366 Meaningful Marriage Minutes'* on Amazon, you'll ensure other couples find this book, and discover the one-minute daily reconnection with their partner, and with God.

I humbly ask if you'll take a moment to leave a book review, and after that, let's continue on this journey toward marital and spiritual rediscovery.

Your voice matters more than you think!

Scan the QR code NOW to write a sentence or two and leave an honest Amazon review that will inspire other couples!

July

IN THE HEAT OF JULY, MAY OUR HEARTS
BURN WITH A PASSIONATE COMMITMENT
TO PURPOSE AND TRUTH. LIKE FIREWORKS
ILLUMINATING THE NIGHT SKY, MAY OUR
ACTIONS INSPIRE AND IGNITE POSITIVE
CHANGE IN THE WORLD, SPREADING LOVE
AND COMPASSION.

July 1

Proverbs 25:11
"A word fitly spoken is like apples of gold in pictures of silver."

What Does This Mean For Us?

Proverbs 25:11 vividly depicts the impact of well-timed and thoughtful words. The verse likens such words to precious ornaments, suggesting that they have the power to enhance and beautify the relationship.

Modern Day Reflection

For spouses, this verse encourages them to be intentional in their communication, choosing words that are not only truthful but also well-timed and considerate. It underscores the beauty and value of words that contribute positively to the atmosphere and dynamics of the marriage.

∼

Prayer For Intentional Communication in Marriage
Dear God, guide us in our communication within our marriage. May our words be fitly spoken, like apples of gold in pictures of silver. Grant us the wisdom to choose our words with care, enhancing the beauty and value of our relationship. Amen.

July 2

James 3:2-4

"For in many things we offend all. If any man offend not in word, the same is a perfect man, and able also to bridle the whole body. Behold, we put bits in the horses' mouths, that they may obey us, and we turn about their whole body. Behold also the ships, which though they be so great, and are driven of fierce winds, yet are they turned about with a very small helm, whithersoever the governor listeth."

What Does This Mean For Us?

The passage compares the tongue to the bit in a horse's mouth or the small helm of a ship, illustrating how something seemingly small can profoundly affect the entire being. It emphasizes the potential for good and harm in words, likening the tongue to a fire that can ignite great destruction.

Modern Day Reflection

In today's world, this passage urges couples to be mindful of the power of their words, recognizing the need for careful and intentional communication to avoid causing harm and promote harmony in their marriage.

Prayer For Kind Words in Marriage

Heavenly Father, may our communication be a force for good, avoiding the destructive power of careless words. Strengthen our commitment to using our tongues for love, understanding, and harmony within our relationship. Amen.

July 3

Matthew 12:36-37

"But I say unto you, That every idle word that men shall speak, they shall give account thereof in the day of judgment. For by thy words thou shalt be justified, and by thy words thou shalt be condemned."

What Does This Mean For Us?

Matthew 12:36-37 underscores the significance of words and the accountability tied to them. The verses emphasize that every word spoken carries weight and will be accounted for.

Modern Day Reflection

Applied to marriage, this passage encourages couples to be intentional and considerate in their communication, recognizing the impact their words can have on the dynamics of the relationship. It highlights the responsibility spouses have to use their words for building up and promoting love rather than contributing to harm.

Prayer For Considerate Communication in Marriage

Dear God, help us be mindful of our words in our marriage. May our communication be intentional and filled with love. Grant us the wisdom to use our words to build each other up and contribute positively to the well-being of our relationship. Amen.

July 4

Colossians 3:13-14

"Forbearing one another, and forgiving one another, if any man have a quarrel against any: even as Christ forgave you, so do ye. And above all these things put on charity, which is the bond of perfectness."

What Does This Mean For Us?

In the context of forgiveness in marriage, Colossians 3:13-14 emphasizes the virtues of forbearance and forgiveness, mirroring Christ's forgiveness of believers. The passage calls for a mutual willingness to forgive, putting on love (charity) as the bond of perfection.

Modern Day Reflection

For a married couple, it encourages you to practice forgiveness, understanding, and to cultivate a love that binds their relationship.

Prayer For Forbearance in Marriage

Heavenly Father, help us live out the spirit of Colossians 3:13-14 in our marriage. May forgiveness and forbearance characterize our relationship, and may the love we share be the bond that perfects and strengthens our commitment to each other. Amen.

July 5

1 Corinthians 7:2

"Nevertheless, to avoid fornication, let every man have his own wife, and let every woman have her own husband."

What Does This Mean For Us?

This verse emphasizes the biblical perspective on marriage as a safeguard against sexual immorality. It encourages individuals to enter into the covenant of marriage, establishing an exclusive relationship between one man and one woman.

Modern Day Reflection

In today's world, this verse underscores the significance of marriage in God's design. It speaks to the importance of the marital relationship as a way to fulfill God's plan for human intimacy and companionship.

Prayer For Companionship in Marriage

Dear Heavenly Father, we thank You for the sacred institution of marriage. Help us to honor and cherish the covenant we share as husband and wife, seeking to fulfill Your design for our union. Amen.

July 6

1 Timothy 5:14

"I will therefore that the younger women marry, bear children, guide the house, give none occasion to the adversary to speak reproachfully."

What Does This Mean For Us?

This verse advises younger women to marry, bear children, and guide the household, emphasizing the importance of family and domestic responsibilities.

Modern Day Reflection

In today's world, this verse can be seen as an encouragement for couples to embrace the responsibilities of marriage and family life. It underscores the value of a stable and loving home environment.

Prayer For Family in Marriage

Lord, bless our marriage and family life. Grant us the strength and wisdom to fulfill our roles with love and commitment. May our home be a place where Your love and grace abound. Amen.

July 7

Ephesians 5:25

"Husbands, love your wives, even as Christ also loved the church and gave himself for it."

What Does This Mean For Us?

This verse speaks directly to husbands, emphasizing love's sacrificial nature within the marriage context.

Modern Day Reflection

This is a clear directive to husbands, placing a special responsibility on them to actively and intentionally love their wives. It sets the tone for a marriage where love is not just an emotion but a deliberate choice and action. In today's world, where relationships can face various challenges, this verse encourages husbands to model their love on the sacrificial love of Christ, seeking the good of their wives above their own desires.

～

Prayer For Enduring Love in Marriage

Dear God, we thank you for the gift of marriage and the love we share. As we navigate the ups and downs of life together, we pray for a love that mirrors Christ's unconditional love for the church. Grant us the ability to love each other without reservation, to forgive as we have been forgiven, and to strengthen our bond through the challenges we may face. May our marriage be a testament to the enduring and sacrificial love you call us to. In Jesus' name, we pray. Amen.

July 8

Romans 8:38-39

"For I am persuaded, that neither death, nor life, nor angels, nor principalities, nor powers, nor things present, nor things to come, Nor height, nor depth, nor any other creature, shall be able to separate us from the love of God, which is in Christ Jesus our Lord."

What Does This Mean For Us?

The verse lists a comprehensive range of circumstances and entities, asserting that nothing in the entire scope of existence—whether life or death, angels or powers—can separate believers from the love of God. In the context of marriage, this underscores the idea that God's love is constant and unwavering, even in the face of life's challenges and uncertainties.

Modern Day Reflection

In today's fast paced world where marriages may face various trials, Romans 8:38-39 assures couples that God's love is a steadfast and unchanging foundation for their relationship.

Prayer For Boundless Love in Marriage

Heavenly Father, Thank you for the promise in Romans 8:38-39 that nothing can separate us from your love. As we continue in this marriage covenant, may your love be the unbreakable bond that sustains us through all seasons of life. Distance, challenges or any circumstance shall not sever our connection in your love. Bless our marriage, Lord, and may it reflect your enduring and boundless love. In Jesus' name, we pray. Amen.

July 9

Proverbs 21:23
"Whoso keepeth his mouth and his tongue keepeth his soul from troubles."

What Does This Mean For Us?

In the context of communication in marriage, Proverbs 21:23 imparts the wisdom of exercising control over one's speech. The verse suggests that being mindful of what one says and how one says it can safeguard the individual from unnecessary troubles.

Modern Day Reflection

In relation to marriage, this passage guides couples to be intentional and wise in their communication, recognizing the potential consequences of careless words. It underscores the importance of fostering a culture of thoughtful and considerate speech within the relationship.

Prayer For Unnecessary Troubles in Marriage
Dear God, help us keep our mouths and tongues in check within our marriage. May our communication be guided by wisdom and intentionality, safeguarding our relationship from unnecessary troubles. Grant us the grace to speak with love and consideration. Amen.

July 10

Galatians 5:22-23

"But the fruit of the Spirit is love, joy, peace, longsuffering, gentleness, goodness, faith, Meekness, temperance: against such there is no law."

What Does This Mean For Us?

This Galatians passage describes the fruit of the Spirit—qualities produced in the lives of believers through the indwelling of the Holy Spirit.

Modern Day Reflection

In the context of marriage, these qualities are foundational for a strong and God-honoring relationship. Love, joy, peace, patience, gentleness, goodness, faith, meekness, and temperance are attributes that contribute to a harmonious and thriving marriage.

~

Prayer For The Spiritual Fruits in Marriage

Gracious God, As we embark on the marriage journey, we seek your Holy Spirit's guidance. May the fruit of the Spirit manifest abundantly in our relationship—love, joy, peace, longsuffering, gentleness, goodness, faith, meekness, and temperance. Grant us the grace to cultivate these qualities in our marriage, creating a foundation of strength and harmony. In your name, we pray. Amen.

July 11

1 Thessalonians 5:15

"See that none render evil for evil unto any man; but ever follow that which is good, both among yourselves, and to all men."

What Does This Mean For Us?

This verse from 1 Thessalonians guides how believers should interact with one another and with others in their conduct. The verse encourages a posture of non-retaliation. In the context of marriage, this suggests that spouses should avoid responding to wrongdoing or hurtful actions with negativity or harm. Instead, it promotes a mindset of forgiveness and grace within the marital relationship.

Modern Day Reflection

The verse advocates for the pursuit of goodness both within the marital relationship and in interactions with others. In the context of marriage, this implies that spouses should actively seek to promote goodness, kindness, and positive actions toward each other and extend these virtues to those around them.

~

Prayer For the Pursuit of Goodness in Marriage

Gracious God, as we stand before you, entering into the covenant of marriage, we are reminded of the wisdom in 1 Thessalonians 5:15. Grant us the grace to refrain from rendering evil for evil and to pursue that which is good actively. May our marriage reflect your goodness, filled with forgiveness and positive actions. In your name, we pray. Amen.

July 12

Proverbs 15:13

"A merry heart maketh a cheerful countenance: but by sorrow of the heart the spirit is broken."

What Does This Mean For Us?

This proverb emphasizes the connection between a joyful heart and a cheerful countenance, contrasting it with the impact of a sorrowful heart that can lead to a broken spirit.

Modern Day Reflection

The verse highlights the correlation between inner joy and outward cheerfulness. In the context of marriage, this suggests that cultivating a joyful and positive heart can contribute to a cheerful and uplifting atmosphere within the relationship. A merry heart becomes a source of radiance that can positively impact the couple's countenance and interactions.

Prayer For Mutual Comfort in Marriage

Heavenly Father, thank you for the wisdom in Proverbs 15:13. As a couple, we pray for the strength to support each other through times of sorrow. May our hearts find solace in your love, preventing the breaking of our spirits. Guide us in being sources of comfort and healing for one another. In Jesus' name, we pray. Amen.

July 13

2 Corinthians 1:3-4

"Blessed be God, even the Father of our Lord Jesus Christ, the Father of mercies, and the God of all comfort; Who comforteth us in all our tribulation, that we may be able to comfort them which are in any trouble, by the comfort wherewith we ourselves are comforted of God."

What Does This Mean For Us?

This passage praises God as the Father of mercies and the source of all comfort. It also emphasizes the idea that the comfort received from God in times of tribulation equips believers to comfort others who are in trouble.

Modern Day Reflection

The opening verse expresses gratitude and recognition of God's role as the ultimate source of mercy and comfort. It encourages couples to turn to God as a source of solace and strength during challenging times. The second verse of the passage highlights the cyclical nature of comfort. As couples experience God's comfort in their own tribulations, they are equipped to extend that comfort to each other and to others in times of trouble.

Prayer For God's Comfort in Marriage

Merciful God, as we journey through the highs and lows of married life, we recognize you as the Father of mercies and the God of all comfort. May your comforting presence be our refuge in times of tribulation. Grant us the strength to draw on your comfort and, in turn, comfort each other in the challenges we face. In your name, we pray. Amen.

July 14

Proverbs 31:26

"She openeth her mouth with wisdom, and in her tongue is the law of
kindness."

What Does This Mean For Us?

This verse describes the virtuous woman in Proverbs 31, emphasizing
her wisdom and the kindness that characterizes her speech. As spouses
communicate with wisdom, they contribute to the growth and strength
of their relationship.

Modern Day Reflection

In today's world, where effective communication and kindness are
essential in marriages, Proverbs 31:26 guides couples to build a strong
and nurturing relationship.

~

Prayer For Nurturing in Marriage
Gracious Lord, as a couple, we seek your guidance in our
communication. Grant us wisdom to choose our words carefully and
speak with understanding. May kindness be the law that governs our
tongues, fostering love and harmony in our marriage. In Jesus' name, we
pray. Amen.

July 15

Philippians 2:1-2

"If there be therefore any consolation in Christ, if any comfort of love, if any fellowship of the Spirit, if any bowels and mercies, Fulfil ye my joy, that ye be likeminded, having the same love, being of one accord, of one mind."

What Does This Mean For Us?

This passage emphasizes the importance of unity, love, and compassion within the Christian community. In the context of marriage, this encourages couples to find their consolation and comfort in Christ. It highlights the significance of spiritual fellowship and compassionate hearts in building a strong marital bond.

Modern Day Reflection

This expresses the joy that comes from unity in love. Marriage, it calls for couples to be like-minded, sharing the same love and being in harmony with one another. It promotes oneness of mind and purpose. Additionally, where marriages may face challenges, Philippians 2:1-2 encourages couples to build their relationship on the foundation of Christ's love and to cultivate unity.

Prayer For Oneness in Marriage

Gracious Lord, as we walk this marital journey, may Your Spirit guide us to be of one accord and one mind. May our love for each other reflect the unity found in Christ. Amen.

July 16

Romans 8:28

"And we know that all things work together for good to them that love God, to them who are the called according to his purpose."

What Does This Mean For Us?

The verse assures couples that, despite challenges and uncertainties, God is at work, orchestrating all things for their ultimate good. It encourages them to trust in God's plan for their marriage.

Modern Day Reflection

Romans 8:28 highlights the importance of aligning one's life, including marriage, with God's purpose. Couples are reminded that their love for God and commitment to His purpose in their marriage assure that all things will work together for good.

❧

Prayer For Trust in God's Plan in Marriage

Heavenly Father, in our marriage journey, help us trust that all things work together for good. May our love for You guide us in aligning with Your purpose, knowing that Your plan is perfect. Amen.

July 17

Psalm 55:22

"Cast thy burden upon the Lord, and he shall sustain thee: he shall never suffer the righteous to be moved."

What Does This Mean For Us?

This verse encourages individuals to entrust their burdens to the Lord, assuring that He will provide support and stability.

Modern Day Reflection

The promise that the righteous will not be moved emphasizes God's faithfulness in providing stability and security. In the context of marriage, it offers the assurance that as couples trust in God and seek His support, they can find a firm foundation, even in the face of life's uncertainties

Prayer For Stability and Trust in Marriage

Heavenly Father, thank you for the wisdom in Psalm 55:22. We trust you and seek your guidance as a couple. In the midst of life's uncertainties, may we find stability in your faithfulness. Uphold us, strengthen us, and assure us that we will not be moved as we lean on you. In Jesus' name, we pray. Amen.

July 18

Proverbs 17:22

"A merry heart doeth good like a medicine: but a broken spirit drieth the bones."

What Does This Mean For Us?

This proverb highlights the positive impact of a joyful heart, likening it to the healing properties of medicine, and contrasts it with the detrimental effects of a broken spirit.

Modern Day Reflection

The verse underscores the therapeutic effect of a joyful and cheerful heart. In the context of marriage, this suggests that maintaining a spirit of joy and positivity can contribute to the overall well-being of the relationship. A joyful heart is likened to a healing medicine, bringing refreshment and vitality to the marriage. In today's world, where couples navigate various challenges, Proverbs 17:22 encourages spouses to prioritize cultivating joy, positivity, and emotional well-being in their marriage.

~

Prayer For Healing and Restoration in Marriage

Heavenly Father, thank you for the wisdom in Proverbs 17:22. As a couple, we pray for healing and restoration in our marriage. May any brokenness be addressed and healed, preventing a spirit of discouragement. Grant us the strength to uplift each other, fostering a healthy and vibrant relationship. In Jesus' name, we pray. Amen.

July 19

Matthew 22: 37-39

"Jesus said unto him, Thou shalt love the Lord thy God with all thy heart, and with all thy soul, and with all thy mind. This is the first and great commandment. And the second is like unto it, Thou shalt love thy neighbour as thyself."

What Does This Mean For Us?

In this passage, Jesus responds to a question about the greatest commandment by emphasizing the centrality of love—love for God and love for others.

Modern Day Reflection

In the contemporary world, where marriages may face various challenges, Matthew 22:37-39 encourages couples to prioritize a love for God and a love for each other

~

Prayer For Mutual Love and and Respect in Marriage

Heavenly Father, thank you for the guidance in Matthew 22:37-39. As a couple, we pray for a love that mirrors your design. May our love for each other reflect our love for you. Help us to love and respect one another as we love ourselves. Bless our marriage with the grace to embody the two greatest commandments. In Jesus' name, we pray. Amen.

July 20

1 Corinthians 14:1

"Follow after charity, and desire spiritual gifts, but rather that ye may prophesy."

What Does This Mean For Us?

This verse from Corinthians encourages the pursuit of love (charity) and spiritual gifts, particularly emphasizing the gift of prophecy. The verse begins with an exhortation to pursue love (charity) and to desire spiritual gifts. The verse additionally singles out the desire for prophecy as a specific emphasis.

Modern Day Reflection

In modern-day marriage, this could be interpreted as a call for couples to seek and share spiritual insights and guidance with each other, fostering a relationship that is centered on God's wisdom and direction.

Prayer For Discernment in Marriage

Heavenly Father, thank you for the wisdom shared in 1 Corinthians 14:1. As a couple, we desire to follow after charity and seek spiritual gifts. Grant us the gift of prophecy in our marriage, that we may share and receive spiritual insights with discernment and understanding. May our relationship be a testament to your wisdom and love. Bless our union, Lord. In Jesus' name, we pray. Amen.

July 21

Psalm 128: 1-4

"Blessed is every one that feareth the Lord; that walketh in his ways. For thou shalt eat the labour of thine hands: happy shalt thou be, and it shall be well with thee. Thy wife shall be as a fruitful vine by the sides of thine house: thy children like olive plants round about thy table. Behold, that thus shall the man be blessed that feareth the Lord."

What Does This Mean For Us?

This psalm celebrates the blessings that come to those who fear the Lord and walk in His ways. It portrays an image of a flourishing family life, with the wife compared to a fruitful vine and the children to olive plants, symbolizing fertility, abundance, and a strong familial bond.

Modern Day Reflection

In the context of God's design for marriage, this passage emphasizes the importance of reverence for the Lord and aligning one's life with His ways. It suggests that such a life leads to prosperity, happiness, and a harmonious family, with each member contributing to the overall well-being of the household.

Prayer For Reverence in Marriage

Lord, guide us in walking in Your ways. Bless our marriage with the richness of Your love, and may our family be a testimony to the joy and prosperity that come from fearing and following You. Amen.

July 22

Genesis 1: 27-28

"So God created man in his own image, in the image of God created he him; male and female created he them. And God blessed them, and God said unto them, Be fruitful, and multiply, and replenish the earth, and subdue it: and have dominion over the fish of the sea, and over the fowl of the air, and over every living thing that moveth upon the earth."

What Does This Mean For Us?

These verses describe the creation of humankind, emphasizing the complementary nature of male and female. God's design for marriage is rooted in the union of a man and a woman, and together, they are blessed to be fruitful, multiply, and have dominion over the earth.

Modern Day Reflection

In today's world, these verses underscore the foundational principles of marriage as a partnership between a man and a woman, marked by collaboration, mutual support, and the shared responsibility of caring for God's creation.

Prayer For Working Together in Marriage

Heavenly Father, thank you for the gift of marriage. Help us, as a couple, to fulfill the purpose You set out for us in our union. May our partnership be fruitful and work together to honor and care for the world You entrusted us. Amen.

July 23

Ecclesiastes 4:9-12

"Two are better than one because they have a good reward for their labor. For if they fall, one will lift up his companion. But woe to him who is alone when he falls, for he has no one to help him up. Again, if two lie down together, they will keep warm; but how can one be warm alone? Though one may be overpowered by another, two can withstand him. And a threefold cord is not quickly broken."

What Does This Mean For Us?

This passage extols the strength and support found in companionship. It emphasizes the benefits of partnership, especially in facing challenges and overcoming difficulties. The imagery of two lying down together and a threefold cord suggests the importance of unity and shared strength in marriage.

Modern Day Reflection

In the modern-day, this passage speaks to the profound impact of a supportive and unified marriage. It encourages couples to face life's challenges together, relying on each other and incorporating a spiritual dimension into their relationship.

Prayer For Unity in Marriage

Lord, bless our marriage with unity and strength. As a couple, may we find solace and support in each other's company. Let Your presence be the third cord in our relationship, making us resilient and unbreakable. Amen.

July 24

Romans 14:19
"Let us therefore follow after the things which make for peace, and
things wherewith one may edify another."

What Does This Mean For Us?

In the context of forgiveness in marriage, Romans 14:19 encourages a
pursuit of peace and actions that build up one another. The verse calls
for a focus on constructive behaviors that contribute to a harmonious
relationship.

Modern Day Reflection

Applied to marriage, it suggests that forgiveness and reconciliation are
essential components for fostering a peaceful and uplifting connection
between partners.

～

Prayer For Connection in Marriage
Dear God, guide us as a couple to follow the wisdom of Romans 14:19
in our marriage. May our actions be centered on peace, and may we
consistently build each other up through forgiveness and
understanding. Amen.

July 25

Proverbs 29:20
"Seest thou a man that is hasty in his words? There is more hope of a
fool than of him."

What Does This Mean For Us?

In the context of communication in marriage, Proverbs 29:20 cautions
against the folly of speaking hastily. The verse suggests that a person
who is quick to speak without thoughtful consideration may be more
challenging to guide and correct than a fool.

Modern Day Reflection

Applied to today's marriage, this passage encourages couples to be
mindful of the words they choose and the speed at which they speak,
emphasizing the importance of thoughtful communication in building
a strong and harmonious relationship.

Prayer For Patient Communication in Marriage
Heavenly Father, teach us the wisdom in Proverbs 29:20 in our
marriage. May we be mindful of the impact of hasty words, choosing
instead to communicate with thoughtfulness and patience. Strengthen
our commitment to building a relationship where words are spoken
with wisdom and love. Amen.

July 26

Proverbs 18:2

"A fool hath no delight in understanding but that his heart may discover itself."

What Does This Mean For Us?

Proverbs 18:2 contrasts the foolishness of one who lacks delight in understanding with the wisdom of seeking mutual understanding. The verse suggests that a fool is more focused on expressing their own thoughts and desires, whereas wisdom lies in valuing and seeking to understand one another.

Modern Day Reflection

This passage guides couples to prioritize mutual understanding in their communication, fostering an environment where both spouses feel heard and valued.

~

Prayer For Mutual Understanding in Marriage

Dear God, grant us the wisdom to delight in understanding within our marriage. May our communication be marked by a genuine desire to comprehend each other, fostering an environment of mutual understanding and respect. Guide us in valuing each other's thoughts and feelings. Amen.

July 27

Proverbs 15:28

"The heart of the righteous studieth to answer: but the mouth of the wicked poureth out evil things."

What Does This Mean For Us?

In the context of communication in marriage, Proverbs 15:28 draws attention to the thoughtful consideration that the righteous give to their responses. It contrasts this with the reckless and harmful speech that characterizes the mouth of the wicked.

Modern Day Reflection

This verse encourages spouses to approach communication with mindfulness, considering the impact of their words on the relationship. It emphasizes the importance of cultivating a heart that seeks to answer with wisdom and kindness.

Prayer For Mindful Communication in Marriage

Heavenly Father, teach us the wisdom found in Proverbs 15:28 in our marriage. May our hearts be righteous, seeking to answer with thoughtfulness and kindness. Strengthen our commitment to mindful communication, fostering an environment of understanding and love within our relationship. Amen.

July 28

Luke 6:37

"Judge not, and ye shall not be judged: condemn not, and ye shall not be condemned: forgive, and ye shall be forgiven."

What Does This Mean For Us?

Luke 6:37 urges individuals, including couples, to refrain from passing judgment and condemnation. The verse emphasizes the principle of reciprocity, suggesting that extending forgiveness opens the door to receiving forgiveness.

Modern Day Reflection

This passage also underscores the importance of cultivating a forgiving, non-judgmental atmosphere to promote harmony and understanding.

Prayer For No Judgement in Marriage

Dear God, help us refrain from judgment and condemnation within our marriage. May our hearts be open to forgiveness, creating a space for understanding and love. Guide us in building a relationship marked by grace and compassion. Amen.

July 29

James 5:16

"Confess your faults one to another, and pray one for another, that ye may be healed. The effectual fervent prayer of a righteous man availeth much."

What Does This Mean For Us?

James 5:16 encourages open communication and mutual confession of faults. The verse highlights the healing power of confessing mistakes to one another and praying for each other.

Modern Day Reflection

Applied to marriage, this emphasizes the importance of vulnerability, transparency, and seeking forgiveness as a means to heal and strengthen the marital bond.

～

Prayer For Healing in Marriage

Heavenly Father, help us embody the wisdom of James 5:16 in our marriage. May we confess our faults, seek forgiveness, and pray for each other's healing. Strengthen our commitment to open communication, vulnerability, and the transformative power of fervent prayer. Amen.

July 30

Luke 17:3-4

"Take heed to yourselves: If thy brother trespass against thee, rebuke him; and if he repent, forgive him. And if he trespass against thee seven times in a day, and seven times in a day turn again to thee, saying, I repent; thou shalt forgive him."

What Does This Mean For Us?

In the context of forgiveness in marriage, Luke 17:3-4 guides the process of forgiveness. The verses encourage addressing grievances and, upon genuine repentance, extending forgiveness.

Modern Day Reflection

As a married couple practicing the repetition of forgiveness, even in the face of repeated offenses, it underscores the importance of a forgiving and understanding attitude within the marital relationship.

Prayer For Forgiveness in Marriage

Heavenly Father, guide us in embodying the principles of Luke 17:3-4. May our marriage be marked by a spirit of forgiveness, understanding, and the willingness to reconcile even in the face of repeated offenses. Strengthen our commitment to a relationship grounded in Your love. Amen.

July 31

Psalm 86:5

"For thou, Lord, art good, and ready to forgive, and plenteous in mercy unto all them that call upon thee."

What Does This Mean For Us?

In the context of forgiveness in marriage, Psalm 86:5 highlights the divine qualities of God's goodness, readiness to forgive, and abundance of mercy. Applied to marriage, it encourages couples to emulate these qualities in their relationship—being ready to forgive one another and extending mercy generously.

Modern Day Reflection

The verse emphasizes the importance of calling upon God in times of difficulty, seeking His guidance and imitating His forgiveness in marital interactions.

~

Prayer For Mercy in Marriage

Dear Lord, may your goodness and readiness to forgive inspire us in our marriage. Help us cultivate a spirit of forgiveness and mercy, and may our relationship reflect the love and grace that you freely offer. Amen.

August

AS THE HARVEST SEASON APPROACHES, MAY AUGUST BE A TIME TO REAP THE FRUITS OF OUR EFFORTS. LET US REFLECT ON THE ABUNDANCE OF LIFE'S BLESSINGS, AND MAY GRATITUDE FILL OUR HEARTS AS WE SHARE THE HARVEST OF LOVE, KINDNESS, AND GENEROSITY.

August 1

James 3:17

"But the wisdom that is from above is first pure, then peaceable, gentle, and easy to be entreated, full of mercy and good fruits, without partiality, and without hypocrisy."

What Does This Mean For Us?

In the context of communication in marriage, James 3:17 outlines the characteristics of wisdom from above. This verse encourages couples to cultivate communication that reflects purity, peaceability, gentleness, and openness to reason. It emphasizes the importance of mercy, good fruits, impartiality, and sincerity in fostering a healthy and harmonious relationship.

Modern Day Reflection

This verse from the Book of James provides a comprehensive description of the wisdom that is heavenly in origin. It outlines the characteristics of such wisdom, emphasizing purity, a peace-loving nature, considerate behavior, humility, mercy, good fruitfulness, impartiality, and sincerity. It offers a standard for discerning true wisdom in contrast to earthly and self-centered perspectives.

Prayer For Sincerity in Marriage

Heavenly Father, grant us the wisdom from above—pure, peace-loving, considerate, and full of mercy. May our actions bear good fruit, and may we approach others with impartiality and sincerity. In our pursuit of wisdom, let Your heavenly guidance shape our thoughts and behaviors.
Amen.

August 2

2 Corinthians 2:7-8

"So that contrariwise ye ought rather to forgive him and comfort him, lest perhaps such a one should be swallowed up with overmuch sorrow. Wherefore I beseech you that ye would confirm your love toward him."

What Does This Mean For Us?

2 Corinthians 2:7-8 speaks to the importance of forgiveness and restoration within the community of believers. The verses encourage a response of forgiveness and comfort to prevent excessive sorrow and emphasize the need to confirm love.

Modern Day Reflection

As it applies to marriage, this passage encourages couples to prioritize forgiveness, comfort each other in times of conflict, and reaffirm their love to strengthen the marital bond.

Prayer For Renewal in Marriage

Heavenly Father, help us to live out the spirit of 2 Corinthians 2:7-8 in our marriage. May forgiveness and comfort be our response to conflicts, and may our love be a constant source of strength and renewal. Strengthen our commitment to a marriage grounded in love and understanding. Amen.

August 3

Matthew 19:4-6

"And he answered and said unto them, Have ye not read, that he which made them at the beginning made them male and female, And said, For this cause shall a man leave father and mother, and shall cleave to his wife: and they twain shall be one flesh? Wherefore they are no more twain, but one flesh. What therefore God hath joined together, let not man put asunder."

What Does This Mean For Us?

This passage emphasizes the divine intention for the unity and indissolubility of marriage. It reaffirms the concept of leaving one's family and cleaving to one's spouse, emphasizing the oneness that God intended for marriage. In the context of forgiveness, maintaining this oneness requires a spirit of forgiveness and understanding.

Modern Day Reflection

In today's world, forgiveness is vital for preserving the unity and sanctity of marriage. Couples face challenges, but forgiveness allows them to overcome obstacles, fostering a bond that reflects the oneness God intended.

Prayer For Forgiveness in Marriage

Lord, help us leave behind any bitterness and embrace forgiveness in our marriage. Bind us together as one, united in Your love. Amen.

August 4

Song Of Soloman 8:6-7

Set me as a seal upon thine heart, as a seal upon thine arm: for love is strong as death; jealousy is cruel as the grave: the coals thereof are coals of fire, which hath a most vehement flame. Many waters cannot quench love, neither can the floods drown it: if a man would give all the substance of his house for love, it would utterly be contemned."

What Does This Mean For Us?

These verses suggest an intimate and enduring connection, likening the bond of love to a seal that signifies permanence and commitment. In the context of marriage, it encourages a commitment that is not only felt emotionally but is also visibly expressed and sealed.

Modern Day Reflection

Where relationships can face various challenges in today's busy times, Song of Solomon 8:6-7 encourages couples to seek a love that is enduring, resilient, and untainted by negative emotions.

Prayer For Enduring Love in Marriage

Gracious God, as we stand together as a couple, we pray for a love as strong as death, sealed upon our hearts and arms. Protect us from harmful emotions, and may our love be resilient against the floods of life. May it endure and withstand the tests of time, growing stronger with each passing day. In your name, we pray. Amen.

August 5

1 Corinthians 13:13

"And now abideth faith, hope, charity, these three; but the greatest of these is charity."

What Does This Mean For Us?

The verse highlights three virtues—faith, hope, and charity (love). While faith and hope are significant, love is declared as the greatest. In the context of marriage, this reinforces the idea that love is the foundational and essential quality that sustains and enriches a marital relationship.

Modern Day Reflection

In today's world, where relationships can face various challenges, 1 Corinthians 13:13 encourages couples to prioritize and cultivate love in their marriage. This verse concludes the famous "Love Chapter" in Corinthians, emphasizing love's enduring nature and supreme importance.

Prayer For Endurance in Marriage

Heavenly Father, Thank you for the gift of love and the guidance found in 1 Corinthians 13:13. As we start this chapter of our lives together, help us to anchor our marriage in faith, sustain it with hope, and let love be the thread that binds us. May our love endure through the highs and lows, always reflecting the greatest of virtues. Bless our journey with enduring and deepening love. In Jesus' name, we pray. Amen.

August 6

Ephesians 5:2

"And walk in love, as Christ also hath loved us, and hath given himself for us an offering and a sacrifice to God for a sweetsmelling savour."

What Does This Mean For Us?

This verse from Ephesians emphasizes the call to walk in love, drawing a parallel to Christ's sacrificial love for humanity. Let's explore its meaning in the context of marriage and God's design.

Modern Day Reflection

The verse begins with a directive to walk in love, signifying that love should be an ongoing and intentional part of one's lifestyle.This verse, as a whole, underscores the idea that Christ's sacrificial love was pleasing and acceptable to God. In the context of marriage, it suggests that selfless and sacrificial love within the marital relationship not only pleases God but also enhances the quality of the relationship.

Prayer For Christ-like Love in Marriage

Gracious Lord, As we embark on the sacred journey of marriage, we are reminded of the profound wisdom in Ephesians 5:2. May our love for each other mirror Christ's selfless and sacrificial love. Help us to walk in love, offering ourselves for the well-being of our spouse. May our love be a sweet fragrance, pleasing to you and strengthening our union. In your name, we pray. Amen.

August 7

John 13:34-35

"A new commandment I give unto you, That ye love one another; as I have loved you, that ye also love one another. By this shall all men know that ye are my disciples, if ye have love one to another."

What Does This Mean For Us?

This passage captures Jesus' instruction to His disciples, emphasizing the centrality of love as a distinguishing characteristic of His followers.

Modern Day Reflection

Jesus introduces a new standard of love, calling His disciples to love one another in a way that mirrors His own love. In the context of marriage, this implies that spouses are called to love each other with selfless and sacrificial love, reflecting the model of Christ's love for humanity given by John 13:34-35 that encourages couples to prioritize a love that reflects Christ's love and serves as a powerful witness to those around them.

Prayer For Guidance in Marriage

Heavenly Father, Thank you for the guidance in John 13:34-35. As a couple, we pray for the strength to live out this new commandment of love in our marriage. May our love be so evident and compelling that it is a powerful witness to your grace and teachings. Help us to display a love that reflects our identity as your disciples. In Jesus' name, we pray. Amen.

August 8

Ephesians 6:4
"And, ye fathers, provoke not your children to wrath: but bring them
up in the nurture and admonition of the Lord."

What Does This Mean For Us?

This verse addresses parents, specifically fathers, urging them not to provoke their children to anger but to raise them in the nurturing and admonition of the Lord.

Modern Day Reflection

The verse advises fathers to avoid behaviors that may provoke or embitter their children. In the context of marriage, this speaks to the importance of parents presenting a united and supportive front to their children, fostering an environment of love and understanding. The verse additionally encourages parents to raise their children in the ways of the Lord, providing guidance, instruction, and discipline that align with biblical principles. In the context of marriage, this emphasizes the parents' shared responsibility in shaping their family's spiritual and moral foundation.

Prayer For Parenthood in Marriage
Gracious Lord, As we embark on the journey of parenthood within our marriage, we seek your guidance in Ephesians 6:4. Grant us the wisdom and unity to parent our children in a way that reflects your love and teachings. Help us to avoid actions that may provoke them, and instead, bring them up in the nurture and admonition of the Lord. In your name, we pray. Amen.

August 9

1 Thessalonians 4:18
"Wherefore comfort one another with these words."

What Does This Mean For Us?

This verse encourages believers to find comfort and solace in the words that have been shared by family, friends, peers, colleagues, and the like. We draw solace and peace within words from our support networks.

Modern Day Reflection

The verse suggests that the shared words are meant to provide comfort and reassurance. In the context of marriage, this encourages spouses to find solace in the words they exchange, especially in times of challenges, uncertainties, or grief.

Prayer For Comforting Words in Marriage
Heavenly Father, Thank you for the wisdom in 1 Thessalonians 4:18. As a couple, we seek your comfort in our words. May our communication be a bond that strengthens our unity, especially in challenging times. Guide us to be a source of support and comfort for each other, leaning on the words of love and encouragement we exchange. In Jesus' name, we pray. Amen.

August 10

Matthew 18:15

"Moreover if thy brother shall trespass against thee, go and tell him his fault between thee and him alone: if he shall hear thee, thou hast gained thy brother."

What Does This Mean For Us?

Matthew 18:15 provides a blueprint for addressing conflicts and seeking reconciliation. The verse encourages individuals, including couples, to address grievances privately and directly with the aim of resolving the issue and restoring the relationship.

Modern Day Reflection

Applied to marriage, this highlights the importance of open communication, addressing faults, and seeking forgiveness in a manner that fosters understanding and unity.

~

Prayer For Reconciliation in Marriage

Heavenly Father, guide us in embodying the principles of Matthew 18:15 in our marriage. May we approach conflicts with love and humility, seeking resolution and reconciliation. Strengthen our commitment to open communication and the restoration of our relationship through forgiveness. Amen.

August 11

Amos 5:24

"But let justice roll on like a river, righteousness like a never-failing stream!"

What Does This Mean For Us?

This powerful verse from Amos emphasizes the importance of justice and righteousness. It serves as a call to maintain a constant and unceasing commitment to justice, allowing it to flow abundantly like a river. The imagery suggests a continuous and unwavering pursuit of what is right and just.

Modern Day Reflection

This is a great verse in the contemporary context of marriage as its overarching theme of justice and righteousness can be applied to various aspects of life, including relationships. It encourages individuals to uphold principles of fairness, integrity, and righteousness in all their dealings, which are foundational qualities in a healthy and just marriage.

~

Prayer For Justice in Marriage

Dear Lord, In Amos 5:24, we are reminded of the call to let justice and righteousness flow like a river in our lives. In our relationships, including marriage, we seek Your guidance to uphold principles of justice, fairness, and righteousness. May our actions and decisions reflect Your unchanging standards. Grant us the strength to navigate challenges with integrity, and may the never-failing stream of righteousness guide our steps. In our pursuit of justice, may our marriages be a testament to Your grace and truth.In Your name, we pray. Amen.

August 12

Ruth 3:10

"The Lord bless you, my daughter,' he replied. 'This kindness is greater than that which you showed earlier: You have not run after the younger men, whether rich or poor."

What Does This Mean For Us?

In this verse, Boaz acknowledges and praises Ruth for her kindness and loyalty. His words reflect appreciation for Ruth's commitment to her mother-in-law Naomi and her decision not to pursue relationships with younger men. The verse highlights qualities of character, faithfulness, and the value placed on virtue and kindness in the context of relationships, making it relevant to themes within marriage.

Modern Day Reflection

In a modern context, Ruth 3:10 speaks to the significance of character and virtue in relationships, including marriage. In a society often influenced by external factors, this verse encourages a reflection on the value of qualities such as loyalty, selflessness, and virtue in choosing life partners. It prompts individuals to prioritize meaningful connections built on character and shared values

Prayer For Vitue in Marriage

Lord, bless our relationship with the virtues of kindness, loyalty, and genuine connection. Help us prioritize character over superficial considerations in pursuing a meaningful and enduring marriage. Amen.

August 13

Galatians 5:1

"It is for freedom that Christ has set us free. Stand firm, then, and do not let yourselves be burdened again by a yoke of slavery."

What Does This Mean For Us?

This verse underscores the liberation that comes through Christ and encourages believers to stand firm in that freedom, avoiding entanglement in burdensome yokes. It encourages spouses to experience and share the freedom of living in Christ's love and grace rather than being bound by human limitations or legalistic standards.

Modern Day Reflection

Galatians 5:1 urges married couples to embrace the freedom that comes through Christ. This freedom involves liberation from the burdens of legalism, unrealistic expectations, and human limitations. In the context of marriage, it encourages partners to build a relationship based on the grace, love, and freedom found in Christ. It calls for a marriage characterized by mutual respect, shared freedom, and the acknowledgment that Christ has set us free to love and support one another in grace.

Prayer For Growth in Marriage

Heavenly Father, As we navigate the complexities of marriage, help us to release burdens and expectations that hinder the fullness of your grace. May our marriage reflect the freedom of your love and grace, fostering an environment where both partners can thrive and grow. Guide us in embracing the freedom you have provided through your Son, Jesus Christ. Amen.

August 14

Philemon 1:17

"If thou count me therefore a partner, receive him as myself."

What Does This Mean For Us?

In this verse, the apostle Paul is appealing to Philemon to welcome Onesimus, the runaway slave who had become a believer in Christ, as a dear brother and partner. The verse underscores the themes of hospitality, reconciliation, and treating others with the same love and acceptance that one would extend to Paul himself.

Modern Day Reflection

While the context is specific to the situation between Philemon and Onesimus, the principle of welcoming others with the love of Christ can be applied to various relationships, including marriage. It encourages an attitude of acceptance, forgiveness, and hospitality within the context of interpersonal relationships.

Prayer For Acceptance in Marriage

Heavenly Father, As we reflect on the message of Philemon 1:17, we seek Your guidance in embodying the spirit of welcome and acceptance in our relationships, including marriage. Teach us to treat each other with the love and kindness You have shown us. May our hearts be open to reconciliation and forgiveness, welcoming one another as partners in life's journey. In Jesus' name, we pray. Amen.

August 15

Ecclesiastes 9:7

"Go thy way, eat thy bread with joy, and drink thy wine with a merry heart; for God now accepteth thy works."

What Does This Mean For Us?

This verse encourages you to enjoy shared meals and experiences as a married couple. It emphasizes the approval of God on the simple pleasures of life, including the companionship found in marriage. The verse suggests that enjoying these moments with a joyful heart is acceptable and aligned with God's approval. In a marital context, it promotes the idea that finding joy and contentment in shared meals and experiences contributes to the overall well-being of the relationship.

Modern Day Reflection

As this applies to your marriage, it promotes the idea that finding joy and contentment in shared meals and experiences contributes to the overall well-being of the relationship.

Prayer For Companionship in Marriage

Gracious Father, We come before you with hearts filled with gratitude for the gift of companionship and shared joy in marriage. We seek Your blessing on the simple moments we share with our spouses—meals, laughter, and the everyday experiences that bring us joy. May our hearts be continually filled with gladness, and may our homes be places of love and approval in Your sight. Grant us the wisdom to appreciate the beauty in these moments and to find contentment in the bond You have blessed us with. In the name of Jesus, we pray. Amen.

August 16

Leviticus 20:7-8

"Sanctify yourselves therefore, and be ye holy: for I am the Lord your God. And ye shall keep my statutes, and do them: I am the Lord which sanctify you."

What Does This Mean For Us?

While these verses primarily focus on the call to holiness and the importance of keeping God's decrees, the principles of consecration and holiness can be applied to the context of marriage. Consecrating oneself and the marital relationship involves dedicating it to God, seeking to align with His values and guidelines for living.

Modern Day Reflection

In the context of marriage, this may include mutual commitment to God, adherence to biblical principles, and the pursuit of a relationship characterized by love, faithfulness, and holiness. The acknowledgment that God is the one who makes us holy emphasizes reliance on His transformative power within the marital bond.

Prayer For Holiness in Marriage

Heavenly Father, We come before you seeking Your guidance and blessings on our marriage. Help us to pursue holiness in our individual lives and, as a couple, rely on Your transformative power to strengthen our bonds. Grant us the wisdom to keep Your commands and the grace to reflect Your holiness in our marriage. May our love and commitment be a testimony to Your faithfulness. In the name of Jesus, we pray.
Amen.

August 17

Numbers 12:3

"Now Moses was a very humble man, more humble than anyone else on the face of the earth."

What Does This Mean For Us?

This verse highlights the exceptional humility of Moses, emphasizing that he was more humble than anyone else on the face of the earth. Despite his significant role as a leader and prophet, Moses demonstrated profound humility before God. In the context of marriage, this verse encourages individuals to cultivate a spirit of humility, recognizing the value of putting others before oneself and approaching relationships with a teachable and selfless attitude.

Modern Day Reflection

In a marital relationship, humility fosters understanding, cooperation, and a willingness to learn and grow together. It serves as a reminder to prioritize humility, acknowledging that strength in a marriage often comes from mutual respect and a humble posture toward one another.

Prayer For Humility in Marriage

Gracious God, teach us to emulate the humility that Moses displayed, putting the needs and well-being of our spouses before our own. May we approach our relationships with open hearts, willing to learn, grow, and serve one another in love. Help us to cultivate humility, recognizing that true strength lies in selflessness and mutual respect. Bless our marriages, O Lord, with the grace of humility. In Your name, we pray. Amen.

August 18

Job 31:1

"I made a covenant with my eyes not to look lustfully at a young woman."

What Does This Mean For Us?

In this verse, Job expresses his commitment to maintaining purity in his thoughts and actions, particularly in the area of lust. He speaks of making a covenant with his eyes, indicating a deliberate decision to guard against inappropriate desires. While Job's context is personal integrity and moral conduct, it emphasizes the importance of faithfulness, self-discipline, and the conscious effort to protect one's heart and commitment within the bounds of a marital relationship.

Modern Day Reflection

It emphasizes the importance of faithfulness, self-discipline, and the conscious effort to protect one's heart and commitment within the bounds of a marital relationship.

Prayer For Purity in Marriage

Heavenly Father, grant us the strength to make similar covenants with our eyes, hearts, and minds as Job did, protecting the sanctity of our relationships. Help us intentionally cultivate purity and resist temptations that may threaten the bond us. May our marriage be grounded in trust, faithfulness, and a commitment to honor one another. Lord, empower us to uphold our sacred vows, seeking Your guidance in every aspect of our relationship. In Your mercy, strengthen our marriage with love, fidelity, and the grace to navigate challenges.
Amen.

August 19

Ezekiel 11:19

"And I will give them one heart, and I will put a new spirit within you; and I will take the stony heart out of their flesh, and will give them an heart of flesh"

What Does This Mean For Us?

In this verse, God speaks about the transformation He will bring to His people, promising to give them an undivided heart and a new spirit. While the context is the restoration of Israel, the concept of an undivided heart and a new spirit has implications for marriage. God's promise reflects the desire for unity and spiritual renewal within relationships.

Modern Day Reflection

In relation to marriage, it encourages spouses to seek an oneness of heart and spirit, allowing God to remove hardness and cultivate a tender, responsive, and united bond between them.

Prayer For Renewed Spirit in Marriage

Heavenly Father, As we reflect on Your promise in Ezekiel 11:19 to give us an undivided heart and a new spirit as we bring our marriage before You. We pray for the transformative work of Your Spirit in our hearts, removing any hardness and granting us unity. Lord, renew our spirits, making us responsive to Your guidance and to the needs of our spouse. We surrender our relationship to Your loving care, trusting in Your transformative power. In Jesus' name, we pray. Amen.

August 20

Hebrews 11:6

"But without faith it is impossible to please him: for he that cometh to God must believe that he is, and that he is a rewarder of them that diligently seek him."

What Does This Mean For Us?

While this verse specifically addresses faith in relation to drawing near to God, the underlying principle of faith can also be applied to marriage. Trust and belief in each other and a shared faith can strengthen the foundation of a marriage and contribute to its overall well-being.

Modern Day Reflection

In the context of modern marriages, Hebrews 11:6 emphasizes the importance of faith. In a marriage, faith involves trust, belief, and confidence in one another.

~

Prayer For Trust in Marriage

Dear God, We come before you with gratitude for the love and companionship you've blessed us with in our marriage. Grant us the strength to trust one another completely, fostering a bond built on mutual confidence and understanding. Help us share common values and beliefs, deepen our connection, and provide a solid foundation for our relationship. In moments of challenge, instill in us the perseverance to continue growing together, both individually and as a couple. May we draw near to you and each other in all that we do. We entrust our marriage into your loving hands, seeking your blessing and guidance every step of the way. Amen.

August 21

3 John 1:8
"We therefore ought to receive such, that we might be fellowhelpers to the truth."

What Does This Mean For Us?

In this verse, the apostle John encourages the practice of hospitality, especially towards those who are involved in spreading the truth of the Gospel. While the context may not directly address marriage, the principle of hospitality can be applied to relationships.

Modern Day Reflection

In a marital context, it suggests a welcoming and supportive atmosphere within the home, where spouses extend warmth, kindness, and a sense of belonging to each other. This verse emphasizes the importance of working together for a common purpose, which may include cultivating a shared commitment to truth, love, and mutual growth in marriage.

Prayer For Open Hearts in Marriage
Heavenly Father, Grant us open, welcoming, and generous hearts toward one another. May our homes be havens of warmth, kindness, and understanding. Lord, help us work together for the truth, aligning our hearts with love, honesty, and mutual support. In moments of togetherness, may we strengthen the bonds of our marriage, always striving to create an atmosphere where Your truth and grace flourish. Guide us, O Lord, as we navigate the journey of marriage with hospitality and love. Amen.

August 22

Matthew 5:44

"But I say unto you, Love your enemies, bless them that curse you, do good to them that hate you, and pray for them which despitefully use you, and persecute you."

What Does This Mean For Us?

Matthew 5:44 challenges us to extend love and forgiveness even to those who may have wronged us.

Modern Day Reflection

The verse encourages couples to cultivate a spirit of forgiveness and compassion, treating each other with love even in challenging moments.

~

Prayer For Compassion in Marriage

Loving God, help us to bless and do good to each other, especially in moments of difficulty. May our marriage reflect Your boundless love, and may our hearts be open to forgiveness and reconciliation. Amen.

August 23

1 Corinthians 13:1

"Though I speak with the tongues of men and of angels, and have not charity, I am become as sounding brass, or a tinkling cymbal."

What Does This Mean For Us?

The verse begins with a powerful hypothetical scenario where one can speak in various languages, even the language of angels, yet lacks charity. "Charity" here refers to selfless, sacrificial love. The verse concludes with a comparison, stating that without love, one's words are like noisy and empty instruments.

Modern Day Reflection

In marriage, this emphasizes that even the most eloquent expressions or actions are meaningless if not rooted in genuine love. Married couples must always remember to speak to each other in kind tones and with loving hearts, no matter the topic of discussion. The verse also encourages couples to prioritize and cultivate selfless, sacrificial love within their marriage.

Prayer For Selfless Love in Marriage

Gracious Lord, As we stand on the threshold of marriage, we are reminded of the profound truth in 1 Corinthians 13:1. May our love for each other go beyond mere words or eloquent expressions. Help us cultivate a selfless and sacrificial love, transcending the superficial. May our actions speak louder than any language, reflecting the depth of our commitment. In your name, we pray. Amen.

August 24

Ephesians 5:28

"So ought men to love their wives as their own bodies. He that loveth his wife loveth himself."

What Does This Mean For Us?

The verse emphasizes the duty of husbands to love their wives as they love their own bodies. This echoes the concept of the two becoming one flesh, highlighting the interconnectedness and unity within marriage.

Modern Day Reflection

The verse exemplifies and encourages husbands to prioritize and care for their wives as an extension of themselves.

~

Prayer For Spousal Care in Marriage

Gracious Lord, As we enter into the marriage covenant, we seek your guidance, as expressed in Ephesians 5:28. May our love for each other reflect the unity and care described in this verse. Help us, as a couple, to prioritize each other's well-being, recognizing that in loving our spouse, we are nurturing and caring for ourselves. In your name, we pray. Amen.

August 25

Psalm 147:3
"He healeth the broken in heart, and bindeth up their wounds."

What Does This Mean For Us?

In the context of marriage, this verse acknowledges that couples may face emotional and relational challenges that can lead to brokenness. It emphasizes God's role as a source of healing, offering comfort and restoration to those who experience heartache within their marriage.

Modern Day Reflection

The imagery of binding wounds signifies God's care and attentiveness to the hurts and pains that couples may endure. As it's relative to marriage, it communicates God's desire to mend and restore the wounds that may result from misunderstandings, conflicts, or hardships.

Prayer For Brokenness in Marriage
Gracious God, In the moments of brokenness within our marriage, we turn to you as the healer of the brokenhearted. Heal our wounds, mend our hearts, and guide us toward reconciliation and understanding. May your love be the balm that restores our relationship. In your name, we pray. Amen.

August 26

Galatians 5:6

"For in Jesus Christ neither circumcision availeth any thing, nor uncircumcision; but faith which worketh by love.."

What Does This Mean For Us?

In this verse, the Apostle Paul emphasizes the importance of faith and love within the Christian context. While the immediate context addresses the issue of circumcision, the broader principle of faith expressing itself through love holds significant implications for various aspects of the Christian life, including relationships.

Modern Day Reflection

To foster love and support in today's marriages, this verse underscores the centrality of genuine faith and the outward expression of that faith through love. It encourages spouses to prioritize love as the foundation of their actions, interactions, and decisions within the marital relationship. Faith and love, intertwined, become the guiding principles that shape a Christ-centered marriage.

❧

Prayer For Prioritizing Love in Marriage

Heavenly Father, a s we ponder the wisdom of Galatians 5:6, we seek Your guidance for our marriages. May our faith find its expression through love in every aspect of our relationship. Grant us the grace to prioritize love in our actions, words, and decisions. Lord, let our marriage be a testament to the transformative power of faith working through love. In Jesus' name, we pray. Amen.

August 27

Hebrews 12:14

"Follow peace with all men, and holiness, without which no man shall
see the Lord."

What Does This Mean For Us?

Hebrews 12:14 advises followers of the Christian faith to seek peace actively in their interactions with everyone and underscores the importance of leading a holy life. The call to "strive for peace with everyone" highlights the value of promoting harmony and avoiding relationship conflicts. At the same time, the second part emphasizes the necessity of moral purity and dedication to God's principles for a profound spiritual connection.

Modern Day Reflection

In modern relationships, the verse encourages individuals to cultivate inner and interpersonal harmony, recognizing that the pursuit of peace and holiness contributes to the overall well-being of individuals and the communities they engage with.

Prayer For Inner Harmony in Marriage

Dear God, grant us the strength to pursue peace in our relationships
and the wisdom to lead lives marked by holiness. Guide us in fostering
understanding and empathy, and may our actions contribute to
harmony in our interconnected world. Amen.

August 28

Amos 5:14

"Seek good, and not evil, that ye may live: and so the Lord, the God of hosts, shall be with you, as ye have spoken."

What Does This Mean For Us?

This verse encourages a life guided by goodness and righteousness, suggesting that by seeking good and avoiding evil, individuals can experience the presence and favor of the Lord. It emphasizes the importance of ethical living and aligning one's actions with God's principles.

Modern Day Reflection

Amos 5:14 is a timeless reminder to prioritize goodness and righteousness in our lives. It encourages married couples to make ethical choices, promote justice, and seek positive actions in their daily interactions. In a world marked by various challenges, this verse calls for a commitment to values that contribute to the well-being of individuals and communities.

~

Prayer For Good in Marriage

Dear Heavenly Father, we seeking to follow the wisdom of Amos 5:14. Help us, Lord, to seek the good in our relationship continually and to shun any path that leads to harm or discord. May our actions be guided by goodness, and may we always choose the path that aligns with your will. Bless our union, Lord, with your presence and grace, that our lives together may be a testimony to your love and a source of inspiration for others. In Jesus' name, we pray. Amen.

Malachi 4:6

"And he will turn the hearts of fathers to their children and the hearts of children to their fathers, lest I come and strike the land with a decree of utter destruction."

What Does This Mean For Us?

This verse highlights the importance of family relationships, specifically the reconciliation and unity between generations. In the context of marriage, it underscores the significance of fostering strong family bonds, where spouses work together to create an environment of love, understanding, and harmony for the well-being of their children.

Modern Day Reflection

In a modern context, Malachi 4:6 encourages us to prioritize and nurture family relationships. The phrase "turn the hearts" suggests a transformative process, urging individuals to invest time and effort in understanding, supporting, and connecting with their family members. In a society often marked by busy schedules and distractions, this verse serves as a reminder to value and invest in the bonds between parents and children, fostering a legacy of love and connection that withstands the challenges of the modern world.

Prayer For Family in Marriage

Heavenly Father, we pray for the grace to turn our hearts towards our family members, fostering love, understanding, and unity. May our relationships, especially within our marriages, be a source of strength and inspiration. Amen.

August 30

Joshua 1:9

"Have not I commanded thee? Be strong and of a good courage; be not afraid, neither be thou dismayed: for the Lord thy God is with thee whithersoever thou goest."

What Does This Mean For Us?

This verse is part of God's charge to Joshua as he takes on the leadership of the Israelites. It encourages strength, courage, and trust in God's presence.

Modern Day Reflection

Joshua 1:9 offers a poignant message for marriages, urging couples to draw strength and courage from their unity. The verse encourages spouses to face challenges without fear, trusting in the presence of the Lord throughout their marital journey. It emphasizes the idea that, as a team, couples can find resilience and bravery in their commitment to one another. The assurance of God's continual presence serves as a foundation for shared faith, fostering a marriage built on trust, courage, and the belief that they can navigate life's complexities together with divine guidance and support.

Prayer For Guidance in Marriage

Dear Lord, as we navigate the journey of marriage, grant us strength and courage. Help us not to be fearful or dismayed but to find solace in the knowledge that You are with us wherever we go. Guide our marriage with Your wisdom and grace, and may our faith in each other and in You deepen with each passing day. In Your name, we pray. Amen.

August 31

Isaiah 40:31

"But they that wait upon the Lord shall renew their strength; they shall mount up with wings as eagles; they shall run, and not be weary, and they shall walk, and not faint."

What Does This Mean For Us?

This verse speaks to the importance of patience and reliance on God. Couples who wait on the Lord, seeking His guidance and strength, will find renewal in their marriage. It encourages them to turn to God in times of weariness or challenges.

Modern Day Reflection

In a marital unit, it signifies that couples, through their reliance on God, will rise above challenges, run their race without weariness, and walk through life without fainting

~

Prayer For Reliance on God in Marriage

Gracious God, renew our strength in this marriage as we wait upon You. Grant us the patience to seek Your guidance, knowing that we find the endurance to rise above challenges in You. Amen.

AS THE AUTUMN LEAVES BEGIN TO FALL, MAY WE GRACEFULLY LET GO OF WHAT NO LONGER SERVES OUR SPIRITUAL GROWTH. LIKE THE TREES SHEDDING THEIR FOLIAGE, MAY SEPTEMBER BE A SEASON OF RELEASE, PAVING THE WAY FOR NEW POSSIBILITIES AND INNER TRANSFORMATION.

September 1

Leviticus 26:3-4

"If ye walk in my statutes, and keep my commandments, and do them;
Then I will give you rain in due season, and the land shall yield her
increase, and the trees of the field shall yield their fruit."

What Does This Mean For Us?

In the context of marriage, Leviticus 26:3 can be applied to emphasize the importance of aligning the relationship with God's principles and commandments. The verse suggests that by walking in God's statutes and observing His commandments, couples can open themselves to His blessings.

Modern Day Reflection

Applying Leviticus 26:3 to marriage involves prioritizing qualities such as love, forgiveness, honesty, and commitment—the principles that God encourages in His commandments. By actively living out these values, couples can create a foundation for a strong and blessed marriage. This verse serves as a reminder that a marriage centered on God's teachings is more likely to thrive and be enriched by His blessings.

Prayer For the Foundation in Marriage

Heavenly Father, grant us the wisdom and strength to live out the values of love, forgiveness, and commitment in our marriage. May our relationship be a reflection of your principles, and may your blessings abound in our lives together. Guide us in the path of righteousness, that our marriage may be a testimony to your grace and love. In Jesus' name, we pray. Amen.

September 2

Job 19:25-26

"For I know that my redeemer liveth, and that he shall stand at the latter day upon the earth: And though after my skin worms destroy this body, yet in my flesh shall I see God."

What Does This Mean For Us?

In the context of Job's story, these verses convey his unwavering trust in a living Redeemer despite his overwhelming adversity. The anticipation of seeing God in the flesh reflects a deep faith in the resurrection and an ultimate restoration beyond his present suffering. It's a powerful declaration of hope in the midst of despair.

Modern Day Reflection

The theme of Job 19:25-26 is of faith, hope, and restoration. In times of difficulty or challenges within a marriage, couples can draw inspiration from Job's unwavering faith in the midst of suffering. The idea of a living Redeemer and the anticipation of seeing God can symbolize the hope for renewal and restoration in a marital relationship. Couples facing trials may find strength in the belief that, even in the face of hardships, there is the possibility of a redeemed and restored marriage.

Prayer For Renewal in Marriage

Dear Lord, grant us the unwavering faith and hope expressed by Job. May we trust in the possibility of renewal and restoration in our marriage, knowing that our Redeemer lives. Guide us through difficulties, strengthen our bond, and lead us to a place of deeper understanding and love. In Your name, we pray. Amen.

September 3

Daniel 2:22

"He revealeth the deep and secret things: he knoweth what is in the
darkness, and the light dwelleth with him.."

What Does This Mean For Us?

Daniel 2:22 emphasizes God's unique ability to bring illumination to the concealed aspects of life, showcasing His wisdom and sovereign knowledge. the verse carries a broad theme of God's capacity to bring light and understanding to hidden circumstances, fostering trust in His wisdom and guidance.

Modern Day Reflection

While this verse is part of Daniel's response to God's revelation of King Nebuchadnezzar's dream, it can be applied to marriage metaphorically. In the context of a marital relationship, it suggests that God has the ability to reveal hidden aspects, bring understanding to challenging situations, and provide insight into the depths of each partner's heart. It encourages spouses to trust in God's guidance, seeking His wisdom to illuminate and strengthen their marriage.

Prayer For God's Guidance in Marriage
Heavenly Father, we acknowledge Your omniscience and Your ability to
unveil hidden mysteries and illuminate the darkness. In our marriage.
Grant us the wisdom to understand each other deeply and the strength
to face any challenges that may arise. May Your divine insight guide us in
our journey together, bringing clarity, love, and unity. Amen.

September 4

1 Corinthians 6:16

"What? know ye not that he which is joined to an harlot is one body? for two, saith he, shall be one flesh."

What Does This Mean For Us?

This verse speaks to the profound nature of physical intimacy, emphasizing that the act of joining with another person in a sexual relationship creates a union, making the two individuals one flesh. In the context of marriage, this verse underscores the exclusivity and sacredness of the marital bond.

Modern Day Reflection

In today's world, this verse encourages couples to recognize the sanctity of the marital relationship and the unique oneness it brings. It emphasizes the importance of fidelity and the understanding that the physical, emotional, and spiritual aspects of marriage are interconnected.

Prayer For Intimacy in Marriage

Heavenly Father, thank you for the gift of intimacy within the bounds of marriage. Help us, as a couple, to honor the sacredness of our union and to cultivate a relationship that reflects the oneness You designed for us. In your name we pray, Amen.

September 5

1 John 4:7
"Beloved, let us love one another: for love is of God, and every one that loveth is born of God and knoweth God."

What Does This Mean For Us?

This verse emphasizes the centrality of love in the Christian life, portraying it as a divine attribute that connects believers with God and with one another. It encourages a selfless and unconditional love that stems from God's nature and is reflected in the relationships among His followers.

Modern Day Reflection

1 John 4:7 holds profound significance by urging couples to embrace a love that mirrors God's unconditional and selfless nature. The verse encourages spouses to cultivate a deep, genuine, and sacrificial love for each other, recognizing that this love originates from God Himself. By embodying this divine love, couples not only strengthen their marital bond but also deepen their connection with God.

Prayer For Unconditional Love in Marriage
Dear Lord, in our marriage, let Your love be our guide. Teach us to love one another as You have loved us—selflessly, unconditionally, and with grace. May our relationship be a reflection of Your divine love, deepening our connection with each other and with You. In Jesus' name, we pray. Amen.

September 6

Proverbs 3:9-10

"Honour the Lord with thy substance, and with the firstfruits of all thine increase: So shall thy barns be filled with plenty, and thy presses shall burst out with new wine."

What Does This Mean For Us?

This passage encourages the act of honoring God with one's possessions and the first and best of one's harvest or income, promising divine blessings in return.

Modern Day Reflection

In a modern context, Proverbs 3:9-10 can be reflected upon in the context of marriage as an encouragement for couples to honor God with the resources and blessings within their marriage. Beyond the material aspects, it suggests the importance of prioritizing each other, expressing gratitude, and offering the best of oneself. By honoring God through mutual respect, generosity, and a commitment to shared values, couples can create a foundation for a flourishing and abundant marriage.

Prayer For Sharing in Marriage

Dear Lord, help us honor You with the fruits of our love and resources. May our commitment to each other and to You be a source of abundance and blessings within our relationship. Guide us in sharing the best of ourselves, and may our union be a testament to Your grace. In Jesus' name, we pray. Amen.

Malachi 2:14

"Yet ye say, Wherefore? Because the Lord hath been witness between thee and the wife of thy youth, against whom thou hast dealt treacherously: yet is she thy companion, and the wife of thy covenant."

What Does This Mean For Us?

This verse highlights the covenantal nature of marriage and addresses the consequences of unfaithfulness within that sacred covenant. It emphasizes God's witness to the commitment made in marriage and underscores the significance of faithfulness to one's spouse.

Modern Day Reflection

Malachi 2:14 speaks to the enduring commitment and covenantal bond within marriage. It serves as a reminder of the sacred promise made between spouses and the gravity of faithfulness in contemporary relationships. The verse prompts reflection on the significance of honoring the commitment to one's partner, recognizing them as a companion and covenantal ally in the journey of life.

Prayer For Faithfulness in Marriage

Heavenly Father, we come before you with gratitude for the marriage covenant you've blessed us with. Grant us the strength to be faithful companions, finding resilience in our commitment to this sacred bond. Heal our wounds, foster our understanding, and deepen our love for each other. May our marriage be a reflection of your enduring faithfulness. In Jesus' name, we pray. Amen.

September 8

Psalm 118:24

"This is the day that the Lord has made; let us rejoice and be glad in it."

What Does This Mean For Us?

Psalm 118:24 encourages us to approach each day with a heart filled with gratitude and joy, recognizing that each day is a gift from the Lord. It invites us to focus on the blessings and opportunities that each day brings, regardless of our circumstances. The verse emphasizes rejoicing in God's providence and sovereignty, acknowledging He controls each moment.

Modern Day Reflection

Within marriage, each day is an opportunity to rejoice in the bond shared between spouses, and to express gratitude for the gift of companionship. This verse encourages couples to celebrate the present moment, finding joy in the shared experiences, challenges overcome together, and the blessings of togetherness. In marriage, each day becomes a reason to rejoice and be glad for the partnership that God has brought together.

Prayer For Our Journey in Marriage

Heavenly Father, we thank You for the precious gift of marriage. May we find joy and gratitude in each shared moment with our spouse, rejoicing in the love You've blessed us with. Grant us the wisdom to appreciate the beauty of today. May our hearts be filled with gladness as we navigate this continued journey of marriage. In Your name, we pray. Amen.

September 9

Ephesians 5:21-25

"Submitting yourselves one to another in the fear of God. Wives, submit yourselves unto your own husbands, as unto the Lord. For the husband is the head of the wife, even as Christ is the head of the church: and he is the saviour of the body. Therefore as the church is subject unto Christ, so let the wives be to their own husbands in every thing. Husbands, love your wives, even as Christ also loved the church, and gave himself for it"

What Does This Mean For Us?

This passage underscores the importance of mutual honor, love, and submission in building a strong and harmonious marital relationship.

Modern Day Reflection

Ephesians 5:21-25 encourages a partnership marked by mutual respect, understanding, and sacrificial love. Husbands are reminded to lead with a love that mirrors Christ's selfless devotion to the church, emphasizing empathy and sacrificial care.

Prayer For Sacrificial Care in Marriage

Heavenly Father, may we embrace the principles of mutual respect and sacrificial love outlined in Ephesians 5. May our relationship be a reflection of Christ's love for the church, marked by understanding, selflessness, and mutual growth. Bless this union, Lord, with the grace to navigate challenges and the joy that comes from honoring each other in love. Amen.

September 10

Ezekiel 16:62

"And I will establish my covenant with thee; and thou shalt know that I am the Lord."

What Does This Mean For Us?

This verse is part of a larger passage where God speaks to Israel using the metaphor of a wayward woman to illustrate the unfaithfulness of the nation. Despite their disobedience and straying from God, this verse emphasizes God's commitment to establishing a covenant with them.

Modern Day Reflection

This verse can inspire couples to approach their marriage with a deep sense of commitment, understanding that true strength in a marriage comes from a foundation built on love, trust, and unwavering dedication to the covenant they've made with each other. It encourages spouses to recognize that, like God's covenant with Israel, their marriage is a sacred bond that should be honored and nurtured.

Prayer For Sacred Bond in Marriage

Dear Heavenly Father, We come before you with gratitude for the covenant of marriage, a sacred bond that reflects Your unwavering commitment to us. Just as You established Your covenant with Israel, we seek Your guidance and strength to uphold the covenant we've made with each other in marriage. Grant us the wisdom to navigate challenges, the grace to forgive, and the humility to always seek reconciliation. Amen.

September 11

1 Corinthians 16:14

"Let all your things be done with charity."

What Does This Mean For Us?

The verse emphasizes the overarching importance of love (charity) in every aspect of life. In the context of marriage, it suggests that love should permeate every action, decision, and interaction within the relationship. This aligns with God's design for marriage, where love is not just an emotion but a guiding principle for every aspect of the union.

Modern Day Reflection

Amidst the hustle and distractions, the call to "do everything in love" serves as a radical reminder to prioritize kindness, understanding, and selfless love in daily interactions and significant decisions. In a culture that often emphasizes individual pursuits, this verse challenges couples to cultivate a love that seeks the well-being of the other, forgives readily, and consistently chooses unity.

Prayer For The Power of Love in Marriage

Dear God, we come before you, seeking the wisdom embedded in 1 Corinthians 16:14. Grant us the grace to "do everything in love" within the sacred covenant of our marriage. In a world that often pulls us in different directions, help us intentionally prioritize the enduring power of love in our shared journey. May our marriage be a testament to the transformative nature of Your love. In Jesus' name, we pray. Amen.

September 12

Mark 10:45

"For even the Son of Man did not come to be served, but to serve, and to give his life as a ransom for many."

What Does This Mean For Us?

In the context of marriage, this verse serves as a profound reminder of the sacrificial and servant-hearted love that Jesus exemplified. It encourages spouses to approach their marriage with a spirit of humility, selflessness, and a willingness to serve each other.

Modern Day Reflection

In the context of modern marriages, Mark 10:45 serves as a timeless guide, urging couples to embrace a counter-cultural approach of selfless service over self-fulfillment. Beyond the romantic ideal, this teaching is particularly relevant in navigating conflicts, inviting couples to approach disagreements with a spirit of understanding and forgiveness.

Prayer For Servitude in Marriage

Dear God, in our marriage journey, let us emulate the example set by Jesus, who came not to be served but to serve. May we approach each day with a heart inclined towards selfless love, seeking opportunities to serve and uplift one another. In moments of joy and challenges, may our actions reflect the sacrificial love that Christ showed, ultimately enriching the bond we share. May our marriage be a testament to the transformative power of serving one another in love. Amen.

<h1 style="text-align:center">September 13</h1>

Matthew 6:33

"But seek ye first the kingdom of God, and his righteousness; and all these things shall be added unto you."

What Does This Mean For Us?

This verse serves as a timeless reminder for couples to prioritize God's kingdom and righteousness in their relationship. It encourages them to seek God's guidance, align their lives with His principles, and trust that their needs and the flourishing of their marriage will be provided for by doing so.

Modern Day Reflection

Matthew 6:33 prompts spouses to align their goals and decisions with divine principles, fostering a shared spiritual path. By seeking God first, couples lay the foundation for a marriage marked by love, forgiveness, and purpose, transcending individual ambitions. It challenges the cultural narrative of prioritizing personal success and material gain, offering a roadmap for couples to find a deeper abundance in their commitment to God's kingdom.

Prayer For Grace in Marriage

As we live daily in our sacred marriage covenant, we invite Your presence to envelop us. May our journey together be guided by Your wisdom, fueled by Your boundless love, and sustained by Your unending grace. Grant us the patience to understand each other truly, the humility to forgive, and the unwavering commitment to prioritize You in every aspect of our lives. Amen.

September 14

Jonah 4:4
"Then said the Lord, Doest thou well to be angry?'"

What Does This Mean For Us?

In Jonah 4:4, God questions Jonah's anger. This verse is part of the narrative where Jonah becomes frustrated and angry because God showed compassion to the repentant people of Nineveh. God's question invites reflection on the nature of Jonah's feelings and serves as a reminder of the importance of mercy and compassion in our interactions with others.

Modern Day Reflection

This verse is an excellent reminder that each spouse needs to be proficient in managing their emotions, understanding God's perspective, and embracing compassion in marriage. It encourages individuals to examine their hearts and responses, fostering an atmosphere of understanding and forgiveness, which can contribute to the strength and harmony of marriages.

~

Prayer For a Compassionate Heart in Marriage
Dear God, In moments of frustration and anger, help us pause and reflect on Your compassionate heart. Guide us to manage our emotions in a way that fosters understanding and kindness in our marriage. May Your love be the foundation of our interactions, and may we always seek to reflect Your mercy in our relationship. Amen.

September 15

Genesis 29:20

"And Jacob served seven years for Rachel; and they seemed unto him but a few days, for the love he had to her."

What Does This Mean For Us?

This verse conveys the powerful and transformative nature of love. Jacob's seven years of labor felt like a short period of time because his love for Rachel was so strong and enduring. It highlights the idea that when love is genuine and profound, it can make challenges and sacrifices seem insignificant in comparison.

Modern Day Reflection

Genesis 29:20 prompts modern-day married couples to reflect on the enduring nature of love. In our fast-paced lives, the verse encourages us to see the sacrifices we make for each other not as burdens but as expressions of a profound love that transcends time. It challenges us to prioritize the strength of our connection, making challenges seem lighter and the passing of time insignificant compared to our enduring bond.

~

Prayer For Strengthening Connection in Marriage

Dear Heavenly Father, as we journey through the seasons of life together, may our love for each other be as deep and enduring as Jacob's love for Rachel. May our commitment to each other make the burdens feel light and the passing of time insignificant, infusing joy and meaning into our marriage. Grant us the strength to prioritize the strength of our connection and the wisdom to navigate life's demands with grace.

Amen.

September 16

Mark 11:25

"And when ye stand praying, forgive, if ye have ought against any: that your Father also which is in heaven may forgive you your trespasses."

What Does This Mean For Us?

For a married couple, this verse holds significance in the context of forgiveness within the relationship. It encourages spouses to prioritize forgiveness and reconciliation in their interactions. he verse suggests that as individuals forgive each other, they open the path for God's forgiveness and blessings in their lives. I

Modern Day Reflection

In the context of forgiveness in marriage, Mark 11:25 emphasizes the connection between forgiveness and prayer. The verse encourages individuals, including couples in marriage, to forgive those they have grievances against, recognizing that forgiveness is intertwined with one's relationship with God. This highlights the importance of fostering a forgiving spirit within the marital relationship.

Prayer For Grievances in Marriage

Dear God, help us forgive one another within our marriage. May our hearts be open to release any grievances and cultivate a spirit of forgiveness. Guide us in building a relationship marked by grace and understanding. Amen.

September 17

Proverbs 19:11

"The discretion of a man deferreth his anger, and it is his glory to pass over a transgression."

What Does This Mean For Us?

Proverbs 19:11 underscores the wisdom of exercising discretion and deferring anger. The verse suggests that choosing not to hold onto anger and passing over a transgression brings glory.

Modern Day Reflection

Applied to marriage, this encourages couples to practice discretion in their reactions, allowing room for forgiveness and understanding rather than harboring resentment. It emphasizes the beauty of letting go and extending grace within the marital relationship.

Prayer For Discretion in Marriage

Heavenly Father, teach us the significance of Proverbs 19:11 in our marriage. May we exercise discretion and defer anger, finding glory in passing over transgressions. Strengthen our commitment to building a marriage grounded in grace, forgiveness, and understanding. Amen.

September 18

Romans 12:19

"Dearly beloved, avenge not yourselves, but rather give place unto wrath: for it is written, Vengeance is mine; I will repay, saith the Lord."

What Does This Mean For Us?

This verse advises against seeking revenge and encourages giving room for divine justice. The verse reminds individuals, including couples, that the responsibility for justice lies with God, freeing them from the burden of retaliation.

Modern Day Reflection

Married couples can reflect on this verse as it emphasizes the importance of letting go of grudges, trusting in divine justice, and focusing on forgiveness rather than seeking vengeance.

~

Prayer For Divine Justice in Marriage

Dear God, as a couple, we reflect on Romans 12:19. Help us release any desire for vengeance and trust in Your divine justice. May our hearts be filled with forgiveness and understanding, allowing Your love to guide our actions. We thank you, Lord God, for your guidance in our marriage. In Jesus name, Amen.

September 19

Luke 23:34

"Then said Jesus, Father, forgive them; for they know not what they do.
And they parted his raiment and cast lots."

What Does This Mean For Us?

In the context of forgiveness in marriage, Luke 23:34 portrays Jesus's profound act of forgiveness on the cross. Despite the injustice and cruelty, Jesus exemplifies unconditional forgiveness, pleading with God to forgive those who were harming Him.

Modern Day Reflection

Applied to marriage, this verse encourages couples to embrace a similar spirit of forgiveness, understanding that forgiveness is not always deserved but is a powerful force that can transform relationships.

Prayer For Forgiveness in Marriage

Lord God, as a couple, help us to emulate the forgiveness shown by Jesus in Luke 23:34. May we cultivate a spirit of forgiveness in our marriage, recognizing its transformative power in our relationship.
Amen.

September 20

Ephesians 1:7
"In whom we have redemption through his blood, the forgiveness of
sins, according to the riches of his grace."

What Does This Mean For Us?

For a married couple, Ephesians 1:7 emphasizes the profound concept
of redemption and forgiveness through the grace of God. In the context
of marriage, it suggests that the foundation of the relationship is rooted
in the grace and forgiveness that God offers.

Modern Day Reflection

In the context of a modern-day marriage, Ephesians 1:7 invites couples
to embrace a profound sense of redemption and forgiveness within their
relationship. It underscores the idea that their union's foundation is
rooted in God's boundless grace. In practical terms, this verse
encourages spouses to approach their marriage with a willingness to
forgive each other's trespasses, recognizing that mistakes can be
opportunities for growth and transformation.

Prayer For Redemption in Marriage
Heavenly Father, help us to live out the message of Ephesians 1:7 in our
marriage. May the forgiveness we extend to each other reflect your
abundant grace, leading to redemption and a stronger, more loving
relationship. Amen.

September 21

Proverbs 28:13

"He that covereth his sins shall not prosper: but whoso confesseth and forsaketh them shall have mercy."

What Does This Mean For Us?

In the context of forgiveness in marriage, Proverbs 28:13 underscores the importance of openness and repentance. The verse suggests that concealing wrongdoing can hinder personal and relational growth, while acknowledging and turning away from mistakes leads to mercy.

Modern Day Reflection

Applied to marriage, it encourages couples to create a space for honesty, confession, and forgiveness, fostering an environment where both partners can experience mercy and growth.

∼

Prayer For Growth in Marriage

Heavenly Father, help us to follow the wisdom of Proverbs 28:13 in our marriage. May we confess our shortcomings, forsake them, and experience the mercy that comes from genuine repentance and forgiveness. Amen.

Micah 7:18-19

"Who is a God like unto thee, that pardoneth iniquity, and passeth by the transgression of the remnant of his heritage? he retaineth not his anger for ever, because he delighteth in mercy. He will turn again, he will have compassion upon us; he will subdue our iniquities; and thou wilt cast all their sins into the depths of the sea."

What Does This Mean For Us?

Micah 7:18-19 highlights the divine nature of forgiveness, portraying God's willingness to pardon and show mercy. This verse encourages couples to emulate God's forgiveness in daily life, recognizing that mercy can subdue wrongs and cast them away.

Modern Day Reflection

In a modern-day reflection for a couple, these verses are a powerful reminder of God's immeasurable mercy and forgiveness. It encourages spouses to emulate this divine compassion in their marriage, recognizing that forgiveness is key to nurturing a lasting and thriving relationship. The verse prompts couples to let go of anger and resentment, just as God does, and to embrace steadfast love and compassion.

Prayer For Mercy in Marriage

Gracious God, inspire us to forgive as You forgive, casting our sins into the depths of understanding and compassion. May our marriage reflect Your mercy, fostering love and healing. Amen.

September 23

Matthew 6:12
"And forgive us our debts, as we forgive our debtors."

What Does This Mean For Us?

Matthew 6:12, part of the Lord's Prayer, emphasizes the reciprocal nature of forgiveness.

Modern Day Reflection

In the context of marriage, this verse encourages couples to acknowledge their own need for forgiveness and to extend that forgiveness to each other. It underscores the importance of a forgiving spirit within the marital relationship, promoting healing and harmony.

Prayer For Forgiveness in Marriage
Loving Father, grant us the strength to forgive as we seek forgiveness. Help us release the debts of the past in our marriage, fostering an atmosphere of grace and understanding. May our love be a testament to your boundless forgiveness. Amen,

September 24

Mark 2:5

"When Jesus saw their faith, he said unto the sick of the palsy, Son, thy sins be forgiven thee."

What Does This Mean For Us?

Mark 2:5 narrates the healing of a paralyzed man by Jesus, highlighting the connection between faith and forgiveness. In the context of marriage, this verse suggests that faith and trust play a crucial role in the process of forgiveness. Just as the paralyzed man experienced physical and spiritual healing, couples can find restoration and renewal through faith and forgiveness.

Modern Day Reflection

The verse underscores the transformative power of faith and forgiveness. It encourages spouses to recognize the significance of faith in their relationship, not only in each other but also in their shared journey. The verse prompts couples to have faith in the healing power of forgiveness, understanding that addressing and forgiving each other's imperfections is essential for emotional and relational well-being. Just as Jesus offered forgiveness and healing, this verse encourages spouses to create an environment of grace and understanding within their marriage.

Prayer For Faith in Marriage

Gracious Lord, help us emulate the forgiveness You showed the paralyzed man. May our faith in each other heal our marriage, and may we find the grace to forgive as we have been forgiven. Amen.

September 25

Isaiah 43:25

"I, even I, am he that blotteth out thy transgressions for mine own sake,
and will not remember thy sins."

What Does This Mean For Us?

This verse speaks of God's forgiveness, emphasizing the act of blotting out transgressions and choosing not to remember sins. It encourages similar forgiveness for married couples to let go of past mistakes for the sake of the relationship's well-being.

Modern Day Reflection

Isaiah 43:25 emphasizes the divine act of forgiveness and the freedom it brings. For spouses, this verse encourages a similar approach within their marriage—forgiving each other's mistakes and shortcomings. It prompts couples to cultivate a mindset where forgiveness is not just about letting go, but about actively choosing not to dwell on past mistakes. This verse invites spouses to create a space in their relationship where the weight of transgressions is lifted, allowing for growth, understanding, and a commitment to a future unburdened by the sins of the past.

Prayer For God's Forgiveness in Marriage

Heavenly Father, as You forgive us, help us to forgive each other. May the act of letting go strengthen our marriage and bring us closer together. Amen.

September 26

Proverbs 17:6

"Children's children are the crown of old men, and the glory of children are their fathers."

What Does This Mean For Us?

This verse highlights the mutual honor and blessing that exist between generations. In the context of God's design for marriage and family, it underscores the interconnectedness and significance of different stages of life.

Modern Day Reflection

In today's world, this verse emphasizes the importance of family legacy and each generation's role in God's marriage design. It suggests that the thriving and honor of both older and younger generations contribute to the overall glory of a family.

∿

Prayer For Family in Marriage

Dear Lord, we thank You for the beauty of family and the connections between generations. May our marriage be a source of blessing to our children and grandchildren. Grant us the wisdom to impart values that honor You and strengthen our family bond. Amen.

September 27

Proverbs 2:16-17

"To deliver thee from the strange woman, even from the stranger which flattereth with her words; Which forsaketh the guide of her youth and forgetteth the covenant of her God."

What Does This Mean For Us?

This passage warns against the allure of an adulterous woman who forsakes the covenant of her God. It underscores the importance of fidelity, commitment, and the preservation of the marital covenant.

Modern Day Reflection

In today's world, where marriages regularly face challenges, this verse encourages couples to remain steadfast in their commitment to each other and to the sacred covenant they entered into before God.

~

Prayer For Fidelity in Marriage

Heavenly Father, guard our hearts and minds from the temptations that may seek to erode the foundation of our marriage. May we, with Your guidance, uphold the covenant we made and cherish the sacred commitment between us. Amen.

1 Corinthians 13:2

"And though I have the gift of prophecy, and understand all mysteries, and all knowledge; and though I have all faith, so that I could remove mountains, and have not charity, I am nothing."

What Does This Mean For Us?

The verse lists remarkable spiritual gifts—prophecy, understanding mysteries, knowledge, and extraordinary faith capable of moving mountains. These gifts, though extraordinary, are presented as insufficient without the presence of love.

Modern Day Reflection

1 Corinthians 13:2 underscores the paramount importance of love in a marriage. It encourages spouses to prioritize love over external achievements or abilities. The verse prompts couples to recognize that even with impressive skills or accomplishments, the essence of their relationship may be lacking without love. In the context of marriage, this verse invites spouses to infuse their interactions with love, patience, kindness, and selflessness. It calls for a conscious effort to nurture a relationship where love is the driving force, creating a foundation for a strong, enduring, and fulfilling marriage.

Prayer For Prioritizing Love in Marriage

Heavenly Father, as a couple, we recognize the importance of love beyond any spiritual gifts or talents we may possess. Grant us the ability to express our love in selfless and meaningful ways. Bless us, Lord, with a love that surpasses all other gifts. In Jesus' name, we pray. Amen.

September 29

John 15:13
"Greater love hath no man than this, that a man lay down his life for his friends."

What Does This Mean For Us?

In this verse, Jesus expresses the ultimate form of love by stating that there is no greater love than willingly laying down one's life for others. While the immediate context is about Jesus' impending sacrifice for humanity, the principle can be applied more broadly to relationships.

Modern Day Reflection

In a contemporary context, the verse encourages us to reflect on the depth and selflessness of love. It suggests that true love involves putting the well-being of others before our own and making sacrifices for the sake of those we care about. In the context of marriage, it emphasizes the idea that a strong and enduring relationship is built on a foundation of selfless love and mutual sacrifice. It challenges us to consider how we can lay down our desires, ego, and personal interests for the sake of our partners, fostering a love that is not only words but also demonstrated through actions and genuine care for one another.

Prayer For Sacrifce in Marriage
Gracious God, may selflessness and sacrifice characterize our love for each other. Help us prioritize our spouse's well-being and happiness above our desires. May our marriage reflect the greatest love—the love that lays down one's life for others. In your name, we pray. Amen.

September 30

1 John 3:18
"My little children, let us not love in word, neither in tongue, but in
deed and in truth."

What Does This Mean For Us?

This verse emphasizes the importance of genuine and practical expressions of love. In a modern context, it encourages us to move beyond mere verbal declarations of love and to demonstrate our love through tangible actions. In relationships, including marriage, the verse prompts us to show our love through deeds, kindness, and sincerity.

Modern Day Reflection

John 3:18 challenges couples to embody love in daily interactions, ensuring that their words align with their actions. Doing so creates a foundation of trust, authenticity, and true connection in our relationships. The verse underscores the idea that love is not just a sentiment expressed in words but a lived experience manifested in our behavior and choices toward others.

Prayer For Sincere Deeds in Marriage
Gracious Lord, we are reminded of the wisdom in 1 John 3:18. May our
love for each other not be confined to words alone, but may it be
genuine, expressed through tangible actions and rooted in truth. Help
us to demonstrate our love in deeds that reflect the sincerity of our
hearts. Bless our marriage with a love that goes beyond mere expressions.
In your name, we pray. Amen.

October

IN THE CRISPNESS OF OCTOBER, LET US
FIND SOLACE IN THE BEAUTY OF CHANGE.
AS NATURE DONS ITS VIBRANT COLORS,
MAY WE ALSO EMBRACE THE COLORS OF
OUR OWN LIVES, ACKNOWLEDGING THE
RICHNESS THAT COMES WITH EMBRACING
DIVERSITY, GROWTH, AND THE CYCLICAL
NATURE OF EXISTENCE.

October 1

1 Thessalonians 3:12

"And the Lord make you to increase and abound in love one toward another, and toward all men, even as we do toward you."

What Does This Mean For Us?

This verse from 1 Thessalonians expresses the Apostle Paul's prayer for the Thessalonian believers, asking the Lord to increase and abound their love for one another and for all people.

Modern Day Reflection

In a modern context, it serves as an inspiration for fostering love not only within a marriage but also extending it to others. It encourages a love that goes beyond boundaries, increasing and overflowing towards both one's partner and the broader community. The verse prompts individuals, especially in the context of marriage, to seek a love that is not stagnant but ever-growing, encompassing a spirit of generosity and compassion toward others. It envisions a love that reflects the abundant and selfless love shown by God, creating a positive ripple effect in relationships and the surrounding community.

Prayer For Abounding Love in Marriage

Gracious Lord, may our love for each other increase and abound, growing beyond measure. Grant us the grace to love not only each other but also all people. May our marriage be a source of love that mirrors the love we have received from others. In your name, we pray. Amen.

<h1 style="text-align:center">October 2</h1>

<h2 style="text-align:center">1 John 4:18</h2>

"There is no fear in love; but perfect love casteth out fear: because fear hath torment. He that feareth is not made perfect in love."

What Does This Mean For Us?

This verse conveys the transformative power of perfect or complete love in overcoming fear. In the context of relationships, particularly marriage, it suggests that when love is genuine, fear diminishes. The verse challenges individuals to cultivate a love that is so profound and secure that it dispels anxiety and apprehension.

Modern Day Reflection

In a contemporary context, it encourages married couples to foster a love that dispels fear and insecurity. It speaks to the idea that a deep, genuine love between partners creates an environment without fear or apprehension. It challenges us to confront any tendencies towards judgment or punishment, advocating for a love that embraces imperfections and nurtures mutual growth.

Prayer For Insecurity in Marriage

Heavenly Father, as a couple, we pray for a love that is perfect and free from fear. May our marriage be a haven of security and peace, rooted in the perfect love that comes from you. Help us to grow in love and cast out any fear that may seek to intrude. In Jesus' name, we pray. Amen.

October 3

Psalm 27:1
"The Lord is my light and my salvation; whom shall I fear? the Lord is the strength of my life; of whom shall I be afraid?"

What Does This Mean For Us?

This verse beautifully expresses trust and confidence in God as the source of light, salvation, and strength.

Modern Day Reflection

In a modern context, it encourages individuals, including married couples, to anchor their lives and relationships in a deep and unwavering trust in God. The verse prompts a reflection on the idea that when God is the stronghold, there is no need to fear external circumstances or challenges.

～

Prayer For God's Strength in Marriage
Almighty God, You are the strength of our lives; in You, we find courage. Grant us the confidence to face challenges without fear, knowing that Your strength empowers us. We place our marriage in Your hands. Amen.

October 4

Deuteronomy 31:6

"Be strong and of a good courage, fear not, nor be afraid of them: for the Lord thy God, he it is that doth go with thee; he will not fail thee, nor forsake thee."

What Does This Mean For Us?

This verse is part of Moses' charge to Joshua and the Israelites as they prepare to enter the Promised Land. It emphasizes strength, courage, and trust in God's unwavering presence.

Modern Day Reflection

This verse offers encouragement and reassurance to face challenges with strength and courage, knowing God is present and steadfast. It encourages a mindset of resilience and faith, trusting that God's presence is constant even in difficult times. In the context of marriage, Deuteronomy 31:6 can inspire couples to support each other, facing challenges together with the confidence that they are not alone. It fosters a relationship built on mutual strength and reliance on God's enduring presence, creating a foundation for enduring love and unity.

Prayer For Strength and Courage in Marriage

Gracious Lord, thank you for the assurance that You will go with us in our marriage. Strengthen our trust in Your unwavering presence. In moments of uncertainty, remind us that You will not fail us nor forsake us. Bless us, Heavenly Father. In your name, we pray, Amen.

October 5

Psalm 34:17-18

"The righteous cry, and the Lord heareth, and delivereth them out of all their troubles. The Lord is nigh unto them that are of a broken heart; and saveth such as be of a contrite spirit."

What Does This Mean For Us?

In the context of couples in the modern world, this suggests that turning to faith and seeking divine intervention can provide solace and assistance during challenging times in their relationship. The verses emphasize the Lord's proximity to the brokenhearted. In practical terms, couples may find strength and support in their faith, fostering resilience and hope in the face of difficulties.

Modern Day Reflection

This passage assures believers that God is attentive to their cries and delivers them from difficulties. In the context of modern relationships, including marriage, Psalm 34:17-18 can be a source of comfort during challenging times. It encourages individuals and couples to turn to God in times of trouble, knowing He is near and ready to offer solace. In the ups and downs of married life, this passage reminds us of God's compassion for the brokenhearted, offering hope and healing for those facing emotional or spiritual challenges. It underscores the idea that, through faith and prayer, couples can find strength and deliverance in God's presence, fostering a resilient and enduring bond in their marriage.

Prayer For Difficulties in Marriage

Gracious God, we cry out to You in our moments of trouble. Hear our prayers and deliver us, O Lord, from the challenges we face in our marriage. Grant us the strength to trust in Your guidance and find healing in Your comforting presence. Amen.

October 6

1 Corinthians 15:58

"Therefore, my beloved brethren, be ye stedfast, unmoveable, always abounding in the work of the Lord, forasmuch as ye know that your labour is not in vain in the Lord."

What Does This Mean For Us?

This verse concludes Paul's discourse on the resurrection, encouraging believers to remain steadfast and devoted to the work of the Lord. In a broader context, this verse encourages believers to remain steadfast and dedicated in their faith and service to God.

Modern Day Reflection

It prompts married couples to commit to enduring faithfulness and dedicated service. In the context of marriage, it should inspire couples to stand firm in their commitment to each other, facing challenges with resilience and giving themselves fully to the growth and well-being of their relationship. Ensuring their efforts in love and partnership are not in vain encourages a sense of purpose and persistence, fostering a marriage built on enduring love, faith, and mutual support.

Prayer For Purpose in Marriage

Gracious Father, grant us the strength to be steadfast and unmovable in our commitment to each other and to You. May our marriage always abound in acts of love and service, reflecting Your grace. Strengthen us, Lord, as we build a marriage that honors You. Amen.

Romans 15:13

"Now the God of hope fill you with all joy and peace in believing, that ye may abound in hope through the power of the Holy Ghost."

What Does This Mean For Us?

Romans 15:13 offers a beautiful prayer for individuals and couples alike. It encourages a deep trust in God, emphasizing the hope, joy, and peace of that trust.

Modern Day Reflection

For married couples, this verse can inspire them to anchor their relationship in faith, finding joy and peace in their shared journey. It encourages spouses to cultivate a relationship filled with hope and guided by the transformative power of the Holy Spirit. Ultimately, Romans 15:13 invites couples to center their marriage on the God of hope, allowing His presence to overflow in their lives and relationships.

Prayer For Faith in Marriage

Loving Lord, We seek the transformative power of the Holy Spirit in our marriage. May the God of hope fill us with joy and peace, leading us to abound in hope as we face life's journey together. Strengthen our faith and renew our hope each day. Amen.

October 8

Psalm 37:4

"Delight thyself also in the Lord, and he shall give thee the desires of thine heart."

What Does This Mean For Us?

In a contemporary context, Psalm 37:4 encourages married couples to find joy and fulfillment in their relationship with God. It suggests that by aligning one's desires with God's will and seeking joy in Him, God will grant the desires of the heart

Modern Day Reflection

In the context of marriage, this verse can inspire couples to prioritize a shared pursuit of spiritual growth and a deep connection with God. By delighting in the Lord together, couples may experience the fulfillment of their shared desires and a harmonious relationship grounded in faith and mutual devotion. Psalm 37:4 emphasizes the transformative power of seeking God first, trusting that He will guide and fulfill the heart's desires in the context of a marriage built on faith and love.

Prayer For Joy in Marriage

Heavenly Father, we desire to delight ourselves in you as a couple. May our relationship with you be the source of joy and strength in our marriage. Align our desires with your will, and, in your grace, grant us the blessings that will fulfill our hearts' desires. In Jesus' name, we pray. Amen.

October 9

Isaiah 41:10

"Fear thou not; for I am with thee: be not dismayed; for I am thy God: I will strengthen thee; yea, I will help thee; yea, I will uphold thee with the right hand of my righteousness."

What Does This Mean For Us?

For married couples, Isaiah 41:10 serves as a powerful reminder of God's constant presence, strength, and support. For individuals or married couples facing challenges, this verse encourages them not to succumb to fear or discouragement. Instead, it prompts a reliance on God's steadfastness and the assurance that He will provide strength and assistance.

Modern Day Reflection

In the context of marriage, Isaiah 41:10 can inspire couples to face difficulties together, trusting that God upholds their relationship with His righteous hand. It fosters a sense of security and confidence, reminding couples that, with God at the center, they can navigate the journey of marriage with faith and resilience.

Prayer For Strength in Marriage

Heavenly Lord, in the journey of our marriage, we cling to the words of Isaiah 41:10. May we not be dismayed, for you are our God. Strengthen us, help us, and uphold us with your righteousness. Grant us confidence in your unwavering support as we face the ups and downs together. In Jesus' name, we pray. Amen.

October 10

1 Peter 5:7

"Casting all your care upon him; for he careth for you."

What Does This Mean For Us?

1 Peter 5:7 offers solace and encouragement for those who may be grappling with worries and stresses, including married couples. It invites a profound trust in God's care and compassion, urging individuals to release their anxieties to Him.

Modern Day Reflection

This verse encourages spouses to share their burdens with God and each other, fostering a relationship built on openness and mutual support. It reminds couples that, in times of stress, turning to God's care can bring comfort and alleviate anxieties, creating a foundation for a marriage marked by trust, communication, and reliance on the unfailing care of a loving God.

~

Prayer For Burdens in Marriage

Gracious God, we come before you casting all our cares upon you. In the challenges and joys of marriage, help us release our burdens and anxieties to your care. We trust that you care for us, and we find comfort in your loving presence. In your name, we pray. Amen.

October 11

Proverbs 15:30

"The light of the eyes rejoiceth the heart: and a good report maketh the bones fat."

What Does This Mean For Us?

In a contemporary context, Proverbs 15:30 encourages married couples to recognize the impact of positivity and encouragement in their relationships. This verse emphasizes the power of a cheerful demeanor and the positive effects it can have on the emotional well-being of others.

Modern Day Reflection

Proverbs 15:30 suggests that small gestures of joy, encouragement, and sharing good news can contribute to the health and vitality of the relationship. The verse additionally inspires couples to cultivate an atmosphere of positivity, appreciation, and mutual support, creating a marriage marked by joy, good news, and the strengthening of emotional bonds.

Prayer For Emotional Bonding in Marriage

Gracious God, As we walk the path of marriage, we seek your guidance in Proverbs 15:30. May the light of our eyes be a source of joy to each other's hearts. Help us approach life with a positive outlook, finding joy in each other and in the journey we share. In your name, we pray. Amen.

October 12

Romans 12:15

"Rejoice with them that do rejoice, and weep with them that weep."

What Does This Mean For Us?

Romans 12:15 prompts couples to share in each other's joys and sorrows. It advocates for a deep emotional connection where spouses genuinely celebrate each other's successes and support one another during challenging times.

Modern Day Reflection

This verse invites couples to be attuned to each other's emotions, fostering a relationship marked by mutual understanding, empathy, and a shared emotional journey. Ultimately, Romans 12:15 encourages a marriage where the highs and lows are faced together, creating a strong bond of companionship and emotional support.

Prayer For Emotional Support in Marriage

Gracious Lord, As we walk the path of marriage, we seek your guidance in Romans 12:15. Grant us the ability to rejoice with each other in moments of celebration. May our hearts be open to share in the joys and triumphs, deepening our bond through shared happiness. In your name, we pray. Amen.

October 13

Colossians 3:16

"Let the word of Christ dwell in you richly in all wisdom; teaching and admonishing one another in psalms and hymns and spiritual songs, singing with grace in your hearts to the Lord."

What Does This Mean For Us?

Colossians 3:16 encourages individuals, including married couples, to cultivate a rich and spiritual atmosphere in their lives and relationships. It suggests incorporating the message of Christ into daily interactions, using wisdom and expressions of gratitude.

Modern Day Reflection

As it applies to marriage, this verse can inspire couples to share spiritual experiences, engage in uplifting conversations, and express gratitude to God together. By incorporating the teachings of Christ into their relationship, couples can create a foundation of shared faith, wisdom, and gratitude, fostering a spiritually enriching and resilient marriage.

∾

Prayer For Strong Worship in Marriage

Heavenly Father, Thank you for the guidance in Colossians 3:16. As a couple, we pray for the grace to teach and admonish one another in psalms, hymns, and spiritual songs. May our shared worship deepen our understanding of your word and strengthen our bond. Guide us in using these expressions of faith as a source of mutual encouragement and growth in our marriage. In Jesus' name, we pray. Amen.

October 14

Hebrews 10:24-25

"And let us consider how we may spur one another on toward love and good deeds, not giving up meeting together, as some are in the habit of doing, but encouraging one another—and all the more as you see the Day approaching."

What Does This Mean For Us?

The verses emphasize the importance of communal encouragement, urging people not to forsake regular gatherings.

Modern Day Reflection

For married couples, this means fostering a supportive environment where spouses spur each other toward love and positive actions. It suggests the value of shared faith experiences, open communication, and encouragement within the marital relationship. By prioritizing mutual support and connection, couples can strengthen their bond and navigate life's challenges together, drawing inspiration from their shared commitment and faith.

Prayer For Mutual Encouragement in Marriage

Dear Lord, we are mindful of the wisdom in Hebrews 10:24-25. Grant us the grace to actively consider and provoke each other unto love and good works. May our marriage be characterized by mutual encouragement, fostering a positive environment of love and virtue. Help us not to neglect the time we spend together but to cherish and exhort one another as we journey together. In your name, we pray. Amen.

October 15

Proverbs 18:21

"Death and life are in the power of the tongue: and they that love it shall eat the fruit thereof."

What Does This Mean For Us?

In a modern context, Proverbs 18:21 highlights the significant impact of words on our lives and relationships. It encourages married couples to be mindful of the power of their words.

Modern Day Reflection

This verse prompts spouses to use their words to uplift, encourage, and speak life into their relationship. It underscores the importance of positive and affirming communication, recognizing that the words we choose can shape the atmosphere of our marriage. Proverbs 18:21 serves as a reminder to cultivate a language of love, support, and kindness within the marital relationship, creating a foundation for a healthy and thriving marriage.

Prayer For Communication in Marriage

Heavenly Father, Thank you for the wisdom in Proverbs 18:21. As a couple, we pray for the strength to love our words wisely. May our communication be a source of life, building up and nourishing our relationship. Guide us in mutual respect and understanding that our words may benefit our marriage. In Jesus' name, we pray. Amen.

October 16

Genesis 3:16

"Unto the woman he said, I will greatly multiply thy sorrow and thy conception; in sorrow thou shalt bring forth children; and thy desire shall be to thy husband, and he shall rule over thee.'"

What Does This Mean For Us?

Genesis 3:16 speaks to the consequences of sin and disobedience, affecting the dynamics of relationships, including marriage. The verse acknowledges challenges and tensions that may arise between spouses.

Modern Day Reflection

This verse serves as a reminder of the fallen nature of humanity and the need for grace and understanding in marital relationships. While the verse points to difficulties, it's essential to approach it with a broader understanding of God's redemptive plan and the importance of mutual respect, love, and cooperation in navigating the complexities of marriage.

Prayer For Mutual Respect in Marriage

Dear Heavenly Father, in the complexities of marriage, we seek Your guidance and grace. As we reflect on the challenges mentioned in Genesis 3:16, we pray for the strength to navigate them with love and understanding. May our relationship be grounded in mutual respect, kindness, and cooperation. Help us overcome difficulties, turning to Your redemptive love as we strive to build a marriage that reflects Your grace. Amen.

October 17

Leviticus 19:14

"Thou shalt not curse the deaf, nor put a stumblingblock before the blind, but shalt fear thy God: I am the Lord."

What Does This Mean For Us?

In modern times, Leviticus 19:14 encourages married couples to practice kindness, empathy, and compassion. It serves as a reminder to treat others respectfully and avoid intentionally causing harm.

Modern Day Reflection

In the context of marriage, this verse should inspire spouses to be considerate of each other's vulnerabilities, to speak words of encouragement, and to refrain from actions that may cause harm or hinder the well-being of their partner. Ultimately, it calls for a relationship built on love, understanding, and reverence for God's commandments.

~

Prayer For Compassion in Marriage

Dear Lord, grant us the wisdom to embody the principles of Leviticus 19:14 in our marriage. Help us to speak words of kindness, to be considerate of each other's vulnerabilities, and to refrain from actions that may cause harm. May our relationship be a reflection of Your love and compassion. Amen.

October 18

Proverbs 12:25

"Heaviness in the heart of man maketh it stoop: but a good word
maketh it glad."

What Does This Mean For Us?

Proverbs 12:25 highlights the impact of words on our emotional well-
being. This verse encourages a married couple to be mindful of the
power of kindness in their communication.

Modern Day Reflection

In the context of marriage, it inspires spouses to offer words of
encouragement, support, and positivity to uplift each other's spirits.
This short verse carries a profound reminder of the influence of our
language on the atmosphere of our relationships, promoting a marriage
filled with kindness and emotional well-being.

~

Prayer For Emotional Well Being in Marriage

Dear God, grant us the wisdom to choose words of kindness in our
marriage. May our communication be a source of encouragement and
upliftment, lightening each other's hearts. Help us create a relationship
filled with positivity and emotional well-being. Amen.

October 19

1 Corinthians 13:8

"Charity never faileth: but whether there be prophecies, they shall fail; whether there be tongues, they shall cease; whether there be knowledge, it shall vanish away."

What Does This Mean For Us?

In a modern context, 1 Corinthians 13:8 underscores the enduring nature of love. This verse encourages individuals, including married couples, to recognize the lasting power of genuine love. In the ebb and flow of life's uncertainties, love stands as a constant and reliable force.

Modern Day Reflection

In the context of marriage, it inspires spouses to build their relationship on the foundation of love, understanding that love transcends the transient nature of other aspects of life. It prompts a commitment to a love that perseveres, overcomes challenges, and remains a steadfast source of strength in the journey of marriage.

Prayer For Constant Love in Marriage

Dear God, bless our marriage with a love that mirrors a constant and reliable force. In moments of uncertainty, may our commitment to each other be unwavering. Help us build a strong foundation of love, transcending challenges and enriching our journey together. Amen.

October 20

Romans 5:8

"But God commendeth his love toward us, in that, while we were yet sinners, Christ died for us."

What Does This Mean For Us?

Romans 5:8 serves as a powerful message of God's unconditional and sacrificial love. Married couples can reflect on the depth of God's love, demonstrated through the sacrifice of Jesus.

Modern Day Reflection

Within the marriage, it inspires spouses to embody a love that mirrors God's love – a forgiving, selfless, and unconditional love. This verse prompts couples to extend grace to one another, recognizing that true love is manifested in moments of vulnerability and imperfection. It encourages a marriage built on the foundation of God's profound and redemptive love.

~

Prayer For Selfless Love in Marriage

Dear Heavenly Father, we thank You for the powerful reminder in Romans 5:8 of Your unconditional and sacrificial love. As we navigate the journey of marriage, help us emulate this love in our relationship. Grant us the strength to love each other, not just in moments of joy, but especially in times of vulnerability and imperfection. May our marriage be a reflection of Your grace and enduring love. In Jesus' name, we pray. Amen.

October 21

Numbers 9:8
"And Moses said unto them, Stand still, and I will hear what
the Lord will command concerning you.'"

What Does This Mean For Us?

In a modern context, Numbers 9:8 underscores the importance of seeking God's guidance before making decisions. In the context of marriage, it encourages couples to seek God's wisdom and direction in their choices and actions.

Modern Day Reflection

This verse prompts spouses to approach decisions together with a willingness to wait for God's guidance, fostering a relationship built on a foundation of faith and trust in His plan. It emphasizes the value of seeking divine counsel, recognizing that God's guidance is paramount in navigating the complexities of married life.

Prayer For Humility in Marriage
Heavenly Father, in the spirit of Numbers 9:8, we come before you
seeking your guidance in our decisions, especially within the sacred
bond of marriage. Grant us patience to wait for your commands,
wisdom to discern your will, and the humility to follow your path. May
our union be a reflection of your divine plan, and may our choices align
with your purpose for our lives together. In your name, we pray. Amen.

Matthew 19:5-6

"And said, For this cause shall a man leave father and mother, and shall cleave to his wife: and they twain shall be one flesh? Wherefore they are no more twain, but one flesh. What therefore God hath joined together, let not man put asunder."

What Does This Mean For Us?

In these verses, Jesus affirms the divine design for marriage, emphasizing the unity and indissolubility of the marital bond. The imagery of leaving one's parents and cleaving to a spouse underscores the sacred nature of the union, suggesting a profound merging of two individuals into one.

Modern Day Reflection

In today's world, this passage highlights the importance of prioritizing and nurturing the marital relationship. It encourages couples to recognize the significance of leaving behind other attachments and forming a strong, unified bond with their spouse. The phrase "What therefore God hath joined together" reinforces the idea that marriage is a sacred covenant established by God.

Prayer For Nurturing in Marriage

Lord, we thank You for the gift of marriage and the unity You've designed for us. Amid life's demands, help us to cleave to each other, leaving behind anything that hinders our connection. May our marriage reflect Your love and purpose. Amen.

October 23

Ephesians 4:26-27

Be ye angry, and sin not: let not the sun go down upon your wrath:
Neither give place to the devil."

What Does This Mean For Us?

In the context of forgiveness in marriage, Ephesians 4:26-27 advises against harboring anger and encourages resolving conflicts promptly. The verses emphasize addressing issues before the day's end, preventing prolonged resentment and the potential harm it can cause.

Modern Day Reflection

These verses prompt spouses to deal with disagreements promptly, fostering open communication and preventing unresolved issues from creating division. By doing so, couples can safeguard their relationship from the detrimental effects of prolonged anger and ensure that their bond remains strong, free from the foothold of negativity and discord.

Prayer For Disagreements in Marriage

Dear God, guide us as a couple to heed the wisdom of Ephesians 4:26-27. May we address our conflicts promptly, not letting anger fester. Grant us the strength to forgive and the wisdom to communicate openly, preventing discord in our marriage. Amen.

October 24

Matthew 5:23-24

"Therefore if thou bring thy gift to the altar, and there rememberest that thy brother hath ought against thee; Leave there thy gift before the altar, and go thy way; first be reconciled to thy brother, and then come and offer thy gift."

What Does This Mean For Us?

In today's context, Matthew 5:23-24 urges married couples to prioritize reconciliation in relationships. This verse prompts spouses to address conflicts and grievances before approaching God in worship. It emphasizes the importance of interpersonal harmony and forgiveness, suggesting that a reconciled relationship takes precedence over religious rituals.

Modern Day Reflection

In the context of marriage, this verse encourages couples to cultivate a spirit of reconciliation, forgiveness, and love, ensuring that their relationship reflects the principles of compassion and understanding in both earthly and spiritual matters.

Prayer For Reconciliation in Marriage

Heavenly Father, guide us in embodying the principles of Matthew 5:23-24 in our marriage. May our hearts be open to reconciliation, and may forgiveness be a cornerstone of our relationship. Strengthen our commitment to a marriage grounded in love and understanding. Amen.

October 25

Proverbs 30:18-19

"There be three things which are too wonderful for me, yea, four which I know not: The way of an eagle in the air; the way of a serpent upon a rock; the way of a ship in the midst of the sea; and the way of a man with a maid."

What Does This Mean For Us?

This proverb uses vivid images to describe the mysterious and wondrous aspects of life, including the interaction between a man and a woman. In the context of God's design for marriage, it acknowledges the complexity and beauty of the relationship between a man and a woman, portraying it as a marvel beyond complete understanding.

Modern Day Reflection

In today's world, this verse encourages couples to recognize the awe-inspiring nature of their union. It suggests that the dynamics of a relationship, like the flight of an eagle or the movement of a ship, are intricate and unique. It prompts couples to approach their marriage with a sense of reverence and appreciation for the mysterious and wonderful aspects of love.

Prayer For Wondrous Design in Marriage

Heavenly Father, as we embark on this journey together, help us to marvel at the wondrous design of love between a man and a woman. May our marriage be a testament to Your creativity and grace. Guide us in understanding and cherishing the beauty of our union. Amen.

October 26

Job 5:17

"Behold, happy is the man whom God correcteth: therefore despise not thou the chastening of the Almighty."

What Does This Mean For Us?

In a contemporary context, Job 5:17 encourages married couples to embrace the lessons that come from God's correction and discipline. It invites a humble and teachable spirit, recognizing that challenges and corrections are opportunities for growth and refinement.

Modern Day Reflection

In the context of marriage, this verse prompts spouses to approach difficulties with a perspective of learning and growth, trusting that God's guidance can strengthen their relationship and character. It encourages a marriage built on resilience, humility, and a willingness to be corrected and refined by the Almighty.

Prayer For Healthy Correction in Marriage

Heavenly Father, as we encounter the challenges and corrections in our journey, we humbly seek Your guidance. Grant us the wisdom to embrace Your discipline with open hearts, knowing that in correction, there is growth. In our marriage, help us to learn from each experience, drawing closer to You and each other. May Your refining touch strengthen our bond and shape us into individuals who reflect Your grace and wisdom. Amen.

Proverbs 24:3-4

"Through wisdom is a house builded, and by understanding it is established: And by knowledge shall the chambers be filled with all precious and pleasant riches."

What Does This Mean For Us?

This passage highlights the importance of wisdom, understanding, and knowledge in building a stable and flourishing household. In the context of God's design for marriage, it suggests that a strong foundation of wisdom and understanding contributes to the establishment and enrichment of a home.

Modern Day Reflection

In a modern context, Proverbs 24:3-4 emphasizes the importance of wisdom, understanding, and knowledge in building a strong and fulfilling life, including marriage. It encourages couples to seek wisdom and understanding in their decisions and actions. In the context of marriage, this verse prompts spouses to build their relationship on a foundation of shared wisdom, fostering a home filled with the treasures of love, mutual understanding, and the richness that comes from a life built on Godly principles.

Prayer For Godly Principles in Marriage

Heavenly Father, grant us the wisdom and understanding to build a strong foundation for our marriage. May our home be filled with the precious and pleasant riches of Your love and guidance. Amen.

October 28

Ecclesiastes 4:11

"Again, if two lie together, then they have heat: but how can one be
warm alone?"

What Does This Mean For Us?

Ecclesiastes 4:11 speaks to the significance of companionship and
mutual support. It suggests that there is comfort and warmth in shared
experiences, especially in the context of a relationship or marriage.

Modern Day Reflection

This verse prompts couples to recognize the value of being together,
offering support and warmth to one another. It underscores the idea
that companionship brings a unique strength and solace that can make
life's journey more bearable and fulfilling.

Prayer For Companionship in Marriage

Dear Lord, we come before you to acknowledge the wisdom in
Ecclesiastes 4:11. In our journey together, help us appreciate the
warmth and support that come from companionship. Grant us the
ability to be a source of comfort to one another, recognizing the
strength that lies in our unity. May our marriage be a testament to the
shared warmth that comes from being together. In your name, we pray.
Amen.

October 29

Proverbs 12:4

"A virtuous woman is a crown to her husband: but she that maketh ashamed is as rottenness in his bones."

What Does This Mean For Us?

This verse highlights the significant role of a virtuous and noble wife in the context of marriage. A virtuous woman is depicted as a crown to her husband, symbolizing her value, honor, and the positive impact she brings to his life. On the other hand, a wife who brings shame is likened to a destructive force, causing decay and distress in the husband's inner being.

Modern Day Reflection

In today's world, this verse encourages couples to recognize the profound influence spouses have on each other. It underscores the importance of qualities like virtue, honor, and mutual respect in fostering a healthy and thriving marriage.

Prayer For Bonding in Marriage

Lord, help us to cultivate virtues in our marriage that bring honor and joy. Guard our hearts against actions that could bring shame, and strengthen the bond between us. Amen.

October 30

1 Corinthians 11:11-12

"Nevertheless neither is the man without the woman, neither the woman without the man, in the Lord. For as the woman is of the man, even so is the man also by the woman; but all things of God."

What Does This Mean For Us?

These verses emphasize the interdependence of men and women in the context of the Lord. The language underscores the idea that neither gender is complete without the other, and both are essential in the divine plan. It acknowledges the mutual origin and dependency between man and woman, with all things ultimately originating from God.

Modern Day Reflection

In today's world, this passage speaks to the complementary nature of marriage. It encourages couples to recognize and honor the equality and mutual dependence of spouses in God's design. The emphasis on "in the Lord" suggests that this interdependence finds its fullest expression within the framework of faith and shared commitment to God.

Prayer For Equality in Marriage

Heavenly Father, we acknowledge Your divine design for marriage, where man and woman are interdependent in You. Help us to honor and support each other, recognizing the completeness we find in our union. May our marriage be a reflection of Your wisdom and love. In your name we pray, Amen.

October 31

Proverbs 10:12

"Hatred stirreth up strifes: but love covereth all sins."

What Does This Mean For Us?

Proverbs 10:12 emphasizes the power of love to heal and reconcile. It encourages individuals, including married couples, to choose love over conflict and animosity.

Modern Day Reflection

In the context of marriage, it inspires spouses to approach disagreements with a spirit of love, seeking understanding and forgiveness. This verse prompts couples to build a relationship where love becomes a covering for mistakes, fostering an atmosphere of grace, humility, and unity within the marriage.

∾

Prayer For Harmonious Love in Marriage

Heavenly Father, we seek guidance in our marriage to cultivate a love that transcends conflicts and shortcomings. Teach us to choose love over hatred, understanding over strife. May our love be a covering for any sins or mistakes, fostering an environment of forgiveness and harmony in our home. Bless our union and help us to reflect your love in our relationship. In Jesus' name, we pray. Amen.

November

AS NOVEMBER WHISPERS THE ARRIVAL OF WINTER, MAY OUR HEARTS BE WARMED BY THE FLAME OF GRATITUDE. IN THIS SEASON OF REFLECTION, LET US GATHER AROUND THE HEARTH OF LOVE, GIVING THANKS FOR THE BLESSINGS OF FAMILY, FRIENDSHIP, AND THE ENDURING SPIRIT OF TOGETHERNESS.

November 1

Romans 12:13

"Distributing to the necessity of saints; given to hospitality."

What Does This Mean For Us?

In a modern context, Romans 12:13 encourages married couples, to cultivate a spirit of generosity and hospitality. It prompts spouses to be open-handed and welcoming, not only within their marriage but also towards those around them.

Modern Day Reflection

This verse encourages couples to share their resources, time, and love with others, fostering a culture of kindness and generosity. In the context of marriage, practicing hospitality can strengthen the bond between spouses as they work together to extend warmth and care to those in need.

~

Prayer For Hospitality in Marriage

Dear Lord, as we reflect on Romans 12:13, we seek Your guidance in embodying the spirit of generosity and hospitality within our marriage. Open our hearts to share with those in need, and may our home be a place of warmth and welcome. Teach us to practice hospitality not only with each other but also with those around us. May our acts of kindness and generosity be a reflection of Your love in our lives. In Your name, we pray. Amen.

November 2

Psalm 28:7

"The Lord is my strength and my shield; my heart trusts in him, and he helps me. My heart leaps for joy, and with my song, I praise him."

What Does This Mean For Us?

In a modern context, Psalm 28:7 serves as a beautiful affirmation of trust and joy in the Lord. In the context of marriage, this verse can be a source of inspiration for couples to rely on God as their strength and protector.

Modern Day Reflection

These verses encourage spouses to trust in God's guidance and find joy in His presence. This verse can be a reminder to turn to God together in times of challenges, finding strength and joy in the journey of marriage through a shared faith.

Prayer For Gratitude in Marriage

Heavenly Father, we thank you for being our strength and shield. As we place our trust in you, may our hearts find joy in your presence. Help us, Lord, to navigate the journey of marriage with the assurance that you are with us, guiding and protecting. In moments of joy and challenge, may our song of praise be a reflection of our gratitude for your constant help. Amen.

November 3

Proverbs 14:29
"He that is slow to wrath is of great understanding: but he that is hasty
of spirit exalteth folly."

What Does This Mean For Us?

In a modern context, Proverbs 14:29 underscores the importance of patience and understanding in relationships, including marriage. This verse encourages individuals, particularly spouses, to cultivate patience as a virtue. It suggests that patience leads to greater understanding, while a quick temper may lead to unwise actions.

Modern Day Reflection

In the context of marriage, this verse prompts couples to approach challenges with a patient and understanding spirit, fostering a relationship built on wisdom, empathy, and enduring love.

Prayer For Patience in Marriage
Heavenly Father, grant us the wisdom to embrace patience in our
marriage, as Proverbs 14:29 teaches. Help us cultivate understanding so
that we may navigate challenges with grace. Guard our hearts against
quick tempers and guide us in building a relationship founded on
wisdom and enduring love. In Your name, we pray. Amen.

November 4

1 Corinthians 13:4-7

"Charity suffereth long, and is kind; charity envieth not; charity vaunteth not itself, is not puffed up, Doth not behave itself unseemly, seeketh not her own, is not easily provoked, thinketh no evil; Rejoiceth not in iniquity, but rejoiceth in the truth; Beareth all things, believeth all things, hopeth all things, endureth all things."

What Does This Mean For Us?

1 Corinthians 13:4-7 encapsulates the essence of genuine love within the context of relationships, offering a profound guide for marriages. Love, as described, is patient and kind, devoid of envy, boasting, and pride. It honors others, is selfless, and avoids easily being angered or keeping records of wrongs. It rejoices in truth, protects, trusts, hopes, and perseveres.

Modern Day Reflection

Today, 1 Corinthians 13:4-7 serves as a profound guide for how love should be expressed within relationships, including marriage. It provides a blueprint for building a strong foundation for a marriage marked by genuine love and mutual respect.

Prayer For Genuine Love in Marriage

Dear Lord, as we reflect on the profound qualities of love outlined in 1 Corinthians 13:4-7, we humbly seek Your guidance. Grant us the strength to embody patience, kindness, humility, and enduring love in our marriage. May our relationship be a testament to the transformative power of selfless and genuine love. Amen.

November 5

1 Timothy 6:10

"For the love of money is the root of all evil: which while some coveted after, they have erred from the faith, and pierced themselves through with many sorrows."

What Does This Mean For Us?

In a modern context, 1 Timothy 6:10 warns against the destructive nature of prioritizing wealth over spiritual values. While money itself is not inherently evil, the verse highlights the dangers of an unhealthy attachment to material possessions.

Modern Day Reflection

In the context of marriage, this verse serves as a reminder for couples to prioritize the foundations of faith, love, and shared values over the pursuit of wealth. It encourages a balanced approach to financial matters within the context of a strong and spiritually grounded relationship.

~

Prayer For Shared Values in Marriage

Dear Heavenly Father, as we reflect on 1 Timothy 6:10, we pray for guidance in our approach to wealth and material pursuits within our marriage. Help us prioritize faith, love, and shared values over the love of money. Guard our hearts from the allure of excessive riches, and may our union be centered on spiritual foundations that bring joy, fulfillment, and harmony. In Your name, we seek wisdom and grace. Amen.

November 6

Psalm 127:3-5

"Lo, children are an heritage of the Lord: and the fruit of the womb is his reward. As arrows are in the hand of a mighty man; so are children of the youth. Happy is the man that hath his quiver full of them: they shall not be ashamed, but they shall speak with the enemies in the gate."

What Does This Mean For Us?

Psalm 127:3-5 expresses the profound idea that children are a blessing and a gift from the Lord. The imagery of arrows in the hand of a warrior emphasizes the strength and purpose that children bring to a family. This passage encourages a perspective that sees children as a source of joy, reward, and strength.

Modern Day Reflection

In the context of marriage, it inspires couples to cherish the gift of children and to view them as a heritage from God. The mention of not being put to shame when speaking with enemies in the gate suggests that a family blessed with children possesses a sense of honor and strength in the community.

~

Prayer For Children in Marriage

Heavenly Father, we come before you with hearts full of gratitude for the beautiful message in Psalm 127:3-5. Thank you for the precious gift of children, who are a blessing and reward from You. Grant us the wisdom and strength to nurture and guide them in Your ways. May our home be a haven where Your presence is felt, and where the bonds of family reflect Your goodness. In Your name, we pray. Amen.

November 7

James 1:5

"If any of you lack wisdom, let him ask of God, that giveth to all men liberally, and upbraideth not; and it shall be given him."

What Does This Mean For Us?

In a modern context, James 1:5 encourages individuals, including married couples, to seek wisdom from God. It emphasizes the generosity of God in granting wisdom without reproach.

Modern Day Reflection

In today's marriage, this verse prompts spouses to turn to God for guidance and insight in navigating the complexities of their relationship. It underscores the importance of seeking divine wisdom in decision-making, conflict resolution, and the overall journey of married life. By relying on God's wisdom, couples can build a strong foundation for their relationship and navigate challenges with grace and understanding.

Prayer For God's Wisdom in Marriage

Dear Heavenly Father, as we ponder James 1:5, we humbly come before You, acknowledging our need for Your wisdom. Grant us the discernment to navigate the intricacies of our marriage with grace and understanding. We seek Your generous wisdom, confident in Your willingness to guide us without reproach. May our decisions and actions be rooted in Your divine insight, and may our marriage reflect the beauty of a union guided by Your wisdom. In Your name, we pray.
Amen.

November 8

Hebrews 13:5

"Let your conversation be without covetousness; and be content with such things as ye have: for he hath said, I will never leave thee, nor forsake thee.'"

What Does This Mean For Us?

In a modern context, Hebrews 13:5 encourages married couples to prioritize contentment over the love of money. It assures believers that God will never leave or forsake them, emphasizing the enduring presence of God as a source of true security and fulfillment.

Modern Day Reflection

In the context of marriage, this verse prompts spouses to find contentment in their relationship and shared experiences, trusting that God's presence is the ultimate source of satisfaction. It encourages a perspective that values the enduring aspects of love and faithfulness over material wealth.

Prayer For Contentment in Marriage

Heavenly Father, in reflection of Hebrews 13:5, we come before You with gratitude for Your promise to never leave nor forsake us. Help us, as a couple, to keep our lives free from the love of money and find contentment in our relationship's richness and Your abiding presence. May our marriage be a testament to the enduring value of love and faithfulness over worldly pursuits. We trust in Your provision and seek contentment in the assurance of Your unwavering presence. In Your name, we pray. Amen.

<h1 style="text-align:center">November 9</h1>

<h2 style="text-align:center">Philippians 2:3-4</h2>

"Let nothing be done through strife or vainglory; but in lowliness of mind let each esteem other better than themselves. Look not every man on his own things, but every man also on the things of others."

What Does This Mean For Us?

Philippians 2:3-4 serves as a powerful guide for relationships, including marriage. It encourages individuals, particularly spouses, to cultivate humility and selflessness. This passage prompts couples to prioritize the well-being and interests of each other above their own.

Modern Day Reflection

For married couples, it fosters an environment of mutual respect, understanding, and sacrificial love. It challenges individuals to set aside selfish ambitions and embrace a mindset that values the needs and desires of their spouse. Applying these principles can contribute to the strength and harmony of a marital relationship.

Prayer For Humility in Marriage

Dear Lord, as we reflect on Philippians 2:3-4, we seek Your guidance and grace. Grant us the humility to put aside selfish ambitions and vain conceit in our marriage. Help us value each other above ourselves, embracing a selfless mindset that considers the interests and needs of our spouse. May our relationship be a testament to the beauty of sacrificial love, and may we continually strive to honor and uplift each other. In Your name, we pray. Amen.

November 10

Proverbs 19:20

Hear counsel, and receive instruction, that thou mayest be wise in thy latter end."

What Does This Mean For Us?

Proverbs 19:20 encourages individuals, including married couples, to be open to advice and willing to accept constructive criticism. It emphasizes the value of learning and growing through wise counsel. In the context of marriage, this verse prompts spouses to actively listen to each other's perspectives, seek guidance when needed, and be open to constructive feedback.

Modern Day Reflection

By embracing a teachable spirit and valuing each other's input, couples can foster a relationship marked by wisdom, understanding, and continual growth.

Prayer For Continuous Improvement in Marriage

Heavenly Father, as we've been taught in Proverbs 19:20, we humbly come before You seeking wisdom and a teachable spirit. Grant us the grace to listen to advice and accept constructive discipline, both in our individual lives and within our marriage. May our hearts be open to growth, and may we be counted among the wise as we learn from each other. Guide us in the path of understanding and continuous improvement. In Your name, we pray. Amen.

November 11

Psalm 113:9

"He maketh the barren woman to keep house and to be a joyful mother of children. Praise ye the Lord."

What Does This Mean For Us?

This verse celebrates God's ability to bring joy and fulfillment to those who have faced challenges in conceiving. It acknowledges God's power to transform barrenness into a source of joy in motherhood.

Modern Day Reflection

If married couples want to start a family, this verse offers hope and encouragement to couples who may be experiencing difficulties in conceiving. It directs our focus toward the divine ability to overcome challenges, reminding us to place our trust in God's timing and plan. It encourages couples to find joy in the journey of parenthood, regardless of the obstacles they may face.

Prayer For Contribution in Marriage

Heavenly Father, we praise You for Your ability to bring joy and fulfillment even in challenging circumstances. Grant us patience and trust as we navigate the journey of starting a family. May Your timing be perfect, and may our hearts find joy in Your plan for our lives. Amen.

November 12

1 Timothy 6:6

"But godliness with contentment is great gain."

What Does This Mean For Us?

1 Timothy 6:6 encourages married individuals to find value in a life characterized by godliness and contentment. It emphasizes that true wealth and gain come from a state of being godly and content rather than pursuing material possessions or wealth.

Modern Day Reflection

In the context of marriage, this verse prompts couples to prioritize spiritual and emotional richness over a relentless pursuit of worldly gain. It fosters an environment where both partners can find contentment in their shared faith and a deeper connection with each other and with God.

~

Prayer For Connection with God in Marriage

Gracious Lord, we seek Your guidance in cultivating a life marked by godliness and contentment. Help us, especially within the sacred bond of marriage, to find true wealth in our shared faith and in the richness of our connection with You. May our hearts be content, and may our pursuit be centered on spiritual and emotional fulfillment rather than the fleeting treasures of the world. In Your name, we pray. Amen.

November 13

1 Thessalonians 5:16-18

"Rejoice evermore. Pray without ceasing. In every thing give thanks: for this is the will of God in Christ Jesus concerning you."

What Does This Mean For Us?

In a modern context, 1 Thessalonians 5:16-18 offers a guide for living a life grounded in faith and gratitude. In the context of marriage, these verses encourage couples to cultivate a spirit of joy, prayer, and thanksgiving.

Modern Day Reflection

It prompts spouses to rejoice in their shared journey, to maintain a constant connection with God through prayer, and to express gratitude in all circumstances. Couples can create a foundation for a resilient and spiritually rich marriage by embodying these principles.

Prayer For Resilience in Marriage

Heavenly Father, with guidance from 1 Thessalonians 5:16-18, we come before You with hearts of gratitude and a desire to align with Your will. Help us, as a couple, to rejoice always in the blessings of our marriage, to maintain a continual connection with You through prayer, and to express thanks in all circumstances. May our relationship be a testament to the joy and gratitude that come from walking in Your ways. In Your name, we pray. Amen.

November 14

Job 42:10

"And the Lord turned the captivity of Job, when he prayed for his friends: also the Lord gave Job twice as much as he had before."

What Does This Mean For Us?

Job 42:10 highlights the transformative power of prayer and the restoration that can come through interceding for others. While the specific circumstances of Job's story are unique, the principle of seeking the well-being of others through prayer resonates.

Modern Day Reflection

In the context of marriage, this verse encourages spouses to not only pray for their own needs but also to intercede for the concerns and well-being of each other and those around them. It reflects the idea that selfless prayers, offered with a heart of compassion, can bring about restoration and abundance.

Prayer For Selfless Prayer in Marriage

Lord, as we reflect onJob 42:10, we are reminded of the transformative power of selfless prayer. May our hearts be open to intercede not only for our own needs but also for the well-being of each other and those around us. Like Job, teach us the beauty of selfless intercession and the restoration that comes from seeking the good of others. In Your name, we pray. Amen.

November 15

Ecclesiastes 4:12
"And if one prevail against him, two shall withstand him; and a threefold cord is not quickly broken."

What Does This Mean For Us?

In a modern context, Ecclesiastes 4:12 emphasizes the strength and resilience found in unity and partnership. In the context of marriage, this verse underscores the idea that a husband and wife, working together and aligned with a shared faith in God as the third strand, create a bond that is not easily broken.

Modern Day Reflection

The verse encourages couples to face challenges with unity, mutual support, and a foundation rooted in their relationship with each other and with God.

~

Prayer For Unity in Marriage
Dear Lord, we acknowledge the strength found in unity. Bless our marriage, Lord, and help us recognize the power of partnership. May we face challenges together, supported by mutual love and a shared faith in You as the third strand in our bond. Grant us the resilience to withstand the storms of life and the wisdom to strengthen our connection with each other and with You continually. In Your name, we pray. Amen.

November 16

Genesis 31:49

"And Mizpah; for he said, The Lord watch between me and thee, when we are absent one from another."

What Does This Mean For Us?

Genesis 31:49 reflects a prayer for God's protection and guidance in relationships, especially during times of separation. It serves as a reminder that God is the ever-watchful presence between them, providing assurance and keeping their connection secure even when they are not together.

Modern Day Reflection

This verse is a beautiful expression of trust and dependence on God in relationships. For couples facing physical separation due to work, travel, or other circumstances, this verse reminds them that the Lord is the constant guardian of their connection. It encourages spouses to lean on God's watchful presence, finding reassurance in the knowledge that, even when apart, their relationship is under the protective gaze of the Almighty.

Prayer For Divine Presence in Marriage

Heavenly Father, may Your watchful presence be a source of comfort and assurance for us, especially when circumstances keep us physically apart. We entrust our relationship to Your care, asking for Your guidance and protection. Lord, keep watch between us, bridging the gaps and maintaining the closeness that distance cannot diminish. In Your name, we pray. Amen.

Leviticus 20:26

"And ye shall be holy unto me: for I the Lord am holy, and have severed you from other people, that ye should be mine."

What Does This Mean For Us?

Leviticus 20:26 underscores the call for holiness and consecration to God. While the specific regulations in Leviticus were given to the Israelites, the principle of being set apart for God's purposes resonates. It prompts spouses to live in a way that reflects God's character and purposes, fostering a relationship grounded in the values of love, righteousness, and devotion to God.

Modern Day Reflection

The verse challenges spouses to set themselves apart for God's divine plan within the unique marriage covenant. This verse additionally prompts couples to cultivate a relationship marked by love, respect, and righteousness, reflecting the character of God.

Prayer For Purpose in Marriage

Heavenly Father, we seek Your guidance in living a life of holiness, both individually and within the sacred union of marriage. May our relationship be set apart for Your divine purposes, reflecting Your character of love and righteousness. Grant us the strength to navigate the world's challenges while upholding moral and spiritual values. Help us continuously strive for a marriage that honors Your standards and is a testament to Your light. In Your name, we pray. Amen.

November 18

Numbers 11:29

"And Moses said unto him, Enviest thou for my sake? would God that all the Lord'S people were prophets, and that the Lord would put his spirit upon them!'"

What Does This Mean For Us?

In a broad context, this verse encourages an open-hearted and inclusive perspective, welcoming the idea that God's Spirit and gifts are not limited but can be poured out on all believers. It's a call for a community where the Spirit empowers everyone to contribute to the work of God.

Modern Day Reflection

This verse encourages a mindset that embraces the diversity of spiritual gifts within the marital union. In the context of marriage, it prompts couples to celebrate and appreciate the unique strengths, talents, and spiritual insights that each partner brings to the relationship.

Prayer For Inclusivity in Marriage

Dear Lord, may Your Spirit be poured out on all Your people, granting each one the gift of prophecy and a deep connection with You. Help us cultivate a community where Your Spirit values, recognizes, and empowers every individual. Let us rejoice in the diverse gifts within our midst, creating a space where Your presence is felt in every heart. In Your inclusive and loving name, we pray. Amen.

November 19

Ruth 4:16

"And Naomi took the child, and laid it in her bosom, and became nurse unto it."

What Does This Mean For Us?

Ruth 4:16 encourages married couples to embrace an inclusive definition of family. It prompts spouses to extend love, care, and support to their biological children and those they consider part of their larger family, whether through marriage, adoption, or close relationships.

Modern Day Reflection

In a contemporary context, Ruth 4:16 invites married couples to reflect on the expansive nature of love within the family unit. It encourages spouses to embrace a mindset that extends beyond biological relationships, fostering an inclusive environment where love, care, and support transcend traditional boundaries. This verse prompts couples to recognize that blood ties do not solely define family but encompasses all those they choose to bring into the circle of their love and care.

Prayer For Family in Marriage

Gracious Father, we bring before You our marriage represented in Your embrace. May our love be expansive, reaching beyond biological ties to encompass all whom we hold dear. Grant us the grace to create a home where love knows no boundaries and where care extends to those brought into our familial circle. May our union be a testament to the inclusivity and warmth of Your divine love. In Your compassionate name, we pray. Amen.

November 20

Philippians 4:4
"Rejoice in the Lord always. I will say it again: Rejoice!"

What Does This Mean For Us?

This verse is a simple yet profound reminder to always find joy in the Lord. The repetition emphasizes the importance of maintaining a spirit of joy, regardless of circumstances. Philippians 4:4 encourages spouses to cultivate a joyful and grateful attitude within their relationship, finding joy not only in their shared moments of happiness but also in the steadfast presence of the Lord in their union.

Modern Day Reflection

Amidst the challenges and triumphs of daily life, this verse prompts spouses to find moments of rejoicing not solely in external circumstances but in God's enduring love and grace that underpins their marriage. It encourages a mindset of gratitude, where the joy of being united is a continuous source of strength, resilience, and celebration.

Prayer For Grateful Attitude in Marriage
Heavenly Father, we come before You with hearts filled with gratitude. In the journey of marriage, we seek Your guidance to cultivate a spirit of unending joy. May our rejoicing be grounded in Your unwavering presence. Grant us the wisdom to find joy not just in moments of happiness but in the constant assurance of Your love. Bless our marriage with a continuous celebration of the sacred bond we share, rooted in faith and gratitude. Amen.

November 21

Hebrews 13:2

"Be not forgetful to entertain strangers: for thereby some have entertained angels unawares."

What Does This Mean For Us?

This verse encourages a spirit of hospitality, emphasizing the potential for divine encounters in our interactions with others as the principle of extending kindness and hospitality can be within and beyond the household.

Modern Day Reflection

Hebrews 13:2 inspires married couples to embrace a lifestyle of hospitality not only within the confines of their home and the broader world. This verse challenges spouses to extend kindness, warmth, and generosity to those around them, recognizing the potential for divine connections in unexpected encounters. The verse also encourages a shared commitment to positively impacting the lives of those they encounter, fostering a marriage that radiates compassion and embodies the spirit of hospitality.

Prayer For Hospitality in Marriage

Gracious Lord, we seek Your guidance in cultivating a spirit of hospitality within our marriage. Teach us to open our hearts and homes to others, recognizing the potential for divine connections in unexpected encounters. May our relationship be a beacon of warmth, kindness, and generosity, extending beyond our union to touch the lives of those we encounter. In Your name we pray. Amen.

November 22

Philippians 4:11-13

"Not that I speak in respect of want: for I have learned, in whatsoever state I am, therewith to be content. I know both how to be abased, and I know how to abound: every where and in all things I am instructed both to be full and to be hungry, both to abound and to suffer need. I can do all things through Christ which strengtheneth me."

What Does This Mean For Us?

This passage from Philippians reflects the Apostle Paul's understanding of contentment in various life circumstances through the strength he derives from his faith in Christ.

Modern Day Reflection

Philippians 4:11-13 offers a profound blueprint for marital contentment. It beckons couples to cultivate a shared understanding of contentment, transcending external circumstances and finding fulfillment in the richness of their union. These verses prompt spouses to navigate the diverse seasons of married life with resilience, gratitude, and unwavering reliance on the strength that emanates from their shared faith and mutual support.

Prayer For Unwavering Reliance in Marriage

Heavenly Father, we seek Your divine guidance and blessings. May our love be a source of strength, resilience, and gratitude. Grant us the grace to navigate challenges with faith, and may the spirit of unity and mutual support prevail in our relationship. In Your holy name, we pray. Amen.

November 23

Philippians 4:6-7

"Be careful for nothing; but in every thing by prayer and supplication with thanksgiving let your requests be made known unto God. And the peace of God, which passeth all understanding, shall keep your hearts and minds through Christ Jesus."

What Does This Mean For Us?

This powerful passage encourages couples to turn to prayer and thanksgiving instead of anxiety. It invites couples to approach challenges hand in hand, seeking divine guidance and finding solace in the assurance that God's peace can prevail in their relationship.

Modern Day Reflection

These verses inspire spouses to turn away from anxiety and unite in prayer, petition, and gratitude. It calls for couples to navigate the complexities of life hand in hand, trusting that, in the sanctuary of prayer and thanksgiving, the tranquility of God will stand guard over their hearts and minds.

Prayer For Challenges in Marriage

Dear Lord, we ask for the strength to cast away anxieties and, with united hearts, present our desires and concerns to You through prayer and thanksgiving. Grant us the wisdom to navigate challenges with grace, the resilience to celebrate joys with gratitude, and the assurance that, in Your divine embrace, we find a source of enduring peace. In Your name, we pray. Amen.

November 24

Numbers 23:19

"God is not a man, that he should lie; neither the son of man, that he should repent: hath he said, and shall he not do it? or hath he spoken, and shall he not make it good?"

What Does This Mean For Us?

This verse emphasizes the trustworthiness and faithfulness of God's promises. It declares that God is not like a human, prone to falsehood or changing His mind. Instead, when God speaks, His words are reliable and will come to fruition.

Modern Day Reflection

Numbers 23:19 affirms God's unwavering faithfulness and truthfulness becoming a foundational pillar for married couples. As they navigate the complexities of life, this verse encourages spouses to anchor their trust in the promises of a God who does not waver or deceive. It prompts couples to build their relationship on the bedrock of divine reliability, finding solace and confidence in the certainty that God's spoken words will be fulfilled.

~

Prayer For Truthfulness in Marriage

Heavenly Father, thank You for being a God of unwavering faithfulness and truth. Strengthen our bond with the certainty that, just as Your promises are steadfast, our commitments to one another can be unwavering. Grant us the grace to build a marriage founded on truth, trust, and the divine promises that endure through all seasons of life. Amen.

November 25

Ecclesiastes 4:9-10

"Two are better than one; because they have a good reward for their labour. For if they fall, the one will lift up his fellow: but woe to him that is alone when he falleth; for he hath not another to help him up."

What Does This Mean For Us?

This passage from Ecclesiastes underscores the strength and support found in companionship. It emphasizes the idea that two individuals working together can achieve more and encourages a partnership marked by collaboration, assistance, and a shared journey through life's challenges.

Modern Day Reflection

This passage calls on couples to recognize the profound strength of their partnership. These verses inspire spouses to view their union as a source of shared labor, where the fruits of their combined efforts are greater than what each could achieve alone. The passage becomes a gentle reminder that, in the inevitable moments of stumbling or adversity, having a companion to help, support, and lift each other is a priceless treasure.

Prayer For Marital Collaboration in Marriage

Heavenly Father, may our marriage be a testament to the strength and support found in companionship. Grant us the grace to labor together, finding joy and fulfillment in our shared endeavors. In moments of challenge or stumbling, be our source of strength, guiding us to lift each other with love and understanding. In Your name, we pray. Amen.

November 26

Ezekial 36:26

"A new heart also will I give you, and a new spirit will I put within you: and I will take away the stony heart out of your flesh, and I will give you an heart of flesh."

What Does This Mean For Us?

This verse speaks of God's transformative power to renew and change the innermost being of individuals. The verse inspires couples to embrace the idea of continual growth and transformation within their relationship.

Modern Day Reflection

Ezekiel 36:26, with its promise of a new heart and spirit, resonates profoundly in the modern context of marriage. The verse inspires couples to embrace the potential for continual transformation and renewal within their relationship. It invites spouses to approach each other with hearts of flesh—softened, understanding, and open to growth. It becomes a reminder that, through divine grace, the ongoing journey of love can be marked by the beauty of evolving hearts and spirits within the sacred bond of marriage.

Prayer For New Spirit in Marriage

Heavenly Father, we seek Your transformative power in our marriage journey to give us new hearts and spirits. May our relationship be a testament to Your grace, with hearts that continually reflect the beauty of evolving love. Grant us the strength to navigate life's changes with resilience and a deepening connection. In Your name, we pray. Amen.

November 27

Daniel 2:23

"I thank thee, and praise thee, O thou God of my fathers, who hast given me wisdom and might, and hast made known unto me now what we desired of thee: for thou hast now made known unto us the king's matter."

What Does This Mean For Us?

This verse is part of Daniel's prayer of gratitude and praise to God for revealing the dream and its interpretation to him. In today's marriage, it can be seen as acknowledging God's guidance, wisdom, and revelation within the union of husband and wife.

Modern Day Reflection

Daniel 2:23 serves as a poignant reminder of the gratitude and praise due to the Lord for the wisdom and guidance bestowed upon a marriage of two souls. This verse prompts couples to reflect on the moments of revelation, understanding and shared dreams that shape their journey together. Daniel 2:23 invites spouses to recognize the hand of God intricately woven into the fabric of their marriage, fostering a spirit of gratitude and praise for the ongoing revelation of shared dreams and purpose.

Prayer For Wisdom and Might in Marriage

Gracious God, we acknowledge Your wisdom and guidance within our marriage. Thank You for the moments of revelation, understanding, and shared dreams that have shaped our journey together. May Your continued presence be a source of strength, love, and purpose in our marriage. In Your holy name, we pray. Amen.

November 28

Jonah 2:9
"But I will sacrifice unto thee with the voice of thanksgiving; I will pay
that that I have vowed. Salvation is of the Lord."

What Does This Mean For Us?

This verse is part of Jonah's prayer of thanksgiving and commitment to fulfill his vows to God after being swallowed by the great fish. In the context of marriage, it can be seen as a declaration of gratitude and acknowledgment that salvation and blessings come from the Lord.

Modern Day Reflection

Jonah 2:9 declares gratitude and commitment to a divine source of salvation and blessings. As couples navigate the depths of their shared journey, this verse inspires them to lift their voices in shouts of grateful praise for the moments of deliverance, grace and shared vows that shape their union. In everyday joys and challenges, Jonah 2:9 prompts spouses to cultivate a spirit of thanksgiving, recognizing the divine hand that orchestrates their salvation and blessings within the sacred marriage covenant.

Prayer For Gratitude in Marriage
Heavenly Father, as we continue our marital journey together, may our
hearts echo Jonah's grateful praise. In moments of joy and challenge,
may we find solace in acknowledging You as the source of our salvation
and blessings. Grant us the grace to fulfill our vows and navigate the
intricacies of married life with gratitude and commitment. In Your
name, we pray. Amen.

November 29

Galatians 5:16

"This I say then, Walk in the Spirit, and ye shall not fulfil the lust of the flesh."

What Does This Mean For Us?

This verse encourages believers to live under the guidance and influence of the Holy Spirit, which leads to a life characterized by spiritual virtues rather than succumbing to the desires of the flesh. It can be seen as a call for couples to seek a relationship guided by the principles of the Spirit, fostering love, patience, and self-control.

Modern Day Reflection

This verse encourages spouses to cultivate a marriage that reflects the fruits of the Spirit—love, joy, peace, patience, kindness, goodness, faithfulness, gentleness, and self-control. It prompts them to seek a union guided by divine principles, fostering a relationship where the desires of the flesh take a back seat to the enduring qualities that strengthen their bond and reflect the beauty of a Spirit-led love.

Prayer For Spirit-led Love in Marriage

Heavenly Father, may the wisdom of Galatians 5:16 guide us and encourage us to walk in the Spirit. Grant us the strength to cultivate a relationship marked by love, joy, and self-control. Bless us with patience, kindness, and a deep understanding of each other. May our union be a testament to the transformative power of a Spirit-led love. In Your name, we pray. Amen.

November 30

Hebrews 12:11

"Now no chastening for the present seemeth to be joyous, but grievous: nevertheless afterward it yieldeth the peaceable fruit of righteousness unto them which are exercised thereby."

What Does This Mean For Us?

This verse emphasizes the transformative nature of discipline, acknowledging its initial difficulty but highlighting its long-term benefits. In the context of marriage, it can be seen as an encouragement for couples to navigate challenges, conflicts, and growth with patience and perseverance, trusting that the process will ultimately yield a harvest of righteousness and peace within their relationship.

Modern Day Reflection

Hebrews 12:11 serves as a profound insight into the dynamics of growth and resilience. This verse encourages couples to view challenges and discipline within their relationship as transformative agents, recognizing that temporary discomfort can lead to a lasting harvest of righteousness and peace.

~

Prayer For Discipline in Marriage

Heavenly Father, we seek Your guidance and grace. In moments of discipline and difficulty, grant us the strength to persevere with patience and resilience. Bless us with a deep understanding of the transformative power of discipline, allowing us to navigate the journey of marriage with wisdom and grace. In Your name, we pray. Amen.

December

AS DECEMBER WRAPS THE YEAR IN A BLANKET OF SNOW, LET US BE REMINDED OF THE PURITY OF OUR INTENTIONS AND THE POTENTIAL FOR A FRESH START. MAY THE LIGHT OF HOPE GUIDE US THROUGH THE WINTER NIGHTS, AND MAY THE SPIRIT OF LOVE SHINE BRIGHTLY, BRINGING WARMTH TO ALL HEARTS.

December 1

Proverbs 15:2

"The tongue of the wise useth knowledge aright: but the mouth of fools poureth out foolishness."

What Does This Mean For Us?

Proverbs 15:2 draws attention to the wise use of knowledge by those with discerning tongues. The verse contrasts this with the foolishness expressed by those who thoughtlessly pour out their words.

Modern Day Reflection

Applied to marriage, this passage guides couples to communicate with wisdom and discernment, using knowledge appropriately. It emphasizes the importance of thoughtful and intentional speech in building a strong and understanding relationship.

Prayer For Knowledge in Marriage

Heavenly Father, teach us the significance of Proverbs 15:2 in our marriage. May our tongues be guided by wisdom, using knowledge appropriately in our communication. Strengthen our commitment to thoughtful and intentional speech, building a relationship where understanding prevails. Amen.

December 2

1 Corinthians 14:33

"For God is not the author of confusion, but of peace, as in all churches of the saints."

What Does This Mean For Us?

This verse emphasizes God's nature as a source of peace rather than confusion. In the context of marriage, it encourages couples to seek harmony, understanding, and peace within their relationship, aligning their actions and decisions with the principles of God's peace.

Modern Day Reflection

1 Corinthians 14:33 underscores the importance of cultivating an atmosphere of peace rather than confusion. The verse encourages couples to approach communication with a mindset of harmony and understanding, recognizing that God desires peace within relationships. It emphasizes the need for clear and constructive communication to avoid misunderstandings and conflicts.

Prayer For Peace in Marriage

Dear God, help us create an atmosphere of peace in our marriage. May our communication be marked by clarity and understanding, aligning with Your desire for harmony. Guide us in resolving conflicts with love and seeking peace in all aspects of our relationship. Amen.

December 3

1 Peter 4:11

"If any man speak, let him speak as the oracles of God; if any man minister, let him do it as of the ability which God giveth: that God in all things may be glorified through Jesus Christ, to whom be praise and dominion forever and ever. Amen."

What Does This Mean For Us?

1 Peter 4:11 encourages couples to speak in alignment with the guidance of God and to serve using their abilities bestowed by God.

Modern Day Reflection

This verse urges couples to approach communication in their marriage with a sense of responsibility and with the intention of glorifying God. It emphasizes the significance of using words that uplift and serve the purpose of building a strong and godly relationship.

Prayer For Healthy Communication in Marriage

Dear Lord, guide us in our communication within our marriage. May our words be aligned with Your wisdom, serving the purpose of building a strong and godly relationship. Help us glorify You in all things through our interactions. Amen.

December 4

Proverbs 20:15
"There is gold, and a multitude of rubies: but the lips of knowledge are a precious jewel."

What Does This Mean For Us?

Proverbs 20:15 uses the imagery of precious jewels to highlight the value of wise and knowledgeable speech. The verse suggests that, like gold and rubies, lips that convey knowledge are a precious jewel.

Modern Day Reflection

This encourages couples to recognize the worth of thoughtful and informed communication in their relationship, emphasizing the beauty and value it adds to their connection.

～

Prayer For Thoughtful Communication in Marriage
Heavenly Father, teach us the significance of Proverbs 20:15 in our marriage. May our communication be a precious jewel, filled with knowledge and wisdom. Strengthen our commitment to expressing thoughtful and informed words, enhancing the value and beauty of our relationship. Amen.

December 5

Matthew 18:21-22

"Then came Peter to him, and said, Lord, how oft shall my brother sin against me, and I forgive him? till seven times? Jesus saith unto him, I say not unto thee, Until seven times: but, Until seventy times seven."

What Does This Mean For Us?

Matthew 18:21-22 recounts Peter's question to Jesus about forgiveness. Jesus responds by emphasizing the limitless nature of forgiveness, suggesting that one should forgive not just seven times but seventy times seven.

Modern Day Reflection

In today's marriage, this conveys the idea that forgiveness should be boundless, encouraging couples to cultivate a forgiving spirit that transcends limitations and promotes ongoing reconciliation.

Prayer For Forgiveness in Marriage

Heavenly Father, teach us the significance of Matthew 18:21-22 in our marriage. May we understand and practice limitless forgiveness, fostering a relationship grounded in grace and understanding. Strengthen our commitment to forgive each other unconditionally, mirroring Your boundless love for us. Amen.

December 6

Proverbs 17:9
"He that covereth a transgression seeketh love; but he that repeateth a matter separateth very friends."

What Does This Mean For Us?

This verse highlights the value of covering transgressions rather than dwelling on them. The verse suggests that seeking to understand, forgive, and move past a wrongdoing fosters love. Conversely, repeatedly bringing up past mistakes can lead to division and separation.

Modern Day Reflection

Applied to marriage, this verse encourages couples to prioritize forgiveness, understanding, and the restoration of love rather than dwelling on past grievances.

~

Prayer For Transgression in Marriage
Almighty God, teach us the significance of Proverbs 17:9 in our marriage. May we choose love by covering transgressions and fostering an environment of forgiveness and understanding. Strengthen our commitment to building a marriage that reflects Your love and grace.
Amen.

<h1 align="center">December 7</h1>

<h2 align="center">Psalm 103:10-12</h2>

"He hath not dealt with us after our sins; nor rewarded us according to our iniquities. For as the heaven is high above the earth, so great is his mercy toward them that fear him.As far as the east is from the west, so far hath he removed our transgressions from us."

<h2 align="center">What Does This Mean For Us?</h2>

Psalm 103:10-12 reflects on the boundless mercy and forgiveness of God. The verses highlight that God does not deal with us based on our sins, and His mercy is vast, removing our transgressions as far as the east is from the west.

<h2 align="center">Modern Day Reflection</h2>

For married couples, this encourages an individual approach to forgiveness with a similar depth of mercy, recognizing the capacity to let go and move forward.

<h2 align="center">Prayer For Boundless Mercy in Marriage</h2>

Dear God, as a couple, we reflect on Your mercy and forgiveness described in Psalm 103:10-12. Help us embody this in our marriage, extending grace and mercy to each other. May our love be a reflection of Your boundless forgiveness. Amen.

December 8

Matthew 5:7
"Blessed are the merciful: for they shall obtain mercy."

What Does This Mean For Us?

This passage encourages a merciful and forgiving attitude. The verse suggests that those who show mercy will receive mercy in return.

Modern Day Reflection

Applied to marriage, this emphasizes the reciprocal nature of forgiveness within the relationship. By cultivating a merciful and forgiving spirit, couples can foster an environment of understanding and grace.

❧

Prayer For Mercy in Marriage

Father in Heaven, guide us in living out the principles of Matthew 5:7 in our marriage. May our hearts be filled with mercy and forgiveness, creating a harmonious and loving environment. Strengthen our commitment to a marriage marked by grace and understanding. Amen.

December 9

1 John 1:9

"If we confess our sins, he is faithful and just to forgive us our sins and to cleanse us from all unrighteousness."

What Does This Mean For Us?

In the context of forgiveness in marriage, 1 John 1:9 emphasizes the importance of confession and God's faithful forgiveness. The verse underscores the idea that acknowledging mistakes and seeking forgiveness is met with divine mercy and cleansing.

Modern Day Reflection

In relation to marriage, this verse encourages couples to foster an environment of honesty, confession, and forgiveness, recognizing that true intimacy is built on mutual understanding and grace.

Prayer For Confession in Marriage

Dear God, guide us as a couple to embrace the principles of 1 John 1:9 in our marriage. May we be open and honest, confessing our mistakes to each other, and may your faithful forgiveness strengthen the bond between us. Amen.

December 10

Matthew 18:35

"So likewise shall my heavenly Father do also unto you if ye from your hearts forgive not every one his brother their trespasses."

What Does This Mean For Us?

Matthew 18:35 encourages couples to cultivate a forgiving spirit that goes beyond surface-level forgiveness and extends to the core of their being.

Modern Day Reflection

Matthew 18:35 underscores the importance of genuine and wholehearted forgiveness. The verse emphasizes that just as God forgives us, we are called to forgive others, including our spouses, from the depths of our hearts.

~

Prayer For a Forgiving Spirit in Marriage

Heavenly Father, help us to embody the spirit of Matthew 18:35 in our marriage. May our hearts be open to forgive each other deeply, fostering a relationship grounded in your love and forgiveness. Amen.

December 11

Isaiah 1:18

"Come now, and let us reason together, saith the Lord: though your sins be as scarlet, they shall be as white as snow; though they be red like crimson, they shall be as wool."

What Does This Mean For Us?

This verse invites a conversation between individuals and God, emphasizing the transformative power of forgiveness. It uses the metaphor of sins being as scarlet and crimson, which can be made as white as snow and wool through divine forgiveness.

Modern Day Reflection

In contemporary reflection, this verse encourages open communication and reasoning together. It suggests that through dialogue and forgiveness, even the deepest stains (symbolized by scarlet and crimson) can be cleansed.

Prayer For Reasoning in Marriage

Loving God, as You transform scarlet into white, transform our hearts and relationships. Grant us the strength to forgive and reason together for a harmonious marriage. Amen.

December 12

Hebrews 13:1

"Let brotherly love continue."

What Does This Mean For Us?

This verse encourages couples to maintain and foster mutual love within their relationships. In the context of marriage, it serves as a reminder for couples to cultivate and sustain a love that is reciprocal, selfless, and enduring.

Modern Day Reflection

In the contemporary landscape of marriage, Hebrews 13:1 stands as a timeless call to prioritize and nurture mutual love. It prompts couples to reflect on the essence of their relationship, encouraging them to let love flourish and endure. This verse serves as a reminder for spouses to intentionally cultivate a love that is reciprocal, selfless, and steadfast.

Prayer For Nurturing Love in Marriage

Heavenly Father, may the essence of Hebrews 13:1 guide our relationship. Grant us the wisdom to nurture a love that is reciprocal, selfless, and enduring. In the midst of life's complexities, may our bond be a beacon of mutual affection and steadfast commitment. Bless our marriage with the grace to let love continue, deepening with each passing day. In Your name, we pray. Amen.

December 13

Malachi 3:6

"For I am the Lord, I change not; therefore ye sons of Jacob are not consumed."

What Does This Mean For Us?

Malachi 3:6 suggests a sense of stability and constancy. The idea that the Lord does not change could be seen as an encouragement for married couples to strive for unwavering commitment and steadfastness in their relationship. It implies a foundation of trust and reliability, much like the unchanging nature of the Lord.

Modern Day Reflection

In a modern context, the verse might encourage married couples to embrace constancy and commitment in their relationship. The idea that God does not change could be seen as a call for couples to remain true to their vows and values despite life's ever-changing circumstances. It inspires a sense of enduring love, loyalty, and resilience in the face of challenges.

Prayer For Loyalty in Marriage

Dear Lord, In the unchanging light of Your love, we stand as a married couple, grateful for the constancy You bring to our lives. Just as You remain steadfast, help us cultivate a love that endures the tests of time. May we find strength in Your unchanging nature to be unwavering in our commitment to one another. Guide us through the seasons of life, reminding us that, in Your love, we are not consumed. Bless our marriage with resilience, trust, and a love that mirrors Your eternal faithfulness. Amen.

December 14

Galatians 6:9

"And let us not be weary in well doing: for in due season we shall reap, if we faint not."

What Does This Mean For Us?

This verse encourages perseverance and steadfastness in doing good deeds and living a righteous life. It advises against becoming weary or discouraged in the face of challenges or setbacks. It's a message of hope and endurance, emphasizing the importance of staying committed to doing what is right even when faced with difficulties.

Modern Day Reflection

Galatians 6:9 can serve as a reminder to stay resilient in the pursuit of kindness and righteousness. It acknowledges the challenges and weariness that may arise but encourages us to persist in doing good, trusting that positive outcomes will eventually manifest.

Prayer For Love and Goodness in Marriage

Dear Lord, In our marriage journey, help us not to grow weary in doing good. May the love we share be a constant source of inspiration and strength. When challenges arise, grant us the resilience to persevere in kindness and righteousness. Let our commitment to each other and to the path of goodness be unwavering. We trust that, in Your perfect timing, we will reap a harvest of joy, love, and shared blessings. Guide us, Lord, as we navigate the complexities of life together, knowing that our efforts in love and goodness are not in vain. Amen.

<h1 style="text-align:center">December 15</h1>

Philemon 1:25

"The grace of the Lord Jesus Christ be with your spirit."

What Does This Mean For Us?

This verse is a closing blessing, expressing the desire for the grace of Jesus Christ to be present in the marriage union. It emphasizes the importance of divine grace and invokes a sense of spiritual well-being. The verse reflects the Christian emphasis on grace as a central and transformative aspect of their faith.

Modern Day Reflection

In a modern context, Philemon 1:25 could be seen as a heartfelt wish for the abiding presence of grace, peace, and spiritual well-being in the lives of individuals and communities. It carries the timeless hope that the transformative power of Christ's grace continues to shape and guide our spirits in today's fast-paced and ever-changing world. The emphasis on spiritual well-being suggests recognizing the importance of inner peace and connection with something greater than ourselves.

Prayer For Transformative Love in Marriage

Dear Lord, In the journey of our marriage, may the grace of our Lord Jesus Christ be an ever-present force in our spirits. As we face life's challenges and joys together, let Your grace guide our actions, words, and hearts. May our union be a testament to Your transformative love. Amen.

December 16

Hebrews 3:13

"But exhort one another every day, as long as it is called 'today,' that none of you may be hardened by the deceitfulness of sin."

What Does This Mean For Us?

Hebrews 3:13 advises couples to encourage one another daily, emphasizing the importance of mutual support in maintaining a steadfast faith. This verse suggests that regular encouragement within a community helps prevent the hardening of hearts and fosters a resilient, enduring faith.

Modern Day Reflection

In a modern context for a married couple, it underscores the significance of constant support and positive affirmation in the relationship. Encouraging one another daily becomes a foundation for building and maintaining a strong marital bond. The verse prompts couples to uplift and inspire each other actively, creating an atmosphere of love, understanding, and shared spiritual growth.

~

Prayer For Positive Affirmation in Marriage

Dear Heavenly Father, grant us the wisdom and compassion to encourage each other daily in our journey together. May our words and actions be a source of strength, preventing any hardening of hearts in times of challenge. Let our marriage be a sanctuary of love, support, and enduring faith. Help us foster an atmosphere of mutual encouragement, understanding, and growth as we navigate life's journey hand in hand.
Amen.

December 17

1 Peter 3:1

"Likewise, ye wives, be in subjection to your own husbands; that, if any obey not the word, they also may without the word be won by the conversation of the wives."

What Does This Mean For Us?

1 Peter 3:1 encourages wives to be submissive to their husbands, emphasizing the potential impact of their behavior in winning over husbands who may not believe in the Christian message. The verse speaks to the transformative power of a wife's conduct and highlights the importance of living out one's faith in a way that draws others closer to God.

Modern Day Reflection

In a modern context for a married couple, this verse reflects on the power of love, respect, and positive influence within the marriage. It doesn't imply blind obedience but rather emphasizes the potential for a wife's actions and demeanor to positively impact her husband, fostering an environment where faith can flourish.

Prayer For Positive Influence in Marriage

Dear Heavenly Father, Grant us the wisdom to understand the essence of 1 Peter 3:1 in the context of our marriage. May our relationship be a reflection of love, respect, and positive influence. Help us, as partners, to support and uplift each other in our journey of faith. May our actions and attitudes draw us closer to You and, in turn, strengthen the bond we share. Guide us in living out our faith in a way that inspires and transforms our hearts. Amen.

December 18

3 John 1:4

"I have no greater joy than to hear that my children walk in truth."

What Does This Mean For Us?

This verse is a statement by the apostle John expressing his joy in knowing that those he cares about are living according to the truth. Additionally, its principle of finding joy in the well-being and righteous path of loved ones can certainly be applied to the context of marital relationships.

Modern Day Reflection

3 John 1:4 inspires couples to find joy in the shared journey of walking in truth. It speaks to the joy that comes from witnessing one another grow spiritually and live in alignment with principles that strengthen the marital bond. The verse invites couples to celebrate personal achievements and the shared commitment to a life grounded in truth, mutual respect, and the enduring love of God.

Prayer For Enduring Love in Marriage

Dear God, In the spirit of 3 John 1:4, our prayer as a married couple is that our journey together brings you joy. May our union be characterized by walking in truth, guided by Your love and principles. As we navigate the complexities of life, grant us the grace to uphold the values that bring joy to us and to Your heart. May our shared commitment to truth and righteousness be a source of joy and fulfillment in our marriage. Amen.

December 19

Hebrews 4:16

"Let us therefore come boldly unto the throne of grace, that we may obtain mercy, and find grace to help in time of need."

What Does This Mean For Us?

The verse assures that in approaching God, we can receive mercy for our failures and find grace to help us in our times of need. Essentially, it invites married couples to confidently seek God's guidance, support, and mercy, knowing that His grace is abundantly available to assist and strengthen them in every aspect of their lives.

Modern Day Reflection

Hebrews 4:16 invites couples to approach God together, seeking His grace and mercy in times of need. It encourages spouses to be confident in bringing their concerns, challenges, and joys before the throne of grace, recognizing that God is a source of strength and support for their journey.

Prayer For Mercy and Grace in Marriage

Dear God, Hebrews 4:16 reminds us to confidently approach Your throne of grace, seeking mercy and finding grace in our times of need. As a married couple, we come before You, acknowledging our dependence on Your guidance and strength. Grant us the confidence to lay our joys and challenges at Your feet, knowing that Your mercy is abundant and Your grace is sufficient. May our union reflect the grace that flows from Your throne, sustaining us in every season of our lives. Amen.

December 20

1 Peter 4:10

"As every man hath received the gift, even so minister the same one to another, as good stewards of the manifold grace of God."

What Does This Mean For Us?

In the context of marriage, this verse encourages spouses to recognize and utilize their individual gifts and talents for the service and benefit of one another.

Modern Day Reflection

1 Peter 4:10 emphasizes the idea of being faithful stewards of God's grace, using the unique qualities and abilities given to each person to contribute positively to the relationship.

Prayer For Mutual Support in Marriage

Dear God, we seek Your guidance in recognizing and utilizing the gifts You have bestowed upon us to serve one another. May our marriage be a testament to the faithful stewardship of Your grace, with each of us contributing our strengths to create a harmonious and loving union. Grant us the wisdom to recognize and appreciate the unique gifts in each other, fostering a relationship marked by mutual support and selfless service. Amen.

December 21

John 15:12

"This is my commandment, That ye love one another, as I have loved you."

What Does This Mean For Us?

This verse emphasizes the profound and selfless love that Jesus calls us to emulate. It serves as a foundational principle for married couples, encouraging them to love one another with the sacrificial and enduring love demonstrated by Christ.

Modern Day Reflection

It challenges couples to embody a love that mirrors the selfless, sacrificial, and unconditional love demonstrated by Jesus. In the complexities of contemporary life, this verse encourages spouses to prioritize kindness, understanding, and forgiveness. It calls for a love that transcends fleeting emotions and perseveres through challenges, fostering a deep connection that reflects the transformative power of Christ's love.

~

Prayer For Embodiment of Love in Marriage

Dear God, we reflect on the command in John 15:12 to love each other as You have loved us. Grant us the strength and wisdom to embody a love that mirrors the selflessness and sacrificial nature of Your love. May our marriage be a testament to the transformative power of Christ's love, radiating kindness, understanding, and forgiveness. In moments of joy and challenges, help us to draw from the well of Your love, creating a bond that reflects Your eternal grace. Amen.

December 22

Hebrews 10:36
"For ye have need of patience, that, after ye have done the will of God, ye might receive the promise."

What Does This Mean For Us?

In the context of marriage, this verse encourages couples to persevere through challenges, trusting that they will receive the promises He has for them as they align their lives with God's will. It speaks to the importance of endurance, faith, and commitment in building a strong and enduring marital relationship.

Modern Day Reflection

This verse encourages spouses to cultivate endurance, faith, and commitment in a world that often emphasizes instant gratification and quick solutions. It speaks to the ongoing process of aligning their lives with God's will, trusting that His promises for their marriage will unfold in due time. In the hustle and bustle of contemporary life, this verse inspires couples to hold onto their faith, remaining steadfast in their commitment to each other and to the divine purpose woven into the fabric of their relationship.

Prayer For Endurance in Marriage
Dear God, Hebrews 10:36 reminds us of the need to persevere in our marriage journey. Grant us the strength to endure challenges, the faith to trust in Your promises, and the commitment to do Your will. In difficult moments, help us lean on Your guidance and trust that Your promises for our union will be fulfilled. In your name, we pray, Amen.

December 23

3 John 1:5

"Beloved, thou doest faithfully whatsoever thou doest to the brethren,
and to strangers"

What Does This Mean For Us?

For married couples, this verse encourages spouses to extend their faithfulness and kindness to each other and those around them. It speaks to the value of selfless actions and hospitality, fostering a spirit of generosity and love within the marriage and beyond.

Modern Day Reflection

3 John 1:5 resonates as a call for couples to extend their faithfulness and kindness beyond the boundaries of their relationship. It encourages spouses to embody a spirit of generosity and hospitality to each other and those they encounter, even if they are strangers.

~

Prayer For Kindness in Marriage

Dear God, In 3 John 1:5, we're taught to be faithful in our actions to each other and those around us. May our marriage be characterized by a selfless love that extends beyond our relationship, reaching out to others with kindness and hospitality. Help us be faithful stewards of the love and grace You've given us, positively impacting those we encounter.
Amen.

December 24

Jonah 1:16
"Then the men feared the Lord exceedingly, and offered a sacrifice unto the Lord, and made vows."

What Does This Mean For Us?

This verse encourages the transformative power of witnessing God's work in challenging situations. It encourages couples to turn to God in awe and reverence, acknowledging His presence and authority and committing to honor Him in their relationship.

Modern Day Reflection

This verse inspires spouses to offer gratitude, commit to honoring God, and strengthen their bond through shared devotion in the sometimes complicated marital union. It calls for a marriage acknowledging God's presence and intentional vows to walk in His ways together.

Prayer For Reverence in Marriage
Dear God, As we contemplate Jonah 1:16, we embrace the transformative power of Your presence in our marriage. May our union be marked by awe and reverence for You, especially in challenging moments. In times of both struggle and triumph, help us offer sacrifices of gratitude and make vows to honor You in our relationship. May our marriage be a living testimony to Your grace and faithfulness.
Amen.

John 4:24

"God is spirit, and his worshipers must worship in the Spirit and in truth."

What Does This Mean For Us?

While this verse primarily addresses worship, it resonates with the idea of transparency and truthfulness in marriage. Couples can find inspiration in the call to be genuine and authentic with each other, fostering a relationship rooted in truth.

Modern Day Reflection

This verse inspires couples to cultivate a relationship grounded in genuine and honest communication. In the midst of a world that often values appearances, it encourages spouses to be true to themselves and each other. Embracing the spirit of worship in marriage involves acknowledging the divine presence in their union and nurturing a connection that reflects the truthfulness and authenticity of their hearts.

Prayer For Truth in Marriage

Dear Lord,we recognize the call to worship in spirit and truth. I n our marriage, may our communication be marked by authenticity and transparency. Help us to be true to ourselves and each other, fostering a relationship that reflects the divine truth at its core. May our worship in marriage be a genuine expression of our hearts, creating a bond that is authentic, honest, and deeply rooted in Your truth. Amen.

December 26

Song of Solomon 2:16
"My beloved is mine and I am his; he browses among the lilies."

What Does This Mean For Us?

This verse encapsulates the intimate connection and mutual possession between lovers. It speaks to the exclusivity and commitment in a marital relationship, emphasizing that each partner belongs to the other.

Modern Day Reflection

In the modern context, Song of Solomon 2:16 reminds married couples of the sacred and exclusive bond they share. It prompts reflection on the idea that amidst life's complexities, they find a place of beauty and exclusivity in the garden of their relationship. The verse invites spouses to cherish the uniqueness of their connection and to recognize the deep sense of belonging they have to each other.

～

Prayer For Sacred Bonds in Marriage
Dear God, As we reflect on Song of Solomon 2:16, we are reminded of the exclusive and sacred bond between us. May our marriage be a garden of beauty and belonging, where we find joy in each other's presence. Help us to cherish the uniqueness of our connection and to honor the commitment we have made to each other. May our love continue to flourish like lilies in the garden of our shared life. Amen.

December 27

Ezekiel 37:27

"My tabernacle also shall be with them: yea, I will be their God, and they shall be my people."

What Does This Mean For Us?

This verse signifies the promise of God's continual presence and intimate relationship with His people. It speaks to the idea of God dwelling among His chosen ones, establishing a covenantal bond where He is their God, and they are His people.

Modern Day Reflection

In the modern context, Ezekiel 37:27 holds the timeless promise of God's abiding presence. For married couples, this verse can serve as a reminder that God is intimately involved in their relationship. It encourages spouses to acknowledge and seek God's presence in their marriage, recognizing that He is the foundation of their union. In the hustle of daily life, this verse inspires couples to build their home on the assurance that God is with them, guiding and sustaining their journey.

Prayer For Continual Holy Presence in Marriage

Dear God, As we reflect on Ezekiel 37:27, we are grateful for the promise of Your dwelling place among us. May Your presence be the cornerstone in our marriage, guiding us and establishing a deep connection with You. We recognize that You are our God, and we are Your people. Grant us the wisdom to seek You in all aspects of our relationship, and may our home be a place where Your love and guidance abound. Amen.

December 28

Numbers 6:27

"And they shall put my name upon the children of Israel, and I will bless them."

What Does This Mean For Us?

God instructs Aaron and his sons to pronounce a blessing over the Israelites. "Putting God's name" on them signifies a divine claim and association, leading to the assurance of God's blessings upon His people.

Modern Day Reflection

In a modern context, Numbers 6:27 speaks to the transformative power of God's name and the blessings that come with His divine presence. For married couples, this verse can serve as a reminder that when God's name is invoked in their relationship, His blessings follow. It prompts reflection on the importance of inviting God into the marriage, seeking His guidance, and acknowledging His authority as the source of blessings and favor.

~

Prayer For Complexities in Marriage

Heavenly Father, we invite Your name into our marriage. May Your presence be a guiding force, and may Your blessings overflow in our relationship. We acknowledge Your authority over our union and seek Your wisdom in navigating the complexities of married life. May our home be a place where Your name is honored. Amen.

December 29

Genesis 18:14

"Is any thing too hard for the Lord? At the time appointed I will return unto thee, according to the time of life, and Sarah shall have a son."

What Does This Mean For Us?

This verse captures the miraculous promise of God's ability to fulfill the seemingly impossible. It underscores the omnipotence of God and His capacity to bring about extraordinary outcomes according to His divine timing.

Modern Day Reflection

In the marital context, Genesis 18:14 encourages married couples to trust in the unlimited power of God. It prompts reflection on the belief that nothing is too difficult for the Lord, including challenges within the marriage or unfulfilled desires. This verse inspires couples to place their faith in God's timing and ability to bring about extraordinary transformations, even in situations that may seem impossible.

Prayer For Power in Marriage

Dear God, we are reminded of Your limitless power and ability to bring about the extraordinary. In our marriage, we surrender our challenges, dreams, and desires to You. Strengthen our faith to believe that nothing is too hard for You. May Your timing be our guide, and may our hearts be open to witnessing the miraculous unfold in our relationship. Amen.

December 30

Ezra 10:11

"Now therefore make confession unto the Lord God of your fathers,
and do his pleasure: and separate yourselves from the people of the land,
and from the strange wives."

What Does This Mean For Us?

This verse from Ezra calls for a commitment to honor God and follow His will, emphasizing the importance of maintaining spiritual fidelity and separation from practices that may lead away from faith. For couples, it highlights the significance of prioritizing a shared commitment to God's principles in their marriage.

Modern Day Reflection

Ezra 10:11 urges married couples to prioritize their spiritual unity. It prompts reflection on the need to align their lives with God's will and intentionally foster a spiritual connection within the marriage. While the cultural context of "foreign wives" may differ today, the essence remains relevant—encouraging couples to keep their faith at the forefront of their relationship.

~

Prayer For Honoring God in Marriage

Dear God, we commit our marriage to honoring You and doing Your will. Help us navigate life's complexities with a shared commitment to Your principles. Grant us the strength to prioritize our spiritual unity and to make choices that align with Your guidance. May our marriage be a testament to Your love and faithfulness. Amen.

December 31

Galatians 6:14

"But God forbid that I should glory, save in the cross of our Lord Jesus Christ, by whom the world is crucified unto me, and I unto the world."

What Does This Mean For Us?

This verse emphasizes a profound shift in priorities, encouraging couples to find their ultimate source of pride and identity in the cross of Jesus Christ. It speaks to a detachment from worldly values and a deep attachment to the transformative power of the cross.

Modern Day Reflection

Galatians 6:14 prompts married couples to reflect on their priorities. It suggests a paradigm shift, encouraging them to find their ultimate pride and identity in the sacrificial love exemplified by the cross. In a world filled with various pursuits, this verse inspires couples to anchor their values, aspirations, and identity in the redemptive message of the cross, fostering a shared perspective that transcends worldly concerns.

Prayer For Pride in Marriage

Dear God, As we meditate on Galatians 6:14, we seek a shift in our priorities as a couple. May our ultimate source of pride be found in the cross of our Lord Jesus Christ. Help us detach from worldly values and attach ourselves to the transformative power of sacrificial love. May our marriage be a reflection of the profound impact of the cross on our lives, guiding us in every aspect of our journey together. Amen.

Final Thoughts

Congratulations, my Brothers and Sisters in Christ! I am so proud to have been on this spiritual journey with you.

As I reflect on your incredible journey through *'366 Meaningful Marriage Minutes'*, my heart swells with gratitude. Thank you from the depths of my being to each of you who welcomed this book into your lives. Your decision to embark on this transformative adventure with me is an honor and a testament to your commitment to your marriage.

First and foremost, I want to express my profound gratitude for trusting the scriptural teachings and methods shared on these pages. Your decision to invest time and energy in your marriage is a powerful declaration of love and dedication. It's a step towards building a foundation that goes beyond the superficial, embracing the profound connection marriage can offer.

Sincere gratitude overflows for your trust in the effectiveness of the *'366 Meaningful Marriage Minutes'* program. Your faith in this journey speaks volumes about your resilience, openness, and willingness to nurture the most important relationship in your life. It's not just a book; it's a shared exploration into the intricacies of marriage, and your trust in the process makes this journey even more meaningful.

As you've completed each daily minute of reflection, I hope you've discovered the beauty in the simplicity of these moments. Marriage is a mosaic of these small, meaningful interactions, and your commitment to dedicating at least one minute each day is a testament to your understanding of their significance. Like droplets in a vast ocean, these moments contribute to the ebb and flow of a thriving marital connection.

Gratitude also extends to the vulnerability you've shown throughout this journey. Marriage is a journey of self-discovery, unveiling the layers that make us who we are. Your willingness to engage with this book's reflections, exercises, and discussions demonstrates courage that is foundational to building a deeply connected and authentic partnership.

In navigating the challenges, celebrating the triumphs, and exploring the nuances of your marriage, you've exemplified resilience. Marriage, like life, is an ever-evolving tapestry of experiences. Your resilience in facing the joys and hardships head-on is the fabric that weaves a story of growth, understanding, and enduring love.

Your contribution to this book's impact on your marriage is a privilege beyond words. Your commitment to growth, dedication to the process, and openness to change have created a ripple effect that extends far beyond the pages of this book. Your journey is a testament to the transformative power of intentional, meaningful moments in shaping the narrative of a marriage.

In closing, I want to express my deepest gratitude once again. Thank you for entrusting me with a small part of your journey. May the insights, reflections, and moments shared in '*366 Meaningful Marriage Minutes*' continue to serve as a guiding light, illuminating the path to a marriage filled with depth, connection, and enduring love. May your journey be adorned with the beauty of shared moments, each minute a brushstroke contributing to the masterpiece that is your unique and cherished marriage.

In His grace and wisdom,

~ London C. Monroe

Help Spread the Word of the Lord!

There's an exciting time in your marriage ahead of you, and you're just at the start of it. This is your chance to help another couple discover their journey that only takes one minute each day!

Simply by sharing your honest opinion of this book and a little about what you found beneficial, you'll help other married couples find the '366 Meaningful Marriage Minutes' foundational spiritual guidance they might not have found otherwise.

Thank you so much for your support. Your review is vital, and I appreciate your HONEST Amazon review tremendously.

Scan the QR code to leave your review on Amazon.

References

Bible Gateway passage: 1 Corinthians 1:10 - King James Version. (2015). Bible Gateway. https://www.biblegateway.com/passage/?search=1+Corinthians+1%3A10& version=KJV

Bible Gateway passage: 1 Corinthians 4:2 - King James Version. (2024). Bible Gateway. https://www.biblegateway.com/passage/?search=1+Corinthians+4%3A2& version=KJV

Bible Gateway passage: 1 Corinthians 6:16 - King James Version. (2015). Bible Gateway. https://www.biblegateway.com/passage/?search=1+Corinthians+6%3A16& version=KJV

Bible Gateway passage: 1 Corinthians 6:18-20 - King James Version. (2015). Bible Gateway. https://www.biblegateway.com/passage/?search=1+Corinthians+6%3A18-20& version=KJV

Bible Gateway passage: 1 Corinthians 7:2 - King James Version. (2015). Bible Gateway. https://www.biblegateway.com/passage/?search=1+Corinthians+7%3A2& version=KJV

Bible Gateway passage: 1 Corinthians 7:3 - King James Version. (2015). Bible Gateway. https://www.biblegateway.com/passage/?search=1+Corinthians+7%3A3& version=KJV

Bible Gateway passage: 1 Corinthians 7:3-4 - King James Version. (2015). Bible Gateway. https://www.biblegateway.com/passage/?search=1+Corinthians+7%3A3-4& version=KJV

Bible Gateway passage: 1 Corinthians 7:3-5 - King James Version. (2024). Bible Gateway. https://www.biblegateway.com/passage/?search=1+Corinthians+7%3A3-5& version=KJV

Bible Gateway passage: 1 Corinthians 7:4 - King James Version. (2015). Bible Gateway. https://www.biblegateway.com/passage/?search=1+Corinthians+7%3A4& version=KJV

Bible Gateway passage: 1 Corinthians 7:10-11 - King James Version. (2015). Bible Gateway. https://www.biblegateway.com/passage/?search=1+Corinthians+7%3A10-11& version=KJV

Bible Gateway passage: 1 Corinthians 7:39 - King James Version. (2015). Bible Gateway. https://www.biblegateway.com/passage/?search=1+Corinthians+7%3A39& version=KJV

Bible Gateway passage: 1 Corinthians 8:9 - King James Version. (2015). Bible Gateway. https://www.biblegateway.com/passage/?search=1+Corinthians+8%3A9& version=KJV

Bible Gateway passage: 1 Corinthians 10:13 - King James Version. (2015). Bible Gateway. https://www.biblegateway.com/passage/?search=1+Corinthians+10%3A13& version=KJV

Bible Gateway passage: 1 Corinthians 10:17 - King James Version. (2015). Bible Gateway.

https://www.biblegateway.com/passage/?search=1+Corinthians+10%3A17&
version=KJV

Bible Gateway passage: 1 Corinthians 10:24 - King James Version. (2015). Bible Gateway.
https://www.biblegateway.com/passage/?search=1+Corinthians+10%3A24&
version=KJV

Bible Gateway passage: 1 Corinthians 11:3 - King James Version. (2015). Bible Gateway.
https://www.biblegateway.com/passage/?search=1+Corinthians+11%3A3&
version=KJV

Bible Gateway passage: 1 Corinthians 11:11-12 - King James Version. (2015). Bible
Gateway.   https://www.biblegateway.com/passage/?search=1+Corinthians+11%
3A11-12&version=KJV

Bible Gateway passage: 1 Corinthians 12:12 - King James Version. (2024). Bible Gateway.
https://www.biblegateway.com/passage/?search=1+Corinthians+12%3A12&
version=KJV

Bible Gateway passage: 1 Corinthians 12:25 - King James Version. (2015). Bible Gateway.
https://www.biblegateway.com/passage/?search=1+Corinthians+12%3A25&
version=KJV

Bible Gateway passage: 1 Corinthians 13:1 - King James Version. (2015). Bible Gateway.
https://www.biblegateway.com/passage/?search=1+Corinthians+13%3A1&
version=KJV

Bible Gateway passage: 1 Corinthians 13:2 - King James Version. (2024). Bible Gateway.
https://www.biblegateway.com/passage/?search=1+Corinthians+13%3A2&
version=KJV

Bible Gateway passage: 1 Corinthians 13:4-5 - King James Version. (2024). Bible Gateway.
https://www.biblegateway.com/passage/?search=1+Corinthians+13%3A4-5&
version=KJV

Bible Gateway passage: 1 Corinthians 13:4-7 - King James Version. (2015). Bible Gateway.
https://www.biblegateway.com/passage/?search=1+Corinthians+13%3A4-7&
version=KJV

Bible Gateway passage: 1 Corinthians 13:6 - King James Version. (2015). Bible Gateway.
https://www.biblegateway.com/passage/?search=1+Corinthians+13%3A6&
version=KJV

Bible Gateway passage: 1 Corinthians 13:7 - King James Version. (2015). Bible Gateway.
https://www.biblegateway.com/passage/?search=1+Corinthians+13%3A7&
version=KJV

Bible Gateway passage: 1 Corinthians 13:8 - King James Version. (2015). Bible Gateway.
https://www.biblegateway.com/passage/?search=1+Corinthians+13%3A8&
version=KJV

Bible Gateway passage: 1 Corinthians 13:13 - King James Version. (2015). Bible Gateway.
https://www.biblegateway.com/passage/?search=1+Corinthians+13%3A13&
version=KJV

Bible Gateway passage: 1 Corinthians 14:1 - King James Version. (2015). Bible Gateway.
https://www.biblegateway.com/passage/?search=1+Corinthians+14%3A1&
version=KJV

Bible Gateway passage: 1 Corinthians 14:33 - King James Version. (2015). Bible Gateway.
https://www.biblegateway.com/passage/?search=1+Corinthians+14%3A33&

version=KJV

Bible Gateway passage: 1 Corinthians 15:33 - King James Version. (2015). Bible Gateway. https://www.biblegateway.com/passage/?search=1+Corinthians+15%3A33& version=KJV

Bible Gateway passage: 1 Corinthians 15:58 - King James Version. (2024). Bible Gateway. https://www.biblegateway.com/passage/?search=1+Corinthians+15%3A58& version=KJV

Bible Gateway passage: 1 Corinthians 16:14 - King James Version. (2015a). Bible Gateway. https://www.biblegateway.com/passage/?search=1+Corinthians+16%3A14& version=KJV

Bible Gateway passage: 1 Corinthians 16:14 - King James Version. (2015b). Bible Gateway. https://www.biblegateway.com/passage/?search=1+Corinthians+16%3A14& version=KJV

Bible Gateway passage: 1 John 1:9 - King James Version. (2015). Bible Gateway. https://www.biblegateway.com/passage/?search=1+John+1%3A9&version=KJV

Bible Gateway passage: 1 John 3:18 - King James Version. (2015). Bible Gateway. https://www.biblegateway.com/passage/?search=1+John+3%3A18&version=KJV

Bible Gateway passage: 1 John 4:7 - King James Version. (2015). Bible Gateway. https://www.biblegateway.com/passage/?search=1+John+4%3A7&version=KJV

Bible Gateway passage: 1 John 4:11 - King James Version. (2015). Bible Gateway. https://www.biblegateway.com/passage/?search=1+John+4%3A11&version=KJV

Bible Gateway passage: 1 John 4:18 - King James Version. (2015). Bible Gateway. https://www.biblegateway.com/passage/?search=1+John+4%3A18&version=KJV

Bible Gateway passage: 1 Peter 2:17 - King James Version. (2015). Bible Gateway. https://www.biblegateway.com/passage/?search=1+Peter+2%3A17&version=KJV

Bible Gateway passage: 1 Peter 3:1 - King James Version. (2015). Bible Gateway. https://www.biblegateway.com/passage/?search=1+Peter+3%3A1&version=KJV

Bible Gateway passage: 1 Peter 3:1-2 - King James Version. (2015). Bible Gateway. https://www.biblegateway.com/passage/?search=1+Peter+3%3A1-2&version=KJV

Bible Gateway passage: 1 Peter 3:5-6 - King James Version. (2015). Bible Gateway. https://www.biblegateway.com/passage/?search=1+Peter+3%3A5-6&version=KJV

Bible Gateway passage: 1 Peter 3:7 - King James Version. (2015a). Bible Gateway. https://www.biblegateway.com/passage/?search=1+Peter+3%3A7&version=KJV

Bible Gateway passage: 1 Peter 3:7 - King James Version. (2015b). Bible Gateway. https://www.biblegateway.com/passage/?search=1+Peter+3%3A7&version=KJV

Bible Gateway passage: 1 Peter 3:8 - King James Version. (2015a). Bible Gateway. https://www.biblegateway.com/passage/?search=1+Peter+3%3A8&version=KJV

Bible Gateway passage: 1 Peter 3:8 - King James Version. (2015b). Bible Gateway. https://www.biblegateway.com/passage/?search=1+Peter+3%3A8&version=KJV

Bible Gateway passage: 1 Peter 4:8 - King James Version. (2015a). Bible Gateway. https://www.biblegateway.com/passage/?search=1+Peter+4%3A8&version=KJV

Bible Gateway passage: 1 Peter 4:8 - King James Version. (2015b). Bible Gateway. https://www.biblegateway.com/passage/?search=1+Peter+4%3A8&version=KJV

Bible Gateway passage: 1 Peter 4:9 - King James Version. (2015). Bible Gateway. https://www.biblegateway.com/passage/?search=1+Peter+4%3A9&version=KJV

Bible Gateway passage: 1 Peter 4:10 - King James Version. (2015). Bible Gateway. https://

www.biblegateway.com/passage/?search=1+Peter+4%3A10&version=KJV

Bible Gateway passage: 1 Peter 4:11 - King James Version. (2015). Bible Gateway. https://www.biblegateway.com/passage/?search=1+Peter+4%3A11&version=KJV

Bible Gateway passage: 1 Peter 5:3 - King James Version. (2015). Bible Gateway. https://www.biblegateway.com/passage/?search=1+Peter+5%3A3&version=KJV

Bible Gateway passage: 1 Peter 5:5 - King James Version. (2015). Bible Gateway. https://www.biblegateway.com/passage/?search=1+Peter+5%3A5&version=KJV

Bible Gateway passage: 1 Peter 5:7 - King James Version. (2015). Bible Gateway. https://www.biblegateway.com/passage/?search=1+Peter+5%3A7&version=KJV

Bible Gateway passage: 1 Thessalonians 3:12 - King James Version. (2015). Bible Gateway. https://www.biblegateway.com/passage/?search=1+Thessalonians+3%3A12&version=KJV

Bible Gateway passage: 1 Thessalonians 4:3-5 - King James Version. (2015). Bible Gateway. https://www.biblegateway.com/passage/?search=1+Thessalonians+4%3A3-5&version=KJV

Bible Gateway passage: 1 Thessalonians 4:9 - King James Version. (2015). Bible Gateway. https://www.biblegateway.com/passage/?search=1+Thessalonians+4%3A9&version=KJV

Bible Gateway passage: 1 Thessalonians 4:18 - King James Version. (2015). Bible Gateway. https://www.biblegateway.com/passage/?search=1+Thessalonians+4%3A18&version=KJV

Bible Gateway passage: 1 Thessalonians 5:11 - King James Version. (2015). Bible Gateway. https://www.biblegateway.com/passage/?search=1+Thessalonians+5%3A11&version=KJV

Bible Gateway passage: 1 Thessalonians 5:15 - King James Version. (2015). Bible Gateway. https://www.biblegateway.com/passage/?search=1+Thessalonians+5%3A15&version=KJV

Bible Gateway passage: 1 Thessalonians 5:16-18 - King James Version. (2015). Bible Gateway. https://www.biblegateway.com/passage/?search=1+Thessalonians+5%3A16-18&version=KJV

Bible Gateway passage: 1 Thessalonians 5:24 - King James Version. (2015). Bible Gateway. https://www.biblegateway.com/passage/?search=1+Thessalonians+5%3A24&version=KJV

Bible Gateway passage: 1 Timothy 2:11-12 - King James Version. (2015). Bible Gateway. https://www.biblegateway.com/passage/?search=1+Timothy+2%3A11-12&version=KJV

Bible Gateway passage: 1 Timothy 3:2 - King James Version. (2015). Bible Gateway. https://www.biblegateway.com/passage/?search=1+Timothy+3%3A2&version=KJV

Bible Gateway passage: 1 Timothy 5:8 - King James Version. (2015). Bible Gateway. https://www.biblegateway.com/passage/?search=1+Timothy+5%3A8&version=KJV

Bible Gateway passage: 1 Timothy 5:14 - King James Version. (2015). Bible Gateway. https://www.biblegateway.com/passage/?search=1+Timothy+5%3A14&version=KJV

Bible Gateway passage: 1 Timothy 6:6 - King James Version. (2015). Bible Gateway. https://www.biblegateway.com/passage/?search=1+Timothy+6%3A6&version=KJV

Bible Gateway passage: 1 Timothy 6:10 - King James Version. (2015). Bible Gateway.

https://www.biblegateway.com/passage/?search=1+Timothy+6%3A10&
version=KJV

Bible Gateway passage: 2 Corinthians 1:3-4 - King James Version. (2015). Bible Gateway.
https://www.biblegateway.com/passage/?search=2+Corinthians+1%3A3-4&
version=KJV

Bible Gateway passage: 2 Corinthians 2:7-8 - King James Version. (2015). Bible Gateway.
https://www.biblegateway.com/passage/?search=2+Corinthians+2%3A7-8&
version=KJV

Bible Gateway passage: 2 Corinthians 9:7 - King James Version. (2015). Bible Gateway.
https://www.biblegateway.com/passage/?search=2+Corinthians+9%3A7&
version=KJV

Bible Gateway passage: 2 Timothy 2:22 - King James Version. (2015). Bible Gateway.
https://www.biblegateway.com/passage/?search=2+Timothy+2%3A22&
version=KJV

Bible Gateway passage: 3 John 4 - King James Version. (2015). Bible Gateway. https://www.
biblegateway.com/passage/?search=3+John+1%3A4&version=KJV

Bible Gateway passage: 3 John 5 - King James Version. (2015). Bible Gateway. https://www.
biblegateway.com/passage/?search=3+John+1%3A5&version=KJV

Bible Gateway passage: 3 John 8 - King James Version. (2015). Bible Gateway. https://www.
biblegateway.com/passage/?search=3+John+1%3A8&version=KJV

Bible Gateway passage: Amos 5:24 - King James Version. (2015). Bible Gateway. https://
www.biblegateway.com/passage/?search=Amos+5%3A24&version=KJV

Bible Gateway passage: Colossians 2:2-3 - King James Version. (2024). Bible Gateway.
https://www.biblegateway.com/passage/?search=Colossians+2%3A2-3&
version=KJV

Bible Gateway passage: Colossians 2:19 - King James Version. (2015). Bible Gateway.
https://www.biblegateway.com/passage/?search=Colossians+2%3A19&version=KJV

Bible Gateway passage: Colossians 3:8 - King James Version. (2015). Bible Gateway. https://
www.biblegateway.com/passage/?search=Colossians+3%3A8&version=KJV

Bible Gateway passage: Colossians 3:9-10 - King James Version. (2015). Bible Gateway.
https://www.biblegateway.com/passage/?search=Colossians+3%3A9-10&
version=KJV

Bible Gateway passage: Colossians 3:13 - King James Version. (2024a). Bible Gateway.
https://www.biblegateway.com/passage/?search=Colossians+3%3A13&version=KJV

Bible Gateway passage: Colossians 3:14 - World English Bible. (2015). Bible Gateway. (Back
Cover)   https://www.biblegateway.com/passage/?search=Colossians+3%3A14&
version=WEB

Bible Gateway passage: Colossians 3:13-14 - King James Version. (2015). Bible Gateway.
https://www.biblegateway.com/passage/?search=Colossians+3%3A13-14&
version=KJV

Bible Gateway passage: Colossians 3:14 - King James Version. (2015). Bible Gateway.
https://www.biblegateway.com/passage/?search=Colossians+3%3A14&version=KJV

Bible Gateway passage: Colossians 3:16 - King James Version. (2015). Bible Gateway.
https://www.biblegateway.com/passage/?search=Colossians+3%3A16&version=KJV

Bible Gateway passage: Colossians 3:18 - King James Version. (2015). Bible Gateway.
https://www.biblegateway.com/passage/?search=Colossians+3%3A18&version=KJV

Bible Gateway passage: Colossians 3:18-19 - King James Version. (2015). Bible Gateway. https://www.biblegateway.com/passage/?search=Colossians+3%3A18-19&version=KJV

Bible Gateway passage: Colossians 3:19 - King James Version. (2015). Bible Gateway. https://www.biblegateway.com/passage/?search=Colossians+3%3A19&version=KJV

Bible Gateway passage: Colossians 3:23 - King James Version. (2015). Bible Gateway. https://www.biblegateway.com/passage/?search=Colossians+3%3A23&version=KJV

Bible Gateway passage: Colossians 4:6 - King James Version. (2015). Bible Gateway. https://www.biblegateway.com/passage/?search=Colossians+4%3A6&version=KJV

Bible Gateway passage: Daniel 2:22 - King James Version. (2015). Bible Gateway. https://www.biblegateway.com/passage/?search=Daniel+2%3A22&version=KJV

Bible Gateway passage: Daniel 2:23 - King James Version. (2015). Bible Gateway. https://www.biblegateway.com/passage/?search=Daniel+2%3A23&version=KJV

Bible Gateway passage: Deuteronomy 7:13 - King James Version. (2015). Bible Gateway. https://www.biblegateway.com/passage/?search=Deuteronomy+7%3A13&version=KJV

Bible Gateway passage: Deuteronomy 31:6 - King James Version. (2015). Bible Gateway. https://www.biblegateway.com/passage/?search=Deuteronomy+31%3A6&version=KJV

Bible Gateway passage: Ecclesiastes 4:9 - King James Version. (2024). Bible Gateway. https://www.biblegateway.com/passage/?search=Ecclesiastes+4%3A9&version=KJV

Bible Gateway passage: Ecclesiastes 4:9-10 - King James Version. (2024). Bible Gateway. https://www.biblegateway.com/passage/?search=Ecclesiastes+4%3A9-10&version=KJV

Bible Gateway passage: Ecclesiastes 4:9-12 - King James Version. (2015). Bible Gateway. https://www.biblegateway.com/passage/?search=Ecclesiastes+4%3A9-12&version=KJV

Bible Gateway passage: Ecclesiastes 4:11 - King James Version. (2015). Bible Gateway. https://www.biblegateway.com/passage/?search=Ecclesiastes+4%3A11&version=KJV

Bible Gateway passage: Ecclesiastes 4:12 - King James Version. (2015). Bible Gateway. https://www.biblegateway.com/passage/?search=Ecclesiastes+4%3A12&version=KJV

Bible Gateway passage: Ecclesiastes 5:4-5 - King James Version. (2015). Bible Gateway. https://www.biblegateway.com/passage/?search=Ecclesiastes+5%3A4-5&version=KJV

Bible Gateway passage: Ecclesiastes 9:7 - King James Version. (2015). Bible Gateway. https://www.biblegateway.com/passage/?search=Ecclesiastes+9%3A7&version=KJV

Bible Gateway passage: Ephesians 1:7 - King James Version. (2015). Bible Gateway. https://www.biblegateway.com/passage/?search=Ephesians+1%3A7&version=KJV

Bible Gateway passage: Ephesians 2:14-15 - King James Version. (2015). Bible Gateway. https://www.biblegateway.com/passage/?search=Ephesians+2%3A14-15&version=KJV

Bible Gateway passage: Ephesians 2:19-22 - King James Version. (2015). Bible Gateway. https://www.biblegateway.com/passage/?search=Ephesians+2%3A19-22&version=KJV

Bible Gateway passage: Ephesians 4:2 - King James Version. (2024). Bible Gateway. https://www.biblegateway.com/passage/?search=Ephesians+4%3A2&version=KJV

Bible Gateway passage: Ephesians 4:3 - King James Version. (2015). Bible Gateway. https://www.biblegateway.com/passage/?search=Ephesians+4%3A3&version=KJV

Bible Gateway passage: Ephesians 4:13 - King James Version. (2015). Bible Gateway. https://www.biblegateway.com/passage/?search=Ephesians+4%3A13&version=KJV

Bible Gateway passage: Ephesians 4:15 - King James Version. (2015). Bible Gateway. https://www.biblegateway.com/passage/?search=Ephesians+4%3A15&version=KJV

Bible Gateway passage: Ephesians 4:25 - King James Version. (2015). Bible Gateway. https://www.biblegateway.com/passage/?search=Ephesians+4%3A25&version=KJV

Bible Gateway passage: Ephesians 4:26-27 - King James Version. (2015). Bible Gateway. https://www.biblegateway.com/passage/?search=Ephesians+4%3A26-27&version=KJV

Bible Gateway passage: Ephesians 4:29 - King James Version. (2015). Bible Gateway. https://www.biblegateway.com/passage/?search=Ephesians+4%3A29&version=KJV

Bible Gateway passage: Ephesians 4:32 - King James Version. (2015). Bible Gateway. https://www.biblegateway.com/passage/?search=Ephesians+4%3A32&version=KJV

Bible Gateway passage: Ephesians 5:2 - King James Version. (2024). Bible Gateway. https://www.biblegateway.com/passage/?search=Ephesians+5%3A2&version=KJV

Bible Gateway passage: Ephesians 5:21 - King James Version. (2015). Bible Gateway. https://www.biblegateway.com/passage/?search=Ephesians+5%3A21&version=KJV

Bible Gateway passage: Ephesians 5:21-25 - King James Version. (2015). Bible Gateway. https://www.biblegateway.com/passage/?search=Ephesians+5%3A21-25&version=KJV

Bible Gateway passage: Ephesians 5:22 - King James Version. (2015). Bible Gateway. https://www.biblegateway.com/passage/?search=Ephesians+5%3A22&version=KJV

Bible Gateway passage: Ephesians 5:25 - King James Version. (2015a). Bible Gateway. https://www.biblegateway.com/passage/?search=Ephesians+5%3A25&version=KJV

Bible Gateway passage: Ephesians 5:25 - King James Version. (2015b). Bible Gateway. https://www.biblegateway.com/passage/?search=Ephesians+5%3A25&version=KJV

Bible Gateway passage: Ephesians 5:25 - King James Version. (2015c). Bible Gateway. https://www.biblegateway.com/passage/?search=Ephesians+5%3A25&version=KJV

Bible Gateway passage: Ephesians 5:28 - King James Version. (2015). Bible Gateway. https://www.biblegateway.com/passage/?search=Ephesians+5%3A28&version=KJV

Bible Gateway passage: Ephesians 5:28-29 - King James Version. (2024). Bible Gateway. https://www.biblegateway.com/passage/?search=Ephesians+5%3A28-29&version=KJV

Bible Gateway passage: Ephesians 5:31 - King James Version. (2015). Bible Gateway. https://www.biblegateway.com/passage/?search=Ephesians+5%3A31&version=KJV

Bible Gateway passage: Ephesians 5:33 - King James Version. (2015). Bible Gateway. https://www.biblegateway.com/passage/?search=Ephesians+5%3A33&version=KJV

Bible Gateway passage: Ephesians 6:4 - King James Version. (2015). Bible Gateway. https://www.biblegateway.com/passage/?search=Ephesians+6%3A4&version=KJV

Bible Gateway passage: Ezekiel 11:19 - King James Version. (2015). Bible Gateway. https://www.biblegateway.com/passage/?search=Ezekiel+11%3A19&version=KJV

Bible Gateway passage: Ezekiel 16:62 - King James Version. (2015). Bible Gateway. https://www.biblegateway.com/passage/?search=Ezekiel+16%3A62&version=KJV

Bible Gateway passage: Ezekiel 36:26 - King James Version. (2015). Bible Gateway. https://www.biblegateway.com/passage/?search=Ezekial+36%3A26&version=KJV

Bible Gateway passage: Ezekiel 37:27 - King James Version. (2015). Bible Gateway. https://www.biblegateway.com/passage/?search=Ezekiel+37%3A27&version=KJV

Bible Gateway passage: Ezra 10:11 - King James Version. (2015). Bible Gateway. https://www.biblegateway.com/passage/?search=Ezra+10%3A11&version=KJV

Bible Gateway passage: Galatians 3:28 - King James Version. (2015). Bible Gateway. https://www.biblegateway.com/passage/?search=Galatians+3%3A28&version=KJV

Bible Gateway passage: Galatians 5:1 - King James Version. (2015). Bible Gateway. https://www.biblegateway.com/passage/?search=Galatians+5%3A1&version=KJV

Bible Gateway passage: Galatians 5:6 - King James Version. (2015). Bible Gateway. https://www.biblegateway.com/passage/?search=Galatians+5%3A6&version=KJV

Bible Gateway passage: Galatians 5:13 - King James Version. (2015a). Bible Gateway. https://www.biblegateway.com/passage/?search=Galatians+5%3A13&version=KJV

Bible Gateway passage: Galatians 5:13 - King James Version. (2015b). Bible Gateway. https://www.biblegateway.com/passage/?search=Galatians+5%3A13&version=KJV

Bible Gateway passage: Galatians 5:16 - King James Version. (2024). Bible Gateway. https://www.biblegateway.com/passage/?search=Galatians+5%3A16&version=KJV

Bible Gateway passage: Galatians 5:22-23 - King James Version. (2015). Bible Gateway. https://www.biblegateway.com/passage/?search=Galatians+5%3A22-23&version=KJV

Bible Gateway passage: Galatians 6:2 - King James Version. (2015). Bible Gateway. https://www.biblegateway.com/passage/?search=Galatians+6%3A2&version=KJV

Bible Gateway passage: Galatians 6:9 - King James Version. (2015). Bible Gateway. https://www.biblegateway.com/passage/?search=Galatians+6%3A9&version=KJV

Bible Gateway passage: Galatians 6:14 - King James Version. (2015). Bible Gateway. https://www.biblegateway.com/passage/?search=Galatians+6%3A14&version=KJV

Bible Gateway passage: Genesis 1:27-28 - King James Version. (2015). Bible Gateway. https://www.biblegateway.com/passage/?search=Genesis+1%3A+27-28&version=KJV

Bible Gateway passage: Genesis 1:28 - King James Version. (2015). Bible Gateway. https://www.biblegateway.com/passage/?search=Genesis+1%3A28&version=KJV

Bible Gateway passage: Genesis 2:18 - King James Version. (2015). Bible Gateway. https://www.biblegateway.com/passage/?search=Genesis+2%3A18&version=KJV

Bible Gateway passage: Genesis 2:24 - King James Version. (2015). Bible Gateway. https://www.biblegateway.com/passage/?search=Genesis+2%3A24+&version=KJV

Bible Gateway passage: Genesis 3:16 - King James Version. (2015). Bible Gateway. https://www.biblegateway.com/passage/?search=Genesis+3%3A16&version=KJV

Bible Gateway passage: Genesis 14:20 - King James Version. (2015). Bible Gateway. https://www.biblegateway.com/passage/?search=Genesis+14%3A20&version=KJV

Bible Gateway passage: Genesis 18:14 - King James Version. (2015). Bible Gateway. https://www.biblegateway.com/passage/?search=Genesis+18%3A14&version=KJV

Bible Gateway passage: Genesis 29:20 - King James Version. (2015). Bible Gateway. https://www.biblegateway.com/passage/?search=Genesis+29%3A20&version=KJV

Bible Gateway passage: Genesis 31:49 - King James Version. (2015). Bible Gateway. https://www.biblegateway.com/passage/?search=Genesis+31%3A49&version=KJV

Bible Gateway passage: Hebrews 3:13 - King James Version. (2015). Bible Gateway. https://www.biblegateway.com/passage/?search=Hebrews+3%3A13&version=KJV

Bible Gateway passage: Hebrews 4:16 - King James Version. (2015). Bible Gateway. https://www.biblegateway.com/passage/?search=Hebrews+4%3A16&version=KJV

Bible Gateway passage: Hebrews 7:2 - King James Version. (2015). Bible Gateway. https://www.biblegateway.com/passage/?search=Hebrews+7%3A2&version=KJV

Bible Gateway passage: Hebrews 10:24-25 - King James Version. (2015). Bible Gateway. https://www.biblegateway.com/passage/?search=Hebrews+10%3A24-25&version=KJV

Bible Gateway passage: Hebrews 10:36 - King James Version. (2024). Bible Gateway. https://www.biblegateway.com/passage/?search=Hebrews+10%3A36&version=KJV

Bible Gateway passage: Hebrews 11:6 - King James Version. (2015). Bible Gateway. https://www.biblegateway.com/passage/?search=Hebrews+11%3A6&version=KJV

Bible Gateway passage: Hebrews 12:11 - King James Version. (2024). Bible Gateway. https://www.biblegateway.com/passage/?search=Hebrews+12%3A11&version=KJV

Bible Gateway passage: Hebrews 12:14 - King James Version. (2024). Bible Gateway. https://www.biblegateway.com/passage/?search=Hebrews+12%3A14&version=KJV

Bible Gateway passage: Hebrews 13:1 - King James Version. (2015). Bible Gateway. https://www.biblegateway.com/passage/?search=Hebrews+13%3A1&version=KJV

Bible Gateway passage: Hebrews 13:2 - King James Version. (2015). Bible Gateway. https://www.biblegateway.com/passage/?search=Hebrews+13%3A2&version=KJV

Bible Gateway passage: Hebrews 13:4 - King James Version. (2015a). Bible Gateway. https://www.biblegateway.com/passage/?search=%C2%A0Hebrews+13%3A4&version=KJV

Bible Gateway passage: Hebrews 13:4 - King James Version. (2015b). Bible Gateway. https://www.biblegateway.com/passage/?search=Hebrews+13%3A4&version=KJV

Bible Gateway passage: Hebrews 13:4 - King James Version. (2015c). Bible Gateway. https://www.biblegateway.com/passage/?search=Hebrews+13%3A4&version=KJV

Bible Gateway passage: Hebrews 13:5 - King James Version. (2015). Bible Gateway. https://www.biblegateway.com/passage/?search=Hebrews+13%3A5&version=KJV

Bible Gateway passage: Isaiah 1:18 - King James Version. (2015). Bible Gateway. https://www.biblegateway.com/passage/?search=Isaiah+1%3A18&version=KJV

Bible Gateway passage: Isaiah 40:31 - King James Version. (2015). Bible Gateway. https://www.biblegateway.com/passage/?search=Isaiah+40%3A31&version=KJV

Bible Gateway passage: Isaiah 41:10 - King James Version. (2015). Bible Gateway. https://www.biblegateway.com/passage/?search=Isaiah+41%3A10&version=KJV

Bible Gateway passage: Isaiah 43:25 - King James Version. (2015). Bible Gateway. https://www.biblegateway.com/passage/?search=Isaiah+43%3A25&version=KJV

Bible Gateway passage: James 1:5 - King James Version. (2015). Bible Gateway. https://www.biblegateway.com/passage/?search=James+1%3A5&version=KJV

Bible Gateway passage: James 1:19 - King James Version. (2015). Bible Gateway. https://www.biblegateway.com/passage/?search=James+1%3A19&version=KJV

Bible Gateway passage: James 3:2-4 - King James Version. (2024). Bible Gateway. https://www.biblegateway.com/passage/?search=James+3%3A2-4&version=KJV

Bible Gateway passage: James 3:17 - King James Version. (2015a). Bible Gateway. https://www.biblegateway.com/passage/?search=James+3%3A17&version=KJV

Bible Gateway passage: James 3:17 - King James Version. (2015b). Bible Gateway. https://www.biblegateway.com/passage/?search=%C2%A0James+3%3A17&version=KJV

Bible Gateway passage: James 4:4 - King James Version. (2015). Bible Gateway. https://www.biblegateway.com/passage/?search=James+4%3A4&version=KJV

Bible Gateway passage: James 4:8 - King James Version. (2015). Bible Gateway. https://www.biblegateway.com/passage/?search=James+4%3A8&version=KJV

Bible Gateway passage: James 5:7-8 - King James Version. (2015). Bible Gateway. https://www.biblegateway.com/passage/?search=James+5%3A7-8&version=KJV

Bible Gateway passage: James 5:12 - King James Version. (2015). Bible Gateway. https://www.biblegateway.com/passage/?search=James+5%3A12&version=KJV

Bible Gateway passage: James 5:16 - King James Version. (2015). Bible Gateway. https://www.biblegateway.com/passage/?search=James+5%3A16&version=KJV

Bible Gateway passage: Jeremiah 29:11 - King James Version. (2015). Bible Gateway. https://www.biblegateway.com/passage/?search=Jeremiah+29%3A11&version=KJV

Bible Gateway passage: Job 5:17 - King James Version. (2015). Bible Gateway. https://www.biblegateway.com/passage/?search=Job+5%3A17&version=KJV

Bible Gateway passage: Job 19:25-26 - King James Version. (2015). Bible Gateway. https://www.biblegateway.com/passage/?search=Job+19%3A25-26&version=KJV

Bible Gateway passage: Job 31:1 - King James Version. (2015). Bible Gateway. https://www.biblegateway.com/passage/?search=Job+31%3A1&version=KJV

Bible Gateway passage: Job 42:10 - King James Version. (2015). Bible Gateway. https://www.biblegateway.com/passage/?search=Job+42%3A10&version=KJV

Bible Gateway passage: John 4:24 - King James Version. (2015). Bible Gateway. https://www.biblegateway.com/passage/?search=John+4%3A24&version=KJV

Bible Gateway passage: John 13:34-35 - King James Version. (2015). Bible Gateway. https://www.biblegateway.com/passage/?search=John+13%3A34-35&version=KJV

Bible Gateway passage: John 15:12 - King James Version. (2015). Bible Gateway. https://www.biblegateway.com/passage/?search=John+15%3A12&version=KJV

Bible Gateway passage: John 15:13 - King James Version. (2015). Bible Gateway. https://www.biblegateway.com/passage/?search=John+15%3A13&version=KJV

Bible Gateway passage: John 17:23 - King James Version. (2015). Bible Gateway. https://www.biblegateway.com/passage/?search=John+17%3A23&version=KJV

Bible Gateway passage: Jonah 1:16 - King James Version. (2015). Bible Gateway. https://www.biblegateway.com/passage/?search=Jonah+1%3A16&version=KJV

Bible Gateway passage: Jonah 2:9 - King James Version. (2015). Bible Gateway. https://www.biblegateway.com/passage/?search=Jonah+2%3A9&version=KJV

Bible Gateway passage: Jonah 4:4 - King James Version. (2015). Bible Gateway. https://www.biblegateway.com/passage/?search=Jonah+4%3A4&version=KJV

Bible Gateway passage: Joshua 1:9 - King James Version. (2024). Bible Gateway. https://www.biblegateway.com/passage/?search=Joshua+1%3A9&version=KJV

Bible Gateway passage: Joshua 24:15 - King James Version. (2015). Bible Gateway. https://www.biblegateway.com/passage/?search=Joshua+24%3A15&version=KJV

Bible Gateway passage: Leviticus 19:14 - King James Version. (2015). Bible Gateway. https://www.biblegateway.com/passage/?search=Leviticus+19%3A14&version=KJV

Bible Gateway passage: Leviticus 19:18 - King James Version. (2015). Bible Gateway. https://www.biblegateway.com/passage/?search=Leviticus+19%3A18&version=KJV

Bible Gateway passage: Leviticus 20:7-8 - King James Version. (2015). Bible Gateway. https://www.biblegateway.com/passage/?search=Leviticus+20%3A7-8&version=KJV

Bible Gateway passage: Leviticus 20:26 - King James Version. (2024). Bible Gateway. https://www.biblegateway.com/passage/?search=Leviticus+20%3A26&version=KJV

Bible Gateway passage: Leviticus 26:3-4 - King James Version. (2015). Bible Gateway. https://www.biblegateway.com/passage/?search=Leviticus+26%3A3-4&version=KJV

Bible Gateway passage: Leviticus 27:30 - King James Version. (2015). Bible Gateway. https://www.biblegateway.com/passage/?search=Leviticus+27%3A30&version=KJV

Bible Gateway passage: Luke 6:37 - King James Version. (2015). Bible Gateway. https://www.biblegateway.com/passage/?search=Luke+6%3A37&version=KJV

Bible Gateway passage: Luke 11:42 - King James Version. (2015). Bible Gateway. https://www.biblegateway.com/passage/?search=Luke+11%3A42&version=KJV

Bible Gateway passage: Luke 17:3-4 - King James Version. (2015). Bible Gateway. https://www.biblegateway.com/passage/?search=Luke+17%3A3-4&version=KJV

Bible Gateway passage: Luke 23:34 - King James Version. (2015). Bible Gateway. https://www.biblegateway.com/passage/?search=Luke+23%3A34&version=KJV

Bible Gateway passage: Malachi 2:14 - King James Version. (2015). Bible Gateway. https://www.biblegateway.com/passage/?search=Malachi+2%3A14&version=KJV

Bible Gateway passage: Malachi 2:14-16 - King James Version. (2024). Bible Gateway. https://www.biblegateway.com/passage/?search=Malachi+2%3A14-16&version=KJV

Bible Gateway passage: Malachi 2:15 - King James Version. (2024). Bible Gateway. https://www.biblegateway.com/passage/?search=Malachi+2%3A15&version=KJV

Bible Gateway passage: Malachi 3:6 - King James Version. (2015). Bible Gateway. https://www.biblegateway.com/passage/?search=Malachi+3%3A6&version=KJV

Bible Gateway passage: Malachi 3:10 - King James Version. (2015). Bible Gateway. https://www.biblegateway.com/passage/?search=Malachi+3%3A10&version=KJV

Bible Gateway passage: Malachi 4:6 - King James Version. (2015). Bible Gateway. https://www.biblegateway.com/passage/?search=Malachi+4%3A6&version=KJV

Bible Gateway passage: Mark 2:5 - King James Version. (2024). Bible Gateway. https://www.biblegateway.com/passage/?search=Mark+2%3A5&version=KJV

Bible Gateway passage: Mark 10:8 - King James Version. (2015). Bible Gateway. https://www.biblegateway.com/passage/?search=Mark+10%3A8&version=KJV

Bible Gateway passage: Mark 10:9 - King James Version. (2015). Bible Gateway. https://www.biblegateway.com/passage/?search=Mark+10%3A9&version=KJV

Bible Gateway passage: Mark 10:14 - King James Version. (2015). Bible Gateway. https://www.biblegateway.com/passage/?search=Mark+10%3A14&version=KJV

Bible Gateway passage: Mark 10:45 - King James Version. (2015). Bible Gateway. https://www.biblegateway.com/passage/?search=Mark+10%3A45&version=KJV

Bible Gateway passage: Mark 11:25 - King James Version. (2015). Bible Gateway. https://www.biblegateway.com/passage/?search=Mark+11%3A25&version=KJV

Bible Gateway passage: Matthew 5:7 - King James Version. (2015). Bible Gateway. https://www.biblegateway.com/passage/?search=Matthew+5%3A7&version=KJV

Bible Gateway passage: Matthew 5:23-24 - King James Version. (2015). Bible Gateway.

Bible Gateway passage: Matthew 5:23-24 - King James Version. https://www.biblegateway.com/passage/?search=Matthew+5%3A23-24&version=KJV

Bible Gateway passage: Matthew 5:28 - King James Version. (2024). Bible Gateway. https://www.biblegateway.com/passage/?search=Matthew+5%3A28&version=KJV

Bible Gateway passage: Matthew 5:32 - King James Version. (2015). Bible Gateway. https://www.biblegateway.com/passage/?search=Matthew+5%3A32&version=KJV

Bible Gateway passage: Matthew 5:44 - King James Version. (2015). Bible Gateway. https://www.biblegateway.com/passage/?search=Matthew+5%3A44&version=KJV

Bible Gateway passage: Matthew 6:12 - King James Version. (2015). Bible Gateway. https://www.biblegateway.com/passage/?search=Matthew+6%3A12&version=KJV

Bible Gateway passage: Matthew 6:14-15 - King James Version. (2015). Bible Gateway. https://www.biblegateway.com/passage/?search=Matthew+6%3A14-15&version=KJV

Bible Gateway passage: Matthew 6:33 - King James Version. (2015). Bible Gateway. https://www.biblegateway.com/passage/?search=Matthew+6%3A33&version=KJV

Bible Gateway passage: Matthew 7:12 - King James Version. (2015). Bible Gateway. https://www.biblegateway.com/passage/?search=Matthew+7%3A12&version=KJV

Bible Gateway passage: Matthew 12:36-37 - King James Version. (2015). Bible Gateway. https://www.biblegateway.com/passage/?search=+Matthew+12%3A36-37&version=KJV

Bible Gateway passage: Matthew 18:15 - King James Version. (2015). Bible Gateway. https://www.biblegateway.com/passage/?search=Matthew+18%3A15&version=KJV

Bible Gateway passage: Matthew 18:21-22 - King James Version. (2015). Bible Gateway. https://www.biblegateway.com/passage/?search=Matthew+18%3A21-22&version=KJV

Bible Gateway passage: Matthew 18:35 - King James Version. (2024). Bible Gateway. https://www.biblegateway.com/passage/?search=Matthew+18%3A35&version=KJV

Bible Gateway passage: Matthew 19:4-6 - King James Version. (2015). Bible Gateway. https://www.biblegateway.com/passage/?search=Matthew+19%3A4-6&version=KJV

Bible Gateway passage: Matthew 19:5 - King James Version. (2015). Bible Gateway. https://www.biblegateway.com/passage/?search=Matthew+19%3A5&version=KJV

Bible Gateway passage: Matthew 19:5-6 - King James Version. (2015). Bible Gateway. https://www.biblegateway.com/passage/?search=Matthew+19%3A5-6&version=KJV

Bible Gateway passage: Matthew 19:6 - King James Version. (2015). Bible Gateway. https://www.biblegateway.com/passage/?search=Matthew+19%3A6&version=KJV

Bible Gateway passage: Matthew 22:37-39 - King James Version. (2015). Bible Gateway. https://www.biblegateway.com/passage/?search=Matthew+22%3A+37-39&version=KJV

Bible Gateway passage: Matthew 23:23 - King James Version. (2015). Bible Gateway. https://www.biblegateway.com/passage/?search=Matthew+23%3A23&version=KJV

Bible Gateway passage: Micah 7:18-19 - King James Version. (2015). Bible Gateway. https://www.biblegateway.com/passage/?search=Micah+7%3A18-19&version=KJV

Bible Gateway passage: Nehemiah 10:38 - King James Version. (2015). Bible Gateway. https://www.biblegateway.com/passage/?search=Nehemiah+10%3A38&version=KJV

Bible Gateway passage: Numbers 6:27 - King James Version. (2015). Bible Gateway. https://www.biblegateway.com/passage/?search=Numbers+6%3A27&version=KJV

Bible Gateway passage: Numbers 9:8 - King James Version. (2015). Bible Gateway. https://www.biblegateway.com/passage/?search=Numbers+9%3A8&version=KJV

Bible Gateway passage: Numbers 11:29 - King James Version. (2015). Bible Gateway. https://www.biblegateway.com/passage/?search=Numbers+11%3A29&version=KJV

Bible Gateway passage: Numbers 12:3 - King James Version. (2015). Bible Gateway. https://www.biblegateway.com/passage/?search=Numbers+12%3A3&version=KJV

Bible Gateway passage: Numbers 23:19 - King James Version. (2015). Bible Gateway. https://www.biblegateway.com/passage/?search=Numbers+23%3A19&version=KJV

Bible Gateway passage: Philemon 17 - King James Version. (2015). Bible Gateway. https://www.biblegateway.com/passage/?search=Philemon+1%3A17&version=KJV

Bible Gateway passage: Philemon 25 - King James Version. (2015). Bible Gateway. https://www.biblegateway.com/passage/?search=Philemon+1%3A25&version=KJV

Bible Gateway passage: Philippians 1:27 - King James Version. (2015). Bible Gateway. https://www.biblegateway.com/passage/?search=Philippians+1%3A27&version=KJV

Bible Gateway passage: Philippians 2:1-2 - King James Version. (2024). Bible Gateway. https://www.biblegateway.com/passage/?search=Philippians+2%3A1-2&version=KJV

Bible Gateway passage: Philippians 2:1-4 - King James Version. (2015). Bible Gateway. https://www.biblegateway.com/passage/?search=Philippians+2%3A1-4&version=KJV

Bible Gateway passage: Philippians 2:2 - King James Version. (2015). Bible Gateway. https://www.biblegateway.com/passage/?search=Philippians+2%3A2&version=KJV

Bible Gateway passage: Philippians 2:3 - King James Version. (2024). Bible Gateway. https://www.biblegateway.com/passage/?search=Philippians+2%3A3&version=KJV

Bible Gateway passage: Philippians 2:3-4 - King James Version. (2015). Bible Gateway. https://www.biblegateway.com/passage/?search=Philippians+2%3A3-4&version=KJV

Bible Gateway passage: Philippians 4:2 - King James Version. (2015). Bible Gateway. https://www.biblegateway.com/passage/?search=Philippians+4%3A2&version=KJV

Bible Gateway passage: Philippians 4:4 - King James Version. (2015). Bible Gateway. https://www.biblegateway.com/passage/?search=Philippians+4%3A4&version=KJV

Bible Gateway passage: Philippians 4:5 - King James Version. (2015). Bible Gateway. https://www.biblegateway.com/passage/?search=Philippians+4%3A5&version=KJV

Bible Gateway passage: Philippians 4:6-7 - King James Version. (2015). Bible Gateway. https://www.biblegateway.com/passage/?search=Philippians+4%3A6-7&version=KJV

Bible Gateway passage: Philippians 4:11-13 - King James Version. (2015). Bible Gateway. https://www.biblegateway.com/passage/?search=Philippians+4%3A11-13&version=KJV

Bible Gateway passage: Philippians 4:13 - King James Version. (2015). Bible Gateway. https://www.biblegateway.com/passage/?search=Philippians+4%3A13&version=KJV

Bible Gateway passage: Proverbs 2:16-17 - King James Version. (2015). Bible Gateway.

https://www.biblegateway.com/passage/?search=Proverbs+2%3A16-17&
version=KJV

Bible Gateway passage: Proverbs 3:3-4 - King James Version. (2015). Bible Gateway.
https://www.biblegateway.com/passage/?search=Proverbs+3%3A3-4&version=KJV

Bible Gateway passage: Proverbs 3:5-6 - King James Version. (2015). Bible Gateway.
https://www.biblegateway.com/passage/?search=%C2%A0Proverbs+3%3A5-6&
version=KJV

Bible Gateway passage: Proverbs 3:7-8 - King James Version. (2015). Bible Gateway.
https://www.biblegateway.com/passage/?search=Proverbs+3%3A7-8&version=KJV

Bible Gateway passage: Proverbs 3:9-10 - King James Version. (2015). Bible Gateway.
https://www.biblegateway.com/passage/?search=Proverbs+3%3A9-10&version=KJV

Bible Gateway passage: Proverbs 4:23 - King James Version. (2015). Bible Gateway. https://
www.biblegateway.com/passage/?search=Proverbs+4%3A23&version=KJV

Bible Gateway passage: Proverbs 5:15-19 - King James Version. (2024). Bible Gateway.
https://www.biblegateway.com/passage/?search=Proverbs+5%3A15-19&
version=KJV

Bible Gateway passage: Proverbs 5:21 - King James Version. (2015). Bible Gateway. https://
www.biblegateway.com/passage/?search=Proverbs+5%3A21&version=KJV

Bible Gateway passage: Proverbs 6:32-33 - King James Version. (2015). Bible Gateway.
https://www.biblegateway.com/passage/?search=Proverbs+6%3A32-33&
version=KJV

Bible Gateway passage: Proverbs 10:12 - King James Version. (2015). Bible Gateway.
https://www.biblegateway.com/passage/?search=Proverbs+10%3A12&version=KJV

Bible Gateway passage: Proverbs 11:13 - King James Version. (2015). Bible Gateway.
https://www.biblegateway.com/passage/?search=Proverbs+11%3A13&version=KJV

Bible Gateway passage: Proverbs 11:24-25 - King James Version. (2015). Bible Gateway.
https://www.biblegateway.com/passage/?search=Proverbs+11%3A24-25&
version=KJV

Bible Gateway passage: Proverbs 12:4 - King James Version. (2015). Bible Gateway. https://
www.biblegateway.com/passage/?search=Proverbs+12%3A4&version=KJV

Bible Gateway passage: Proverbs 12:22 - King James Version. (2015a). Bible Gateway.
https://www.biblegateway.com/passage/?search=Proverbs+12%3A22&version=KJV

Bible Gateway passage: Proverbs 12:22 - King James Version. (2015b). Bible Gateway.
https://www.biblegateway.com/passage/?search=Proverbs+12%3A22&version=KJV

Bible Gateway passage: Proverbs 12:25 - King James Version. (2015). Bible Gateway.
https://www.biblegateway.com/passage/?search=Proverbs+12%3A25&version=KJV

Bible Gateway passage: Proverbs 14:1 - King James Version. (2015). Bible Gateway. https://
www.biblegateway.com/passage/?search=Proverbs+14%3A1&version=KJV

Bible Gateway passage: Proverbs 14:21 - King James Version. (2015). Bible Gateway.
https://www.biblegateway.com/passage/?search=Proverbs+14%3A21&version=KJV

Bible Gateway passage: Proverbs 14:22 - King James Version. (2015). Bible Gateway.
https://www.biblegateway.com/passage/?search=Proverbs+14%3A22&version=KJV

Bible Gateway passage: Proverbs 14:29 - King James Version. (2024). Bible Gateway.
https://www.biblegateway.com/passage/?search=Proverbs+14%3A29&version=KJV

Bible Gateway passage: Proverbs 15:1 - King James Version. (2015a). Bible Gateway.
https://www.biblegateway.com/passage/?search=Proverbs+15%3A1&version=KJV

Bible Gateway passage: Proverbs 15:1 - King James Version. (2015b). Bible Gateway. https://www.biblegateway.com/passage/?search=Proverbs+15%3A1&version=KJV

Bible Gateway passage: Proverbs 15:2 - King James Version. (2015). Bible Gateway. https://www.biblegateway.com/passage/?search=Proverbs+15%3A2&version=KJV

Bible Gateway passage: Proverbs 15:13 - King James Version. (2015). Bible Gateway. https://www.biblegateway.com/passage/?search=Proverbs+15%3A13&version=KJV

Bible Gateway passage: Proverbs 15:18 - King James Version. (2015). Bible Gateway. https://www.biblegateway.com/passage/?search=Proverbs+15%3A18&version=KJV

Bible Gateway passage: Proverbs 15:22 - King James Version. (2015). Bible Gateway. https://www.biblegateway.com/passage/?search=Proverbs+15%3A22&version=KJV

Bible Gateway passage: Proverbs 15:28 - King James Version. (2015). Bible Gateway. https://www.biblegateway.com/passage/?search=Proverbs+15%3A28&version=KJV

Bible Gateway passage: Proverbs 15:30 - King James Version. (2024). Bible Gateway. https://www.biblegateway.com/passage/?search=Proverbs+15%3A30&version=KJV

Bible Gateway passage: Proverbs 16:3 - King James Version. (2015). Bible Gateway. https://www.biblegateway.com/passage/?search=Proverbs+16%3A3&version=KJV

Bible Gateway passage: Proverbs 16:9 - King James Version. (2015). Bible Gateway. https://www.biblegateway.com/passage/?search=Proverbs+16%3A9&version=KJV

Bible Gateway passage: Proverbs 16:24 - King James Version. (2015). Bible Gateway. https://www.biblegateway.com/passage/?search=Proverbs+16%3A24&version=KJV

Bible Gateway passage: Proverbs 17:1 - King James Version. (2015). Bible Gateway. https://www.biblegateway.com/passage/?search=Proverbs+17%3A1&version=KJV

Bible Gateway passage: Proverbs 17:6 - King James Version. (2015). Bible Gateway. https://www.biblegateway.com/passage/?search=Proverbs+17%3A6&version=KJV

Bible Gateway passage: Proverbs 17:9 - King James Version. (2024). Bible Gateway. https://www.biblegateway.com/passage/?search=Proverbs+17%3A9&version=KJV

Bible Gateway passage: Proverbs 17:14 - King James Version. (2015). Bible Gateway. https://www.biblegateway.com/passage/?search=Proverbs+17%3A14&version=KJV

Bible Gateway passage: Proverbs 17:17 - King James Version. (2015). Bible Gateway. https://www.biblegateway.com/passage/?search=Proverbs+17%3A17&version=KJV

Bible Gateway passage: Proverbs 17:22 - King James Version. (2015). Bible Gateway. https://www.biblegateway.com/passage/?search=Proverbs+17%3A22&version=KJV

Bible Gateway passage: Proverbs 18:2 - King James Version. (2024). Bible Gateway. https://www.biblegateway.com/passage/?search=Proverbs+18%3A2&version=KJV

Bible Gateway passage: Proverbs 18:13 - King James Version. (2015). Bible Gateway. https://www.biblegateway.com/passage/?search=Proverbs+18%3A13&version=KJV

Bible Gateway passage: Proverbs 18:21 - King James Version. (2015). Bible Gateway. https://www.biblegateway.com/passage/?search=Proverbs+18%3A21&version=KJV

Bible Gateway passage: Proverbs 18:22 - King James Version. (2015a). Bible Gateway. https://www.biblegateway.com/passage/?search=Proverbs+18%3A22&version=KJV

Bible Gateway passage: Proverbs 18:22 - King James Version. (2015b). Bible Gateway. https://www.biblegateway.com/passage/?search=Proverbs+18%3A22&version=KJV

Bible Gateway passage: Proverbs 19:11 - King James Version. (2015). Bible Gateway. https://www.biblegateway.com/passage/?search=Proverbs+19%3A11&version=KJV

Bible Gateway passage: Proverbs 19:14 - King James Version. (2015). Bible Gateway. https://www.biblegateway.com/passage/?search=Proverbs+19%3A14&version=KJV

Bible Gateway passage: Proverbs 19:20 - King James Version. (2015). Bible Gateway. https://www.biblegateway.com/passage/?search=Proverbs+19%3A20&version=KJV

Bible Gateway passage: Proverbs 19:21 - King James Version. (2015). Bible Gateway. https://www.biblegateway.com/passage/?search=Proverbs+19%3A21&version=KJV

Bible Gateway passage: Proverbs 20:6-7 - King James Version. (2015). Bible Gateway. https://www.biblegateway.com/passage/?search=Proverbs+20%3A6-7&version=KJV

Bible Gateway passage: Proverbs 20:15 - King James Version. (2015). Bible Gateway. https://www.biblegateway.com/passage/?search=Proverbs+20%3A15&version=KJV

Bible Gateway passage: Proverbs 20:22 - King James Version. (2015). Bible Gateway. https://www.biblegateway.com/passage/?search=Proverbs+20%3A22&version=KJV

Bible Gateway passage: Proverbs 20:25 - King James Version. (2015). Bible Gateway. https://www.biblegateway.com/passage/?search=Proverbs+20%3A25&version=KJV

Bible Gateway passage: Proverbs 21:19 - King James Version. (2015). Bible Gateway. https://www.biblegateway.com/passage/?search=Proverbs+21%3A19&version=KJV

Bible Gateway passage: Proverbs 21:23 - King James Version. (2015). Bible Gateway. https://www.biblegateway.com/passage/?search=Proverbs+21%3A23&version=KJV

Bible Gateway passage: Proverbs 22:6 - King James Version. (2024). Bible Gateway. https://www.biblegateway.com/passage/?search=Proverbs+22%3A6&version=KJV

Bible Gateway passage: Proverbs 24:3-4 - King James Version. (2015). Bible Gateway. https://www.biblegateway.com/passage/?search=Proverbs+24%3A3-4&version=KJV

Bible Gateway passage: Proverbs 25:11 - King James Version. (2015). Bible Gateway. https://www.biblegateway.com/passage/?search=Proverbs+25%3A11&version=KJV

Bible Gateway passage: Proverbs 25:19 - King James Version. (2015). Bible Gateway. https://www.biblegateway.com/passage/?search=Proverbs+25%3A19&version=KJV

Bible Gateway passage: Proverbs 28:10 - King James Version. (2015). Bible Gateway. https://www.biblegateway.com/passage/?search=Proverbs+28%3A10&version=KJV

Bible Gateway passage: Proverbs 28:13 - King James Version. (2015). Bible Gateway. https://www.biblegateway.com/passage/?search=Proverbs+28%3A13&version=KJV

Bible Gateway passage: Proverbs 28:20 - King James Version. (2015a). Bible Gateway. https://www.biblegateway.com/passage/?search=Proverbs+28%3A20&version=KJV

Bible Gateway passage: Proverbs 28:20 - King James Version. (2015b). Bible Gateway. https://www.biblegateway.com/passage/?search=Proverbs+28%3A20&version=KJV

Bible Gateway passage: Proverbs 29:20 - King James Version. (2015). Bible Gateway. https://www.biblegateway.com/passage/?search=Proverbs+29%3A20&version=KJV

Bible Gateway passage: Proverbs 30:18-19 - King James Version. (2015). Bible Gateway. https://www.biblegateway.com/passage/?search=Proverbs+30%3A18-19&version=KJV

Bible Gateway passage: Proverbs 31:10-12 - King James Version. (2024). Bible Gateway. https://www.biblegateway.com/passage/?search=Proverbs+31%3A10-12&version=KJV

Bible Gateway passage: Proverbs 31:11 - King James Version. (2015). Bible Gateway. https://www.biblegateway.com/passage/?search=Proverbs+31%3A11&version=KJV

Bible Gateway passage: Proverbs 31:12 - King James Version. (2015). Bible Gateway. https://www.biblegateway.com/passage/?search=Proverbs+31%3A12&version=KJV

Bible Gateway passage: Proverbs 31:26 - King James Version. (2015). Bible Gateway. https://www.biblegateway.com/passage/?search=Proverbs+31%3A26&version=KJV

Bible Gateway passage: Proverbs 31:26-27 - King James Version. (2015). Bible Gateway. https://www.biblegateway.com/passage/?search=Proverbs+31%3A26-27&version=KJV

Bible Gateway passage: Psalm 27:1 - King James Version. (2015). Bible Gateway. https://www.biblegateway.com/passage/?search=Psalm+27%3A1&version=KJV

Bible Gateway passage: Psalm 28:7 - King James Version. (2015). Bible Gateway. https://www.biblegateway.com/passage/?search=Psalm+28%3A7&version=KJV

Bible Gateway passage: Psalm 34:17-18 - King James Version. (2015). Bible Gateway. https://www.biblegateway.com/passage/?search=Psalm+34%3A17-18&version=KJV

Bible Gateway passage: Psalm 37:4 - King James Version. (2015). Bible Gateway. https://www.biblegateway.com/passage/?search=Psalm+37%3A4&version=KJV

Bible Gateway passage: Psalm 37:5 - King James Version. (2015). Bible Gateway. https://www.biblegateway.com/passage/?search=Psalm+37%3A5&version=KJV

Bible Gateway passage: Psalm 55:22 - King James Version. (2015). Bible Gateway. https://www.biblegateway.com/passage/?search=Psalm+55%3A22&version=KJV

Bible Gateway passage: Psalm 86:5 - King James Version. (2015). Bible Gateway. https://www.biblegateway.com/passage/?search=Psalm+86%3A5&version=KJV

Bible Gateway passage: Psalm 90:12 - King James Version. (2015). Bible Gateway. https://www.biblegateway.com/passage/?search=Psalm+90%3A12&version=KJV

Bible Gateway passage: Psalm 101:2-3 - King James Version. (2015). Bible Gateway. https://www.biblegateway.com/passage/?search=Psalm+101%3A2-3&version=KJV

Bible Gateway passage: Psalm 103:10-12 - King James Version. (2015). Bible Gateway. https://www.biblegateway.com/passage/?search=Psalm+103%3A10-12&version=KJV

Bible Gateway passage: Psalm 113:9 - King James Version. (2015). Bible Gateway. https://www.biblegateway.com/passage/?search=Psalm+113%3A9&version=KJV

Bible Gateway passage: Psalm 118:24 - King James Version. (2015). Bible Gateway. https://www.biblegateway.com/passage/?search=Psalm+118%3A24&version=KJV

Bible Gateway passage: Psalm 127:3-5 - King James Version. (2015). Bible Gateway. https://www.biblegateway.com/passage/?search=+Psalm+127%3A3-5&version=KJV

Bible Gateway passage: Psalm 128:1-4 - King James Version. (2015). Bible Gateway. https://www.biblegateway.com/passage/?search=Psalm+128%3A+1-4&version=KJV

Bible Gateway passage: Psalm 128:3 - King James Version. (2015). Bible Gateway. https://www.biblegateway.com/passage/?search=Psalm+128%3A3&version=KJV

Bible Gateway passage: Psalm 133:1 - King James Version. (2015). Bible Gateway. https://www.biblegateway.com/passage/?search=Psalm+133%3A1&version=KJV

Bible Gateway passage: Psalm 141:3 - King James Version. (2015). Bible Gateway. https://www.biblegateway.com/passage/?search=Psalm+141%3A3&version=KJV

Bible Gateway passage: Psalm 147:3 - King James Version. (2015). Bible Gateway. https://www.biblegateway.com/passage/?search=Psalm+147%3A3&version=KJV

Bible Gateway passage: Revelation 2:10 - King James Version. (2015). Bible Gateway. https://www.biblegateway.com/passage/?search=Revelation+2%3A10&version=KJV

Bible Gateway passage: Romans 5:8 - King James Version. (2015). Bible Gateway. https://www.biblegateway.com/passage/?search=Romans+5%3A8&version=KJV

Bible Gateway passage: Romans 8:28 - King James Version. (2015). Bible Gateway. https://www.biblegateway.com/passage/?search=Romans+8%3A28&version=KJV

Bible Gateway passage: Romans 8:28 - King James Version. (2024). Bible Gateway. https://www.biblegateway.com/passage/?search=Romans+8%3A28&version=KJV

Bible Gateway passage: Romans 8:38-39 - King James Version. (2024). Bible Gateway. https://www.biblegateway.com/passage/?search=Romans+8%3A38-39&version=KJV

Bible Gateway passage: Romans 12:5 - King James Version. (2015). Bible Gateway. https://www.biblegateway.com/passage/?search=Romans+12%3A5&version=KJV

Bible Gateway passage: Romans 12:10 - King James Version. (2015). Bible Gateway. https://www.biblegateway.com/passage/?search=Romans+12%3A10&version=KJV

Bible Gateway passage: Romans 12:11 - King James Version. (2015). Bible Gateway. https://www.biblegateway.com/passage/?search=Romans+12%3A11&version=KJV

Bible Gateway passage: Romans 12:13 - King James Version. (2015). Bible Gateway. https://www.biblegateway.com/passage/?search=Romans+12%3A13&version=KJV

Bible Gateway passage: Romans 12:15 - King James Version. (2015). Bible Gateway. https://www.biblegateway.com/passage/?search=Romans+12%3A15&version=KJV

Bible Gateway passage: Romans 12:16 - King James Version. (2024). Bible Gateway. https://www.biblegateway.com/passage/?search=Romans+12%3A16&version=KJV

Bible Gateway passage: Romans 12:18 - King James Version. (2015). Bible Gateway. https://www.biblegateway.com/passage/?search=Romans+12%3A18&version=KJV

Bible Gateway passage: Romans 12:19 - King James Version. (2015). Bible Gateway. https://www.biblegateway.com/passage/?search=Romans+12%3A19&version=KJV

Bible Gateway passage: Romans 13:10 - King James Version. (2015). Bible Gateway. https://www.biblegateway.com/passage/?search=Romans+13%3A10&version=KJV

Bible Gateway passage: Romans 14:19 - King James Version. (2015). Bible Gateway. https://www.biblegateway.com/passage/?search=Romans+14%3A19&version=KJV

Bible Gateway passage: Romans 15:1-2 - King James Version. (2015). Bible Gateway. https://www.biblegateway.com/passage/?search=Romans+15%3A1-2&version=KJV

Bible Gateway passage: Romans 15:5-6 - King James Version. (2015). Bible Gateway. https://www.biblegateway.com/passage/?search=Romans+15%3A5-6&version=KJV

Bible Gateway passage: Romans 15:7 - King James Version. (2015). Bible Gateway. https://www.biblegateway.com/passage/?search=%C2%A0Romans+15%3A7&version=KJV

Bible Gateway passage: Romans 15:13 - King James Version. (2015). Bible Gateway. https://www.biblegateway.com/passage/?search=Romans+15%3A13&version=KJV

Bible Gateway passage: Ruth 1:16-17 - King James Version. (2015). Bible Gateway. https://www.biblegateway.com/passage/?search=Ruth+1%3A16-17&version=KJV

Bible Gateway passage: Ruth 3:10 - King James Version. (2015). Bible Gateway. https://www.biblegateway.com/passage/?search=Ruth+3%3A10&version=KJV

Bible Gateway passage: Ruth 4:16 - King James Version. (2024). Bible Gateway. https://www.biblegateway.com/passage/?search=Ruth+4%3A16&version=KJV

Bible Gateway passage: Song of Solomon 2:16 - King James Version. (2015). Bible Gateway. https://www.biblegateway.com/passage/?search=Song+of+Solomon+2%3A16&version=KJV

Bible Gateway passage: Song of Solomon 6:3 - King James Version. (2015). Bible Gateway. https://www.biblegateway.com/passage/?search=Song+of+Solomon+6%3A3&version=KJV

Bible Gateway passage: Song of Solomon 8:6-7 - King James Version. (2015). Bible Gateway.

https://www.biblegateway.com/passage/?search=Song+Of+Soloman+8%3A6-7&
version=KJV

Bible Gateway passage: Titus 1:6 - King James Version. (2015). Bible Gateway. https://
www.biblegateway.com/passage/?search=Titus+1%3A6&version=KJV

Bible Gateway passage: Titus 2:4-5 - King James Version. (2015). Bible Gateway. https://
www.biblegateway.com/passage/?search=Titus+2%3A4-5&version=KJV